Board Review Series

Behavioral Science
2nd edition

Board Review Series

Behavioral Science
2nd edition

Barbara Fadem, Ph.D.
Associate Professor of Psychiatry
Department of Psychiatry
University of Medicine and Dentistry of New Jersey
New Jersey Medical School
Newark, New Jersey

Harwal Publishing

Philadelphia • Baltimore • Hong Kong • London • Munich • Sydney • Tokyo

A Waverly Company

Harwal

Acquisitions Editor: Elizabeth A. Nieginski
Managing Editor: Susan E. Kelly
Production: Laurie Forsyth, Joan Leary

Library of Congress Cataloging-in-Publication Data

Fadem, Barbara.
    Behavioral science / Barbara Fadem. — 2nd ed.
        p.   cm. — (Board review series)
    Includes bibliographical references and index.
    ISBN 0-683-02953-3
    1. Psychiatry—Outlines, syllabi, etc.   2. Psychology—Outlines,
syllabi, etc.   3. Psychiatry—Examinations, questions, etc.
4. Psychology—Examinations, questions, etc.   I. Title.
II. Series.
    RC457.2.F34   1994
    616.89'0076—dc20
DNLM/DLC
for Library of Congress   93-39958
                                                                         CIP

10 9 8 7 6 5 4 3

Contents

Section III.   BEHAVIOR OF THE INDIVIDUAL

Section VII. THE DOCTOR-PATIENT RELATIONSHIP

20 Doctor-Patient Communication   165

21 Emotional Reactions to Illness   173

Section VIII. HEALTH CARE DELIVERY

22 Epidemiology and Statistical Methods   181

23 Systems of Health Care Delivery   195

Preface to the Second Edition

In medicine, the relationship between the body and the mind is of supreme importance to the physical and mental health of an individual. Those who teach behavioral science and psychiatry in medical schools, while keenly aware of this relationship, are also aware of the overwhelming amount of information that students must assimilate for the United States Medical Licensing Examination (USMLE) Step 1. Therefore, this concise review has been prepared as a learning tool, which will help students rapidly recall information that they have learned in behavioral science, psychiatry, epidemiology, and other related courses they have taken in the first two years of medical school.

The second edition of **BRS Behavioral Science** contains 8 sections divided into 24 chapters. Each chapter has been updated to include the most current information and demographic statistics. A total of 500 questions and answers with detailed explanations are presented after each chapter and in the Comprehensive Examination at the end of the book. This examination serves as a practice exam and self-assessment tool to help students assimilate information and evaluate their mastery of facts and concepts relating to behavioral science. All questions reflect the new USMLE format and include clinically oriented information. Fifty-four tables are included throughout the book to access essential information for quick recall.

Preface to the Second Edition

Acknowledgments

The author wishes to thank Susan Kelly, Managing Editor of the Board Review Series, whose great patience, hard work, and good humor helped so much to bring this second edition into being. The author also acknowledges with thanks the assistance of faculty members at New Jersey Medical School, University of Medicine and Dentistry of New Jersey, who reviewed sections of manuscript, including Dr. Henry Kalir and Dr. Cheryl Kennedy of the Department of Psychiatry, and Dr. Allan Siegel of the Department of Neuroscience. Special thanks to Dr. Marian Passannante of the Department of Preventive Medicine and Community Health for her generous contributions of time and knowledge. Most of all, the author thanks Dr. Steven Simring, Director of Medical Student Education of the Department of Psychiatry, for his scholarly assistance, encouragement, and friendship.

1

Genetic Bases of Psychiatric Disorders

I. Genetic Studies

A. Pedigree and family risk studies

- Pedigree studies use a **family tree** to show the occurrence of traits and diseases within a family.
- A pedigree helps to assess whether **genetic factors** are involved and, if so, the mode of inheritance of a trait or disease.
- **Family risk studies** compare how frequently a disease occurs in the relatives of the **proband,** or affected individual, with how frequently it occurs in the general population.

B. Adoption studies

- Adoption studies using twins reared together or apart are used to distinguish the effects of genetic factors from environmental factors in disease.
  - Twin studies may involve **monozygotic twins** (derived from a single fertilized ovum) or **dizygotic twins** (derived from two fertilized ova).
  - If genetic in origin, a disorder may be expected to occur more often in monozygotic twins than in dizygotic twins. If both twins have a trait, they are **concordant** for that trait.
- **Heritability** is the degree (percentage) to which genetic factors are responsible for an illness.

II. Genetic Origins of Schizophrenia

A. Incidence and prevalence of schizophrenia

- Incidence of schizophrenia is about **0.5 per 1000 persons per year**.
- The chances of a person becoming schizophrenic in his lifetime (**lifetime prevalence**) are about **1.5%**.
- The prevalence of schizophrenia is approximately **equal in men and women**.
- Although previous studies reported that more African Americans (hereafter referred to as blacks) than whites were schizophrenic, the prevalence of schizophrenia is now thought to be **equivalent in whites and blacks**.

B. Genetic factors

- Although environmental factors most likely affect the expression of genetic factors in schizophrenia, these factors are probably outweighed by genetic influences.

1

Table 1-1. Risk of Developing Schizophrenia in Relatives of Schizophrenics

Group	Concordance Rate (%)
Dizygotic twin of a person with schizophrenia	9–26
Children who have one parent with schizophrenia	10–13
Children who have two parents with schizophrenia	30–40
Monozygotic twin of a person with schizophrenia	35–58

– Persons with a **close genetic relationship** to a patient with schizophrenia are more likely than those with a more distant relationship to be concordant for, or to develop, the disorder (Table 1-1).
– Increased severity of the disorder is directly related to a high concordance rate for schizophrenia occurring in twins.
– In some studies, markers on **chromosome 5** have been associated with schizophrenia.

III. Genetic Origins of Affective (Mood) Disorder

– The **affective disorders** include both unipolar and bipolar disorders (see Chapter 11). Genetic factors appear to be involved in the etiology of both conditions.

A. Unipolar disorder

– Unipolar disorder is characterized by single or multiple episodes of **depressed mood (depression)**.
– The **lifetime prevalence** of unipolar disorder is about **10% in men and 15%–20% in women**.

B. Bipolar disorder

– Episodes of both **elevated mood** (mania) and **depression** are seen in bipolar disorder. The **lifetime prevalence** of bipolar disorder is about **1%** and is equal in men and women.
– Markers on the **X chromosome** have been associated with bipolar disorder.
– Although evidence of genetic markers on chromosome 11 had been identified in bipolar disorder, recent studies suggest a weaker relationship between these markers and this condition than originally believed.

C. Relationship between unipolar disorder and bipolar disorder

– The **concordance rate** for bipolar disorder is higher than that for unipolar disorder.
– About 50% of persons with bipolar disorder have a parent with a mood disorder.
– The degree of relatedness to persons with bipolar illness is related to the incidence of mood disorders (Table 1-2).

Table 1-2. Incidence of Mood Disorder in Specific Populations

Group	Concordance Rate (%)
Dizygotic twin of a person with bipolar disorder	14–20
Children who have one parent with bipolar disorder	27
Children who have two parents with bipolar disorder	50–75
Monozygotic twin of a person with bipolar disorder	65–67

Table 1-3. Psychiatric Conditions Observed in Relatives of Patients with Personality Disorders

Personality Disorder of Patient	Problems Seen in Relatives
Antisocial	Alcoholism; somatization disorder (Briquet's syndrome)
Avoidant	Anxiety disorder
Borderline	Mood disorder
Histrionic	Somatization disorder
Obsessive-compulsive	Depression
Schizoid, schizotypal, paranoid	Schizophrenia

IV. Genetic Origins of Personality Characteristics and Disorders

A. Temperament and intelligence

- Responsiveness to stimulation, fearfulness, activity level, and distractibility have a higher concordance rate in monozygotic twins than in dizygotic twins.
- **Intelligence quotient (IQ)** is concordant in about 85% of monozygotic twins even if they are raised apart.
- IQ is concordant in about 50% of dizygotic twins.

B. Personality disorders

- Evidence indicates that **genetic factors** play a role in antisocial, obsessive-compulsive, schizotypal, histrionic, and schizoid personality disorders (see Chapter 14).
  - In personality disorders, the concordance rate is higher in monozygotic twins than in dizygotic twins.
  - Relatives of patients with specific personality disorders have demonstrated characteristic psychiatric problems (Table 1-3).

V. Genetic Origins of Neuropsychiatric Disorders

A. Alzheimer's disease

- There appears to be a **genetic component** in Alzheimer's disease, a progressive deterioration of cognitive functioning. In many cases, there is a family history of Alzheimer's disease.
- There is also a high concordance rate for Alzheimer's disease in monozygotic twins.
- **Chromosome 21,** the chromosome associated with **Down's syndrome,** has been found to be defective in patients with **Alzheimer's disease**.
- Persons with Down's syndrome who live beyond age 40 develop symptoms resembling Alzheimer's disease.

B. Other disorders

- **Tourette's syndrome, Huntington's disease, Wilson's disease,** and **infantile autism** also have genetic components.
- **Huntington's disease,** which usually shows its first signs in individuals aged 35–45 years, exhibits an **autosomal dominant** pattern of inheritance; if one parent has the disease, each child has a 50% chance of inheriting the disease (Table 1-4).
- Forms of mental retardation with genetic components include the following syndromes: **Down's** and **fragile X** (the first and second most common genetic causes of mental retardation, respectively), **Klinefelter's, Turner's, cri du chat,** and **Lesch-Nyhan** (see Table 1-4).

Table 1-4. Genetic Defects that Occur in Neuropsychiatric Diseases

Syndrome or Disease	Genetic Defect
Alzheimer's disease	Anomaly on chromosome 21
Cri du chat syndrome	Part of chromosome 5 missing
Down's syndrome	Nondisjunction or trisomy (more common) of chromosome 21
Huntington's disease	Abnormal gene on short arm of chromosome 4
Klinefelter's syndrome	More than one X chromosome; one Y chromosome
Lesch-Nyhan syndrome	X-linked transmission
Turner's syndrome	One X chromosome

VI. Genetic Origins of Alcoholism

- Studies indicate that a genetic component is involved in alcohol abuse.
- Alcoholism is **four times more prevalent** in children of alcoholics than in children of nonalcoholics. This ratio persists even if the children are raised by adoptive parents.
- The **concordance rate** for alcoholism in monozygotic twins may be as much as two times greater than in dizygotic twins.
- **Sons of alcoholics** are at **greater risk than daughters** of alcoholics. The genetic influence is strongest in males who abuse alcohol prior to age 20.

Review Test

Directions: Each of the numbered items or incomplete statements in this section is followed by answers or by completions of the statement. Select the **one** lettered answer or completion that is **best** in each case.

1. Which of the following statements about patients with affective disorders is true?

(A) The lifetime prevalence of unipolar disorder is approximately equivalent in men and women
(B) In bipolar disorder, episodes of elevated mood are more common than episodes of depression
(C) The lifetime prevalence of bipolar disorder is approximately equivalent in men and women
(D) Patients with bipolar disorder rarely have relatives with unipolar illness
(E) The concordance rate for unipolar disorder is higher than for bipolar disorder

2. Which of the following personality disorders has been linked to alcoholism in relatives?

(A) Histrionic
(B) Borderline
(C) Obsessive-compulsive
(D) Avoidant
(E) Antisocial

3. Which of the following statements about the incidence and origins of personality disorders is true?

(A) High incidence of schizoid personality disorder occurs in families of patients with mood disorders
(B) High incidence of schizotypal personality disorder occurs in families of patients with mood disorders
(C) The concordance rate for personality disorders is equivalent in monozygotic twins and in dizygotic twins
(D) Evidence for genetic factors is seen in antisocial personality disorder

4. All of the following statements about the genetics of neuropsychiatric disorders are true EXCEPT

(A) in cri du chat syndrome, part of chromosome 5 is missing
(B) a high concordance rate for Alzheimer's disease is seen in twins
(C) an anomaly on chromosome 21 has been linked to Alzheimer's disease
(D) Lesch-Nyhan syndrome involves autosomal dominant transmission
(E) there is probably a genetic component in infantile autism

5. Which of the following statements about the genetics of alcoholism is true?

(A) The concordance rate for alcoholism is higher in dizygotic twins than in monozygotic twins
(B) Alcoholism is about two times more prevalent in the children of alcoholics than in the children of nonalcoholics
(C) Adopted children tend to drink as much alcohol as their adoptive, rather than their biologic, parents
(D) Sons of alcoholics are more at risk of developing alcoholism than daughters of alcoholics
(E) The genetic effects of alcoholism are strongest in females under age 20

6. The second most common genetic cause of mental retardation is

(A) Huntington's disease
(B) cri du chat syndrome
(C) Klinefelter's syndrome
(D) fragile X syndrome
(E) Lesch-Nyhan syndrome

5

Answers and Explanations

1–C. The lifetime prevalence of bipolar disorder is about equal in women and men.

2–E. Alcoholism is seen among relatives of patients with antisocial personality disorders.

3–D. Genetic factors are involved in many personality disorders, including antisocial personality disorder.

4–D. Lesch-Nyhan syndrome involves X-linked transmission.

5–D. Sons of alcoholics are more at risk of developing alcoholism than daughters.

6–D. Down's syndrome is the most common genetic cause of mental retardation. Fragile X syndrome is the second most common.

2

Anatomy and Biochemistry of Behavior

I. Anatomy of the Nervous System

A. Neuron

- Neurons (nerve cells) are the basic units of the nervous system and generally have two types of projections: **axons** and **dendrites**.

1. The **axon** usually carries messages away from the neuron, is covered with a **myelin sheath**, and has a terminal enlargement called the **axon terminal**, or bouton.
   - **Myelin** increases the conduction efficiency of the axon.
   - The **axon terminal** is one site for the synaptic vesicles that contain neurotransmitters.

2. Many, few, or no **dendrites** may emerge from the neuron cell body.
   - Dendrites often consist of many branches and contain spikes known as **dendritic spines**.
   - The dendritic spines are sites of reception of neurotransmitter messages from the axons of other neurons.

B. Glial cells

- Glial cells, including astrocytes, ependymal cells, oligodendrocytes, microglia, Schwann cells, and satellite cells, are non-neuronal cells in the central nervous system (CNS) and in the peripheral nervous system (PNS). These cells contribute to the **blood–brain barrier**, which prevents substances from passing from the blood into the nervous system.

C. Central and peripheral nervous systems

- The human nervous system consists of the CNS, which contains the **brain and spinal cord**, and the PNS, which contains the **spinal nerves, cranial nerves**, and the **peripheral ganglia**.
  - The PNS carries **sensory** information to the CNS, and it carries **motor** information away from the CNS.

D. Autonomic nervous system

- The autonomic nervous system (ANS), which consists of **sympathetic** and **parasympathetic** divisions, innervates the internal organs.

7

Table 2-1. Neuropsychiatric Consequences of Brain Lesions

Location of Lesion	Consequences
Frontal lobes	Labile or shallow affect, depression, reduction in motivation, problems with attention and memory, inappropriate behavior; dominant lesions result in poor expressive speech (Broca's aphasia)
Temporal lobes	Impaired memory, psychomotor seizures; dominant lesions result in poor verbal comprehension (Wernicke's aphasia)
Hippocampus	Poor new learning; implicated specifically in Alzheimer's disease
Amygdala	Docility and increased sexual behavior (Klüver-Bucy syndrome)
Parietal lobes	Problems with intellectual processing of sensory (nondominant lesions) and verbal (dominant lesions) information
Occipital lobes	Visual hallucinations and illusions; blindness; disturbances of spatial orientation
Thalamus	Increased pain perception; impaired memory and arousal
Basal ganglia	Disorders of movement, thought, affect, and cognition; Parkinson's disease and Huntington's disease
Cerebellum	Atrophy may be seen in schizophrenia, bipolar disorder, epilepsy, and autism
Reticular system	Sleep-arousal mechanisms affected
Limbic system	Emotion; memory; mediation between cortex and lower centers affected
Hypothalamus	Problems with eating, sexual activity, body temperature regulation, and sleep-wake cycle

- The ANS mediates emotions with visceral responses such as heart rate, blood pressure, and size of pupils.

II. Functional Brain Anatomy and Psychopathology

A. Cerebral cortex

- The cerebral cortex can be divided as follows:
  - **Anatomically** into four lobes: frontal, temporal, parietal, and occipital.
  - **By arrangement** of neuron layers or cryoarchitecture.
  - **Functionally** into motor, sensory, and association areas.

B. Cerebral hemispheres

- The brain has two cerebral hemispheres, which are connected by the corpus callosum, anterior commissure, hippocampal commissure, posterior commissure, and habenular commissure. The two hemispheres are **lateralized** with respect to function.

1. The **right**, or **nondominant**, hemisphere is associated with **spatial relations**, musical ability, facial recognition, and the perception of social cues.

2. The **left**, or **dominant**, hemisphere is associated with **language function** in almost all right-handed persons and in about 70% of left-handed persons.

C. Brain lesions

- Brain lesions caused by accident, illness, or surgery are associated with particular behavioral and cognitive deficits (Table 2-1).

Table 2-2. Psychiatric Conditions and Associated Neurotransmitters

Psychiatric Condition	Neurotransmitter
Schizophrenia	Dopamine
Depression	Norepinephrine, serotonin, dopamine
Anxiety	GABA, norepinephrine, serotonin
Alzheimer's disease	Acetylcholine

III. Neurotransmission

A. Synapses and neurotransmitter

- Information in the nervous system is transferred across synapses or spaces between the axon terminal of the presynaptic neuron and the dendrite of the postsynaptic neuron. The space between the synapses is the **synaptic cleft**.
- When the presynaptic neuron is stimulated, a **neurotransmitter** (chemical messenger) is released, travels across the synaptic cleft, and acts on receptors on the postsynaptic neuron.

B. Receptors

- Receptors are proteins present in the membrane of the neuron and can recognize specific neurotransmitters.
  - **Presynaptic receptors** act to bind neurotransmitters.
  - **Postsynaptic receptors** may change the ionic conduction of membranes.
- The changeability of number or affinity of receptors for specific neurotransmitters (**neuronal plasticity**) can regulate the responsiveness of neurons.

C. Second messengers

- When stimulated by neurotransmitters, postsynaptic receptors may alter the metabolism of the neuron by the use of second messengers, which include **cyclic AMP**, **lipids** such as diacylglycerol, and Ca^{2+}.

D. Classification of neurotransmitters

- The three major classes of neurotransmitters are **biogenic amines** (monoamines), **amino acids**, and **peptides**.

E. Mechanism of action of neurotransmitters

- Neurotransmitters can be **excitatory** if they increase the chances that a neuron will fire; they are **inhibitory** if they decrease these chances.
- After release by the presynaptic neuron, neurotransmitters are removed from the synaptic cleft by reuptake by the presynaptic neuron or by degradation by enzymes such as **monoamine oxidase (MAO)**.
  - If this reuptake or enzyme degradation is blocked, a higher concentration of neurotransmitter is available in the synaptic cleft.

F. Clinical correlations of neurotransmitters

- Availability of specific neurotransmitters is associated with common psychiatric and neuropsychiatric conditions (Table 2-2).

IV. Biogenic Amines

- The biogenic amines, or monoamines (which include catecholamines, indolamines, ethylamines, and quaternary amines), are synthesized in the axon terminal and are involved in 10% or less of brain synapses.

A. Dopamine

1. **Role of dopamine**

   – Dopamine, a catecholamine, is involved in the pathophysiology of **schizophrenia, Parkinson's disease,** and **mood disorders**.

      – A **hyperdopaminergic state** may be involved in the etiology of **schizophrenia**. The clinical success of antipsychotic drugs that block dopamine receptors supports this hypothesis.

      – The brains of people with schizophrenia show increased numbers of dopamine receptors at autopsy. This increase in the number of dopamine receptors may be secondary to and thus confounded by antipsychotic drug treatment that the patient with schizophrenia may have received.

      – **Manic patients** may show **dopamine hyperactivity**; **depressed patients** may show **dopamine hypoactivity**.

2. **Synthesis and storage**

   – The amino acid tyrosine is converted to the precursor for dopamine by the action of **tyrosine hydroxylase**.

   – Following synthesis, dopamine is stored in synaptic vesicles.

3. **Dopaminergic tracts**

   a. The **nigrostriatal tract** is involved in the regulation of muscle tone and movement.

      – This tract **degenerates in Parkinson's disease**.

      – Treatment with antipsychotic drugs, which block postsynaptic dopamine receptors receiving input from the nigrostriatal tract, can result in parkinsonism-like symptoms.

   b. Dopamine acts on the **tuberoinfundibular tract** to inhibit the secretion of prolactin from the anterior pituitary.

      – Blockade of dopamine receptors by antipsychotic drugs prevents the inhibition of prolactin release and results in **elevated prolactin** levels.

   c. The **mesolimbic–mesocortical tract** may have a role in expression of **mood** since it projects into areas of the brain that are involved in emotional behavior.

4. **Metabolism of dopamine**

   – Free dopamine is metabolized by **MAO**.

      – **Homovanillic acid (HVA)** is a metabolite of dopamine that is often measured in psychiatric research (Table 2-3).

      – Higher levels of plasma HVA are seen in unmedicated schizophrenics than in medicated schizophrenics or normal controls.

      – Decreased HVA levels can be seen when patients improve clinically following treatment with neuroleptic drugs.

5. **Tardive dyskinesia**

   – Tardive dyskinesia, **abnormal movements** primarily of the face and tongue, is a serious and permanent adverse effect caused by **long-term use of antipsychotic drugs**.

   – This disorder may occur when the postsynaptic dopamine receptors become supersensitized after they have been blockaded over an extended period by antipsychotic drugs.

Table 2-3. Metabolites of Monoamines Commonly Measured in Psychiatric Research

Neurotransmitter	Metabolite	Disease State	Direction (measured in)
Dopamine	HVA (homovanillic acid)	Schizophrenia	Increased (plasma)
		Parkinson's disease, ADHD*, Tourette's syndrome	Decreased (CSF; plasma)
Norepinephrine	MHPG (3-methoxy-4-hydroxyphenylglycol)	Severe depression, attempted suicide	Decreased (CSF; urine)
	VMA (vanillylmandelic acid)	Adrenal medulla tumor (pheochromocytoma)	Increased (CSF)
Serotonin	5-HIAA (5-hydroxyindole-acetic acid)	Severe depression, aggressiveness, impulsiveness, violence	Decreased (CSF)

*ADHD = Attention-deficit hyperactivity disorder.

B. Norepinephrine

1. Role of norepinephrine and its metabolites

– Norepinephrine, a **catecholamine**, may play a role in the physiologic functions of the **sleep-wake cycle, arousal, anxiety, learning, memory,** and **pain**.
– It also plays a role in **mood and anxiety disorders**.
  – The most important metabolite of norepinephrine is **3-methoxy-4-hydroxyphenylglycol (MHPG)** [see Table 2-3]. Elevated MHPG in the cerebrospinal fluid (CSF) has been seen in some patients with schizophrenia.
  – Another important metabolite of norepinephrine is **vanillylmandelic acid (VMA)** [see Table 2-3].

2. Synthesis and storage

– Like dopaminergic neurons, noradrenergic neurons synthesize dopamine.
– **β-hydroxylase**, present in noradrenergic neurons, converts dopamine to norepinephrine.
– Most noradrenergic neurons (approximately 10,000 per hemisphere in the brain) are located in the **locus ceruleus**.

3. Noradrenergic receptors

– α_1-Receptors are postsynaptic, and α_2-receptors are mainly presynaptic.
– β_1-Receptors and β_2-receptors are usually postsynaptic; they may be important for receiving locus ceruleus input.

C. Serotonin

1. Role of serotonin and its metabolites

– Serotonin, an **indolamine**, is involved in the pathophysiology of **affective disorders**. It also is involved in **anxiety** and **violence**.

- The **monoamine theory of mood disorder** hypothesizes that lowered noradrenergic or serotonergic activity results in depression.
- High levels of serotonin are associated with **decreased sexual activity**; low levels are associated with **depression** and **violence**.
- Serotonin is involved in the function of **sleep**. If the **dorsal raphe nucleus**, which contains most of the serotonergic cell bodies in the brain, is destroyed, sleep is reduced for a period of time.
- Serotonin is metabolized by MAO to **5-hydroxyindoleacetic acid (5-HIAA)** [see Table 2-3].

2. **Synthesis and storage**
   - Conversion of the amino acid tryptophan to serotonin (also known as 5-hydroxytryptamine [5-HT]) is accomplished by the enzyme tryptophan hydroxylase as well as by an amino acid decarboxylase.
     - In the synaptic cleft, binding of serotonin to serotonergic receptors occurs.
     - Deactivation of serotonin is achieved by its reuptake into the presynaptic terminals.

3. **Antidepressants and serotonin**
   - Heterocyclic antidepressants, selective serotonin reuptake inhibitors, and MAO inhibitors may increase the presence of norepinephrine and serotonin in the synaptic cleft.
     - **Heterocyclics** and **selective serotonin reuptake inhibitors** such as fluoxetine [Prozac] **block reuptake** of serotonin by the presynaptic neuron.
     - **MAO inhibitors prevent** the **degradation** of serotonin and norepinephrine by MAO.

D. **Histamine**

1. **Role of histamine**
   - Histamine, an **ethylamine**, is involved in the control of **sleep** and **waking**.
     - Histamine cells are present in the hypothalamus. Projections of these cells go to the thalamus, cerebral cortex, and limbic system.
     - Abnormalities in histamine metabolism have been observed in patients with schizophrenia.

2. **Blockade of histamine receptors**
   - Blockade of H_1 **receptors** is the mechanism of action of **antihistamines** (allergy medication).
   - Because H_2 **receptor blockade** may lead to **weight gain**, cyproheptadine, which blocks H_2 receptors, has been used in the treatment of anorexia nervosa.

E. **Acetylcholine (ACh)**

1. **Role of ACh**
   - ACh, a **quaternary amine**, is the transmitter used by **nerve-skeleton-muscle junctions**. It has been implicated in mood and sleep disorders.
     - Cholinergic neurons synthesize ACh from acetyl coenzyme A and choline using **choline acetyltransferase**.
     - Acetylcholinesterase (AChE) breaks ACh into choline and acetate.
     - Degeneration of cholinergic neurons is associated with **Alzheimer's disease, Down's syndrome**, and **movement disorders**.

2. ACh receptors

– Cholinergic receptors are divided into two main types: nicotinic and muscarinic receptors.

  – **Blockade of muscarinic receptors** with drugs such as antipsychotics and tricyclic antidepressants results in the classic "anticholinergic" adverse effects seen with use of these drugs, including dry mouth, blurred vision, urinary hesitancy, and constipation.

  – Blockade of **cholinergic receptors** can result in **delirium**.

V. Amino Acid Neurotransmitters

– Amino acid neurotransmitters are involved in nearly two-thirds of the synapses in the brain. These neurotransmitters include γ-aminobutyric acid (GABA), glycine, and glutamic acid.

A. Amino acid neurotransmitters and neuropsychiatric illness

– Decreased activity of **GABA** may be implicated in the development of epilepsy and anxiety.

  – Loss of GABA-ergic neurons has been observed in **Huntington's disease** and **Parkinson's disease**.

– **Glycine** is an inhibitory neurotransmitter.

– **Glutamic acid** is an excitatory neurotransmitter and may be involved in epilepsy and neurodegenerative illnesses.

B. GABA

– GABA is the principal neurotransmitter involved in presynaptic inhibition in the CNS.

– GABA is also intimately involved in the action of psychoactive drugs.

1. Benzodiazepines (e.g., diazepam [Valium]) are antianxiety drugs that act through GABA receptors.

– They increase the affinity of GABA for its binding site, allowing more chloride to enter the neuron. The chloride-laden neurons become hyperpolarized and inhibited, decreasing neuronal firing.

2. Barbiturates (e.g., secobarbital [Seconal]) may also act through GABA receptors.

VI. Neuropeptides

A. Neuroactive peptides

– A peptide is a **protein** consisting of fewer than **100 amino acids**. About 50 neuroactive peptides have been identified but many more exist.

– Peptides are synthesized in the body of some neurons and are carried to the axon terminals.

B. Endogenous opioids

– Endogenous opioids are associated with the effects of **pain** and **stress**.

  – **Enkephalins** and **endorphins** are endogenous opioids that affect thermoregulation, seizure induction, alcoholism, and schizophrenia.

Table 2-4. Neuropeptides and Possible Associated Psychopathology

Neuropeptide	Psychopathology
Cholecystokinin	Schizophrenia; eating and movement disorders
Neurotensin	Schizophrenia
Somatostatin	Huntington's disease; Alzheimer's disease; mood disorders
Substance P	Pain; Huntington's disease; mood disorders
Vasopressin	Mood disorders
Vasoactive intestinal peptide	Dementia; mood disorders

C. Other neuropeptides

– The peptides adrenocorticotropic hormone (**ACTH**) and corticotropin-releasing hormone (**CRH**) may mediate the regulation of stress, memory, and mood.

– Other neuropeptides also have been implicated in psychopathology (Table 2-4).

Review Test

Directions: Each of the numbered items or incomplete statements in this section is followed by answers or by completions of the statement. Select the **one** lettered answer or completion that is **best** in each case.

1. A 25-year-old male patient sustains a serious head injury in an automobile accident. He had been aggressive and assaultive, but after the accident he is placid and cooperative. He makes continual suggestive gestures and comments and masturbates a great deal. The patient's injury is most likely to affect what portion of the brain?

(A) Frontal lobes
(B) Temporal lobes
(C) Parietal lobes
(D) Occipital lobes
(E) Basal ganglia

2. Sleep-arousal mechanisms are affected by damage to the

(A) cerebellum
(B) basal ganglia
(C) thalamus
(D) reticular system
(E) amygdala

3. Increased pain perception is associated with damage to what area of the brain?

(A) Thalamus
(B) Corpus callosum
(C) Basal ganglia
(D) Reticular system
(E) Hypothalamus

4. Parkinson's disease is associated with damage to what area of the brain?

(A) Cerebellum
(B) Hypothalamus
(C) Basal ganglia
(D) Frontal lobes
(E) Temporal lobes

5. What is the major area of the brain implicated in Alzheimer's disease and amnestic disorders?

(A) Amygdala
(B) Parietal lobes
(C) Hippocampus
(D) Thalamus
(E) Basal ganglia

6. All of the following statements about neurotransmission are true EXCEPT

(A) receptors are proteins in the membranes of neurons
(B) presynaptic receptors bind neurotransmitters
(C) postsynaptic receptors change the ionic conduction of membranes
(D) neurotransmitters exert their effects only on postsynaptic neurons
(E) postsynaptic receptors bind neurotransmitters

7. Which of the following statements about neurotransmission is true?

(A) Amino acid neurotransmitters account for 15% of the synapses in the human brain
(B) The biogenic amines are involved in 50% of the synapses in the brain
(C) Dopamine is a second messenger
(D) Diacylglycerol is a second messenger
(E) Reuptake of neurotransmitters by the presynaptic neuron does not occur

8. Which of the following statements about dopamine is true?

(A) At autopsy, the brains of schizophrenics show decreased numbers of dopamine receptors
(B) Blockade of dopamine receptors results in decreased prolactin levels
(C) Antipsychotic drugs that block postsynaptic dopamine receptors may cause Parkinson-like symptoms
(D) Dopamine enhances the release of prolactin
(E) Patients with mania show dopamine hypoactivity

15

9. Which of the following statements about GABA is true?

(A) It is primarily an excitatory neurotransmitter
(B) It is an amino acid neurotransmitter
(C) It mediates postsynaptic inhibition in the CNS
(D) Increased GABA activity has been reported in Huntington's disease
(E) Increased GABA activity is seen in epilepsy

10. All of the following statements about the endogenous opioids are true EXCEPT

(A) they are associated with effects of stress and pain
(B) alterations in opioid levels may be involved in seizures
(C) they include the enkephalins
(D) they include glutamic acid
(E) alterations in opioid levels may be involved in alcoholism

11. Which of the following neuropeptides has been implicated in the pathology of schizophrenia?

(A) Somatostatin
(B) Neurotensin
(C) Substance P
(D) Vasopressin
(E) Vasoactive intestinal peptide

12. Which of the following neuropeptides has been implicated in the psychopathology of pain?

(A) Cholecystokinin
(B) Vasopressin
(C) Substance P
(D) Somatostatin
(E) Vasoactive intestinal peptide

13. The left hemisphere of the brain is thought to be associated with which one of the following functions?

(A) Perception of social cues
(B) Musical ability
(C) Spatial relations
(D) Language
(E) Facial recognition

14. All of the following structures connect the two cerebral hemispheres EXCEPT

(A) the corpus callosum
(B) the anterior commissure
(C) the hippocampal commissure
(D) the posterior commissure
(E) the amygdala

15. Which of the following statements about neurotransmitters and their metabolites is true?

(A) MHPG levels in urine are increased in patients with severe depressive disorders
(B) MHPG is increased in the cerebrospinal fluid of patients who have attempted suicide
(C) 5-HIAA is decreased in aggressive, violent individuals
(D) MHPG is a metabolite of serotonin
(E) VMA is a metabolite of serotonin

16. Blockade of H_2 receptors is associated primarily with

(A) depression
(B) weight gain
(C) increased anxiety
(D) epilepsy

17. Degeneration of cholinergic neurons is involved primarily in

(A) mania
(B) depression
(C) movement disorders
(D) anxiety
(E) sleep disorders

18. Which of the following statements about monoamines and their metabolites is true?

(A) Mania is associated with dopamine hypoactivity
(B) Free dopamine is metabolized by 5-HIAA
(C) There is more plasma monoamine oxidase (MAO) in unmedicated schizophrenics than in controls
(D) There is no association between levels of MHPG and suicidal behavior
(E) Decreased HVA is seen with clinical improvement in patients treated with neuroleptics

Directions: The group of items in this section consists of lettered options followed by a set of numbered items. For each item, select the **one** lettered option that is most closely associated with it. Each lettered option may be selected once, more than once, or not at all.

Questions 19–23

Match the chemical characteristic or clinical correlation with the appropriate neurotransmitter.

(A) Serotonin
(B) Norepinephrine
(C) Dopamine
(D) GABA
(E) Acetylcholine (ACh)

19. Major neurotransmitter implicated in Alzheimer's disease

20. Major neurotransmitter implicated in schizophrenia

21. Indolamine

22. Metabolized to MHPG

23. Metabolized to 5-HIAA

Answers and Explanations

1–B. The patient is suffering from Klüver-Bucy syndrome, which includes hypersexuality and docility and is associated with damage to the temporal lobes.

2–D. Sleep-arousal mechanisms are affected by damage to the reticular system.

3–A. Damage to the thalamus is associated with increased pain perception.

4–C. Parkinson's disease is associated with damage to the basal ganglia.

5–C. The major area of the brain implicated in Alzheimer's disease and amnestic disorders is the hippocampus.

6–D. Neurotransmitters exert their effects on specific presynaptic or postsynaptic receptors.

7–D. The biogenic amines are involved in up to 10% of the synapses of the human brain; amino acid neurotransmitters account for up to 60% of the synapses. Reuptake of neurotransmitter by the presynaptic neuron can occur. Second messengers include cyclic AMP, Ca^{2+}, and diacylglycerol.

8–C. Blockade of postsynaptic dopamine receptors results in Parkinson-like symptoms.

9–B. GABA is an inhibitory amino acid neurotransmitter and the principal neurotransmitter mediating presynaptic inhibition in the CNS. Decreased GABA activity may occur in epilepsy, and loss of GABA-ergic neurons has been seen in Huntington's disease and Parkinson's disease.

10–D. The endogenous opioids include the enkephalins and endorphins. *anxiety*

11–B. Neurotensin and cholecystokinin have been implicated in the pathology of schizophrenia.

12–C. Substance P has been implicated in pain disorders.

13–D. Dominance for language in both right-handed and left-handed people is usually in the left hemisphere of the brain.

14–E. The corpus callosum and the anterior, hippocampal, and posterior commissures connect the two hemispheres of the brain; the amygdala does not.

15–C. Levels of 5-HIAA, a metabolite of serotonin, have been shown to be decreased in violent, aggressive, impulsive individuals.

16–B. Blockade of H_2 receptors is associated with weight gain.

17–C. Degeneration of cholinergic neurons is typically seen in movement disorders.

18–E. Decreased HVA can be seen in patients who improve clinically following treatment with neuro-leptic agents.

19–E. ACh is the major neurotransmitter implicated in Alzheimer's disease.

20–C. Dopamine is the major neurotransmitter implicated in schizophrenia.

21–A. Serotonin is an indolamine; norepinephrine and dopamine are catecholamines.

22–B. Norepinephrine is metabolized to MHPG.

23–A. Serotonin is metabolized to 5-HIAA.

3

Pharmacology of Behavior and Electroconvulsive Therapy

I. Antipsychotic Agents

A. Overview

- Drugs used in the treatment of psychosis are known as **antipsychotics** (also called neuroleptics or major tranquilizers).
  - Antipsychotic drugs are used primarily in the treatment of **schizophrenia** as well as to treat psychosis associated with other psychiatric and physical diseases.

B. Classification

- The three most important classes of antipsychotic drugs are **phenothiazines** (which include aliphatics, piperazines, and piperidines), **thioxanthenes**, and **butyrophenones**.
- Each of these agents can be classified by **potency** (Table 3-1).

C. Action and use

- Most antipsychotic drugs act by **blocking central D_2-receptors**.
- Significant improvement is seen in approximately 70% of patients following treatment with these drugs.
- Although negative symptoms of schizophrenia, such as withdrawal, may improve with continued treatment, antipsychotic agents are **most effective against positive symptoms** such as hallucinations and thought disorders.

D. Adverse effects and drug interactions

- **Low-potency** antipsychotic drugs are associated with **non-neurologic** adverse effects (Table 3-2).
- **High-potency** drugs are associated with **neurologic** adverse effects (Table 3-3) such as **tardive dyskinesia**.
- Drug interactions occur between antipsychotic and antidepressant agents, central nervous system (CNS) depressants, antihypertensives, anticholinergics, antacids, nicotine, epinephrine, propranolol, and warfarin.

II. Other Agents Used to Treat Psychosis

A. Agents such as **carbamazepine, lithium, propranolol, benzodiazepines, and reserpine** are used to treat psychosis, usually when patients are unable to use conventional antipsychotics.

Table 3-1. Potencies of Common Antipsychotic Drugs

Drug	Classification	Potency
Thioridazine [Mellaril]	Piperidine phenothiazine	Low
Chlorpromazine [Thorazine]	Aliphatic phenothiazine	Low
Haloperidol [Haldol]	Butyrophenone	High
Perphenazine [Trilafon]	Piperazine phenothiazine	High
Trifluoperazine [Stelazine]	Piperazine phenothiazine	High

B. Clozapine [Clozaril]

– Patients resistant to or those suffering severe adverse effects from other antipsychotic agents should be considered for treatment with clozapine.

– In contrast to other antipsychotic agents, the **major mechanism of action** of clozapine appears to be on **serotonergic systems**. Clozapine also affects dopaminergic systems, primarily as a D_1-receptor antagonist.

– Clozapine may be **more effective** than other antipsychotics when used to treat the **negative symptoms** of schizophrenia (see Chapter 10).

– Unlike other antipsychotics, clozapine is not associated with tardive dyskinesia, neuroleptic malignant syndrome, or extrapyramidal effects.

– Serious adverse effects of clozapine include **agranulocytosis** (decreased number of certain types of white blood cells) and **seizures**.

III. Antidepressant Agents

A. Classification

– **Heterocyclic antidepressants** (tricyclic and tetracyclic), **monoamine oxidase (MAO) inhibitors**, selective **serotonin reuptake inhibitors, sympathomimetic agents** (amphetamines), and other agents are used to treat depression.

– **Heterocyclic antidepressant agents and MAO inhibitors** have little or no effect as euphoriants or stimulants in nondepressed people.

Table 3-2. Non-neurologic Adverse Effects of Antipsychotic Drugs

Adverse Effects	Comments
Organ systems	
Circulatory	Electrocardiogram abnormalities; piperidines most cardiotoxic in overdose; orthostatic hypotension (more common with chlorpromazine and thioridazine)
Endocrine	Increase in prolactin results in breast enlargement, galactorrhea, impotence, amenorrhea, decreased libido
Hematologic	Leukopenia, agranulocytosis (usually appear in first 3 months of treatment)
Hepatic	Jaundice, elevated liver enzymes (usually appear in first month; more common with chlorpromazine)
Skin	Skin eruptions, photosensitivity, blue-gray skin discoloration with chlorpromazine
Ophthalmologic	Irreversible retinal pigmentation from thioridazine; deposits in lens and cornea from chlorpromazine
Other effects	
Anticholinergic	
Peripheral	Dry mouth, blurred vision, constipation, and urinary retention
Central	Severe agitation, disorientation
Weight gain and sedation	Common negative effects; chlorpromazine most sedating

Table 3-3. Neurologic Adverse Effects of Antipsychotic Drugs

Adverse Effects	Manifestations and Incidence
Parkinsonian effects	Muscle rigidity, shuffling gait, stooped posture, drooling, tremor, mask-like facial expression; occurs in 15% of patients within 3 months of initiation of treatment
Tardive dyskinesia	Abnormal movements of tongue, head, face, body; usually occurs after at least 6 months of treatment; more common in women
Neuroleptic malignant syndrome	High fever, sweating, increased pulse and blood pressure, muscular rigidity; more common in men; mortality rate 15%–25%
Akathisia	Motor symptoms, subjective feeling of agitation
Dystonias	Slow, prolonged muscular spasms; most common in men under age 40
Seizures	Slowing and increased synchronization of the electrocardiogram, decreased seizure threshold

- **Amphetamines** are only used as antidepressants in treatment-resistant persons and in those at risk from the adverse effects of other antidepressants or electroconvulsive therapy (ECT).

B. Heterocyclics

- **Tricyclic antidepressant agents,** which structurally resemble phenothiazines, are the primary drugs used to treat depression.
  Generally, heterocyclics **block reuptake of norepinephrine and serotonin** at the synapse, increasing the availability of these neurotransmitters and causing various adverse effects (Table 3-4).
- These drugs also block muscarinic acetylcholine and histamine receptors, resulting in **anticholinergic effects** such as **dry mouth, blurred vision, urine retention, constipation,** and **sedation.**
- Other adverse effects include precipitation of manic episodes, orthostatic hypotension, neurologic effects such as tremor, cardiac effects, allergic reactions, weight gain, and sexual dysfunction.
- **Overdoses** of heterocyclics may be **fatal.**

C. MAO inhibitors

1. Use

- These drugs may be particularly useful in the treatment of **eating disorders, pain syndrome, agoraphobia with panic attack,** and **posttraumatic stress syndrome.**

Table 3-4. Effects of Heterocyclic Antidepressants

Drug	Comments
Imipramine [Tofranil, others]	Strongly anticholinergic *Bed wetting treatment*
Desipramine [Norpramin, others]	Least sedating
Amitriptyline [Elavil, others]	Strongly sedating and anticholinergic
Nortriptyline [Pamelor, others]	Least likely to cause orthostatic hypotension
Amoxapine [Asendin]	Parkinsonian symptoms, galactorrhea, sexual dysfunction; most serious in overdose
Doxepin [Sinequan, Adapin]	Strongly sedating and anticholinergic

2. Mechanism of action

– MAO inhibitors inhibit MAO in an irreversible reaction, **increasing norepinephrine and serotonin availability** at the synaptic cleft.
– At least two **subtypes** of MAO inhibitors exist: **MAO-A** and **MAO-B;** MAO-A is more specific for serotonin and norepinephrine, and MAO-B is more specific for dopamine.

3. Effects and adverse reactions

– MAO inhibitors are as safe as heterocyclics if **dietary precautions** are followed: Ingestion of tyramine-rich foods (beer and wine, broad beans, aged cheese, beef or chicken liver, orange pulp, and smoked or pickled meats or fish) can lead to a **hypertensive crisis** in patients taking MAO inhibitors.
– MAO-Bs are less likely than MAO-As to cause a hypertensive crisis.
– Adverse effects are similar to those of the heterocyclics and include anticholinergic effects, sedation, and cardiac complications.

D. Selective serotonin reuptake inhibitors

– These agents include **fluoxetine** [Prozac], **sertraline** [Zoloft], and **paroxetine** [Paxil].
– They selectively block the reuptake of serotonin but have little effect on dopamine or norepinephrine availability.
– When compared with tricyclic antidepressants, they are equivalent in efficacy, have **minimal anticholinergic** and **cardiovascular adverse effects**, and may cause **weight loss.**

E. Other antidepressants

– **Trazodone** [Desyrel] is less anticholinergic and has a greater margin of safety than other antidepressants. It may be used as an adjunct to tricyclic agents.
– **Alprazolam** [Xanax] has antidepressant activity but is used mainly as an antianxiety agent.

F. Drugs used to treat mania

1. Lithium

– Although **lithium carbonate** or **lithium citrate** are used primarily to treat the **mania** of bipolar disorder, they also have antidepressant activity. Either form may be used in combination with other antidepressants in patients with unipolar disorder.
– The mechanism of action is uncertain.
– Adverse effects from chronic use of lithium include **renal dysfunction, cardiac conduction abnormalities, gastric distress, tremor, mild cognitive impairment, hypothyroidism, and congenital anomalies.**
– Accurate blood levels of lithium must be maintained.

2. Carbamazepine and other anticonvulsants

– **Carbamazepine**, used to treat mania, may be associated with severe adverse effects such as **aplastic anemia** and **agranulocytosis**.
– Other anticonvulsants, including **valproic acid** [Depakene, Depakote] and **clonazepam** [Klonopin], are also effective in treating mania.
– **Valproic acid** may be particularly useful for treating bipolar symptoms resulting from an organic brain syndrome or in bipolar disorder characterized by **rapid mood changes** (rapid cycling).

IV. Antianxiety Agents

A. Classification

– **Antianxiety agents** (also known as anxiolytics or minor tranquilizers) include the following classes: benzodiazepine, carbamate, azaspirodecanedione, and barbiturate.

B. Benzodiazepines

– These drugs can be short-, intermediate-, or long-acting and may also be used to treat disorders other than anxiety disorders (Table 3-5).
– Benzodiazepines commonly cause **sedation**; less common adverse effects include blurred vision, weakness, nausea and vomiting.
– **Tolerance and dependence** may occur with chronic use of these drugs.

C. Carbamates

– These drugs include meprobamate, ethinamate, and carisoprodol, which have been used in the past as anxiolytics.
– They have **more potential for abuse** and are more likely to induce dependence than the benzodiazepines.
– Carbamate therapy is indicated only when use of benzodiazepines is not possible.

D. Azaspirodecanediones

– **Buspirone** [BuSpar], an azaspirodecanedione, is unrelated to the benzodiazepines.
– It is unique among anxiolytics in that it is **nonsedating** and is **not associated with dependence, abuse, or withdrawal** problems.

E. Barbiturates

– Barbiturates have **greater potential for abuse** and a **lower therapeutic index** (the ratio of minimum toxic dose to maximum effective dose) than the benzodiazepines; they are thus less frequently used as antianxiety drugs.
– Adverse effects include sedation and respiratory depression; **overdose** of barbiturates may be **lethal**.
– **Tolerance and dependence** develop with chronic use.

Table 3-5. Characteristics of Benzodiazepines

Drug	Duration of Action	Other Uses
Midazolam [Versed]	Short	Anesthesia
Oxazepam [Serax]	Short	Alcohol withdrawal
Triazolam [Halcion]	Short	Insomnia
Alprazolam [Xanax]	Intermediate	Antidepressant, panic attacks
Clonazepam [Klonopin]	Intermediate	Seizures, mania, panic attacks
Lorazepam [Ativan]	Intermediate	Psychotic agitation
Chlordiazepoxide [Librium]	Long	Alcohol withdrawal
Diazepam [Valium]	Long	Muscle relaxant, analgesia
Flurazepam [Dalmane]	Long	Insomnia
Halazepam [Paxipam]	Long	. . .
Prazepam [Centrax]	Long	. . .
Temazepam [Restoril]	Long	Insomnia

V. Electroconvulsive Therapy (ECT)

A. Uses of ECT

- ECT is an effective and safe treatment for some psychiatric disturbances. It is most commonly used to treat **major depression**; it may be indicated for acute mania and schizophrenia with acute, catatonic, or affective symptoms.
- ECT involves inducing a generalized seizure by passing an electric current across the brain.
- It may alter neurotransmitter function in a manner similar to that of treatment with antidepressant drugs.
- Signs of improvement typically begin after a few ECT treatments. A maximum response to ECT is usually seen after 5–10 treatments.

B. Problems associated with ECT

- Most problems associated with ECT, such as broken bones, have been virtually eliminated with judicious use of **general anesthesia** and **muscle relaxants** administered prior to treatment.
- Unilateral electrode placement has also reduced problems.
- The major adverse effect of ECT is **retrograde amnesia** for past events. In most patients being treated with ECT, memory impairment resolves 6 months after treatment concludes.
- The mortality rate associated with ECT is comparable to that associated with the induction of general anesthesia.

Review Test

Directions: Each of the numbered items or incomplete statements in this section is followed by answers or by completions of the statement. Select the **one** lettered answer or completion that is **best** in each case.

1. The antipsychotic drug producing the greatest sedative effect is

(A) haloperidol
(B) chlorpromazine
(C) perphenazine
(D) thioridazine
(E) trifluoperazine

2. A 45-year-old male employed as an air traffic controller presents for treatment of depression. Which of the following heterocyclic agents is least likely to cause sedation in this patient?

(A) Desipramine
(B) Imipramine
(C) Amitriptyline
(D) Doxepin
(E) Amoxapine

3. Which of the following statements about the characteristics of tardive dyskinesia is true?

(A) It is more common in men than in women
(B) It includes abnormal movements of the tongue
(C) It usually occurs within 3 months of beginning drug treatment
(D) It occurs more often in treatment using clozapine than treatment using other antipsychotic agents
(E) It is a consequence of antidepressant drug treatment

4. Parkinsonian-like symptoms are associated mainly with which one of the following antidepressants?

(A) Desipramine
(B) Imipramine
(C) Amitriptyline
(D) Amoxapine
(E) Nortriptyline

5. Which of the following statements about electroconvulsive therapy (ECT) is true?

(A) The most common indication is in the treatment of schizophrenia
(B) It involves induction of a generalized seizure
(C) It is associated with considerable risk
(D) It is an effective treatment for anxiety
(E) Maximum response is usually seen after two to four treatments

6. A 25-year-old patient who has taken haloperidol for the past 2 years is brought to the hospital with a temperature of 104° F, blood pressure of 190/110, and muscular rigidity. What is the most likely diagnosis?

(A) Tardive dyskinesia
(B) Negative symptoms of schizophrenia
(C) Adverse effect of antipsychotic drug therapy
(D) Adverse effect of antidepressant drug therapy
(E) Massive overdose of haloperidol

7. Which of the following statements about the characteristics of antidepressant agents is true?

(A) They structurally resemble the anxiolytic agents
(B) They frequently induce euphoria in nondepressed patients
(C) They rarely have anticholinergic effects
(D) The heterocyclics block reuptake of serotonin at the synapse
(E) A common side effect of heterocyclic agents is weight loss

8. Which one of the following statements about MAO inhibitors is true?

(A) The inhibition of MAO is reversible
(B) MAO inhibitors are used to treat depression
(C) Adverse effects of MAO inhibitors are distinct from those of heterocyclic agents
(D) MAO-Bs are more likely than MAO-As to cause a hypertensive crisis

9. A patient with bipolar disorder is being treated with lithium. Which adverse effect is this patient least likely to experience?

(A) Cardiac conduction abnormalities
(B) Gastric distress
(C) Tremor
(D) Mild cognitive impairment
(E) Food allergy

10. Antipsychotic agents are usually associated with all of the following adverse effects EXCEPT

(A) orthostatic hypotension
(B) dry mouth
(C) amenorrhea
(D) weight loss
(E) breast enlargement

11. Which of the following antipsychotic agents is least likely to cause parkinsonian effects?

(A) Chlorpromazine
(B) Haloperidol
(C) Perphenazine
(D) Trifluoperazine
(E) Pimozide

Directions: The group of items in this section consists of lettered options followed by a set of numbered items. For each item, select the **one** lettered option that is most closely associated with it. Each lettered option may be selected once, more than once, or not at all.

Questions 12–15

Match the indication or contraindication with the appropriate agent.

(A) Buspirone
(B) Diazepam
(C) Haloperidol
(D) Chlorpromazine
(E) Lithium
(F) Fluoxetine
(G) Amoxapine

12. Heterocyclic antidepressant to be avoided in suicidal patients

13. Antidepressant that is particularly useful in overweight patients

14. Used mainly to treat mania

15. Antianxiety agent that is particularly useful in patients with a history of abuse of antianxiety drugs

Answers and Explanations

1–B. Chlorpromazine is the most sedating of the antipsychotic drugs.

2–A. Desipramine is the agent least likely to cause sedation. Imipramine, amitriptyline, doxepin, and amoxapine all cause sedation.

3–B. Tardive dyskinesia includes abnormal tongue movements, is more common in women than in men, and usually occurs after 6 months of treatment with an antipsychotic drug. Clozapine is associated with fewer motor problems (e.g., tardive dyskinesia) than the neuroleptic agents.

4–D. Treatment with amoxapine may result in parkinsonian-like symptoms.

5–B. ECT involves induction of a seizure. It is most commonly indicated in the treatment of major depression.

6–C. Neuroleptic malignant syndrome (including high fever, sweating, increased pulse and blood pressure, and muscular rigidity) is a serious adverse effect of treatment with neuroleptic agents. The mortality rate with this syndrome is 15%–25%.

7–D. The heterocyclic antidepressants block reuptake of serotonin and norepinephrine at the synapse.

8–B. MAO inhibitors are used to treat depression and may also be useful in treating eating disorders, pain, panic attacks, and posttraumatic stress disorder.

9–E. Cardiac conduction abnormalities, gastric distress, and tremor are common adverse effects of lithium treatment. Food allergy is not an adverse effect of lithium use.

10–D. Orthostatic hypotension, dry mouth, amenorrhea, breast enlargement, and weight gain (not weight loss) are adverse effects of the antipsychotic drugs.

11–A. Chlorpromazine, a low-potency antipsychotic, is less likely to cause parkinsonism, a neurologic adverse effect.

12–G. Amoxapine [Asendin] is the most dangerous antidepressant in overdose.

13–F. Fluoxetine [Prozac] is associated with weight loss.

14–E. Lithium is used mainly to treat mania.

15–A. Buspirone [BuSpar] is a nonsedating antianxiety agent with less potential for abuse than benzodiazepines.

4

Beginning of Life, Growth, and Development

I. Pregnancy

A. Conception

– Child development begins at conception and is influenced by factors that occur during pregnancy and childbirth as well as postnatal life.

– Approximately 90% of children result from **planned pregnancies**.

B. Emotions

– A woman's sense of **maternal competence** is strongly influenced by her own mother as a role model.

– **Mood swings** are common during pregnancy.

– Concerns over loss of physical attractiveness increase as pregnancy progresses.

– **Pseudocyesis (false pregnancy)**, accompanied by many symptoms of pregnancy, may occur in women who have a strong wish to be pregnant or a strong fear of pregnancy.

C. Sexuality

– Some pregnant women have an **increased sex drive**, possibly due to pelvic vasocongestion.

– In other women, **sex drive may be reduced** because of physical discomfort, the association of motherhood with decreased sexual activity, or fears of harming the fetus.

– Diminution of sexual activity can put a strain on the marriage.

– **Husbands' extramarital affairs**, if they occur, are most likely during the last three months of the wife's pregnancy.

– Many obstetricians suggest cessation of sexual intercourse about four weeks prior to the expected date of delivery.

D. Teenage pregnancy

– Teenage pregnancy is a severe social problem in the United States; American teenagers give birth to about 600,000 babies and have about 400,000 abortions annually.

– Nearly 50% of **unmarried mothers** are teenagers.

– **First sexual intercourse** in the United States occurs on average at **16 years** of age; by age 19, 80% of males and 70% of females have had sexual intercourse.

– Teenagers are **erratic** in the use of **contraceptives**.

- Numerous factors predispose adolescent girls to pregnancy, including depression, low academic achievement and goals, poor planning for the future, and divorced parents.
- Pregnant teenagers are at high risk for **obstetric complications**.

II. Childbirth

A. Birth rate and infant mortality

- The birth rate in the United States was approximately 16 per 1000 population in 1989 (3,830,000 babies born).
- The rate of **cesarean birth** increased from 5% in the 1960s to 20% in the 1980s, partly because of physicians' fears of malpractice suits.
- The United States ranks twentieth in the world in infant mortality; the rate was **9.2 per 1000** live births in **1990**.
- **Low socioeconomic status** correlates with high infant mortality.
- The mortality rate for black infants is 2.4 times higher than that for white infants; the mortality rate for Native American infants is 14.4 per 1000. For Chinese-American and Japanese-American infants, the mortality rate is 7.6 and 6.4 per 1000, respectively.

B. Prematurity

- Prematurity is defined as **gestation of less than 34 weeks** or **birth weight under 2500 g**.
- Prematurity occurs in about 7% of all births and correlates with teenage pregnancy, low socioeconomic status, and poor maternal nutrition.
- Prematurity puts the child at greater risk of emotional and behavioral problems, mental retardation, learning problems such as dyslexia, and child abuse.

C. The mother-infant relationship

- **Bonding** between mother and infant may be adversely affected if the child is of **low birth weight**, is **ill**, is **separated from the mother** after delivery, or if there are problems in the mother-father relationship.
- Women **prepared for childbirth** by such training regimens as Dick-Read's "natural childbirth" or Lamaze's "psychoprophylactic childbirth" have shorter labors and fewer medical complications, need less medication, and have better initial relationships with their infants.

D. Postpartum reactions

- One-third to one-half of women develop a short-lived depressed mood known as **baby blues** or **postpartum blues** following the birth of a child. Postpartum blues result from changes in hormone levels, the stress of childbirth, awareness of increased responsibility, disappointment over the child's appearance, and fatigue.
- **Major depression** affects 5%–10% of women after childbirth. About 0.1%–0.2% of these severely depressed women will develop a **postpartum psychosis** characterized by hallucinations or delusions and severe anxiety.
- Social factors related to long-lasting postpartum reactions include **lack of child care experience** and **lack of social support** from husband and relatives.

III. Infancy: Birth to 15 Months

A. Attachment

– The principal psychological task of infancy is the **formation of an intimate attachment** to the mother or primary caregiver.

1. Separation of mother and infant

– If separated from the mother or primary caregiver between 6–12 months of age, the child initially protests loudly at the loss.
– With continued absence of the mother, the infant is at risk for **anaclitic depression,** in which the infant becomes **withdrawn** and **unresponsive**.

2. Studies of attachment

    a. Harry Harlow demonstrated that infant monkeys reared in relative isolation by **surrogate artificial mothers** do not develop normal mating, maternal, and social behaviors as adults.

        – **Males** may be **more affected** than females by such isolation.
        – Young monkeys raised in isolation for less than 6 months can be rehabilitated by playing with normal young monkeys.
        – **No recovery** is possible if young monkeys are **isolated** for **more than 6 months.**

    b. John Bowlby demonstrated that maintenance of a continuous relationship, including **physical contact** between mother and infant, is crucial to the child's development.

    c. René Spitz documented that children without proper mothering (such as those in institutions) show severe **developmental retardation, poor health,** and higher death rates (**"hospitalism"**) in spite of adequate physical care.

B. Characteristics of the infant

1. Physical development

– At birth, the infant possesses simple reflexes such as the **startle** reflex (Moro's reflex), the **palmar grasp** reflex, **Babinski's** reflex, and the **rooting** reflex.
– These reflexes disappear at 2 months (palmar grasp), between 3–6 months (Moro's), and at 12 months (Babinski's).
– Turning over typically occurs at about 5 months, sitting alone at 6 months, and walking unassisted at 12 months of age.

2. Social development

    a. At birth, infants can visually follow (track) a human face; **socialization** of the child thus begins **at birth.**

    b. Although there is a reflexive smile present at birth, the **social smile** that develops between **5–8 weeks** of age is one of the first markers of the infant's responsiveness and attachment to another individual.

    c. Stranger anxiety is the infant's tendency to cry and cling to the mother when a stranger approaches.

        – In normal infants, stranger anxiety develops between **7–9 months** of age and signals the infant's specific attachment to the mother and the ability to distinguish her from a stranger.
        – Infants exposed to multiple caregivers are less likely to show stranger anxiety than those exposed to only one caregiver.

Table 4-1. Stages of Human Development: Major Theorists

| Age (years) | Stage | | | Characteristics |
	Freud	Erikson	Piaget	
0–1	Oral	Basic trust vs mistrust	Sensorimotor (0–2 years)	Stranger anxiety
1–3	Anal	Autonomy vs shame and doubt	Preoperational (2–7 years)	Separation anxiety
3–5	Phallic-oedipal	Initiative vs guilt	Preoperational (2–7 years)	Imaginary companions
6–11	Latency *sch..of age*	Industry vs inferiority	*speci fr* Concrete operations (7–11 years)	Logical thought
11–20	Genital *Adolescence*	Identity vs diffusion	Formal operations role (11–20 years)	Abstract thought *general principles*

C. Individual differences

– It is likely that there are **endogenous differences** in infants in **temperament** and reactivity to stimuli.
– Differences between infants have been described in activity level, cyclic behavior patterns such as sleeping, approach or withdrawal to new stimuli, adaptability, reactivity, responsiveness, mood, distractibility, and attention span.
– In many people, these differences are quite stable for the first 25 years.

D. Developmental theorists (Table 4-1)

1. Sigmund Freud and Erik Erikson

– According to Freud, the major site of gratification for the child during the first year of life is the **mouth** (**oral phase**).
– Erik Erikson noted that children establish a sense of **basic trust versus** a sense of **mistrust** by the end of the first year.
– In order to establish trust, a child must have the expectation that its basic needs will be taken care of and that it can rely on its caregivers to respond to its signals in a fairly consistent manner.

2. Margaret Mahler

– Margaret Mahler described early development as a sequential process of separation from the mother or primary caregiver.

a. Normal autistic phase (0–1 month)

– In this stage, the infant has little interaction with the environment.

b. Symbiotic phase (1–5 months)

– The infant shares a sense of oneness with the mother or caregiver.

c. Separation-individuation phase (5–16 months)

– The first phase of separation-individuation is the **period of differentiation** from 5–9 months when the mother is first perceived as a separate individual.
– In the **practicing phase**, which occurs from 10–16 months, the child moves away from the mother but returns from time to time.

3. Jean Piaget

- Piaget described the period from birth to 2 years as the **sensorimotor stage**. In this phase, mastery of the child's environment comes through **assimilation**, the ability to understand new stimuli in the environment, and **accommodation**, the ability to alter one's behavior when a new stimulus is presented.
- The capacity to maintain internal representations without currently seeing the object, **object permanence**, develops between 12–24 months of age.

IV. The Toddler Years: 15 Months to 2½ Years

A. Attachment

- The **major theme** of the second year of life is to **separate from the mother** or primary caregiver.

1. The child develops physical and emotional distance from the mother and begins to behave like a separate person by about 18 months of age; however, the process of separation-individuation is not complete until about age 3.

2. Mahler called the period of moving away and returning for comfort and reassurance from 16–24 months **rapprochement**.

3. **Separation anxiety** peaks at 18 months.

B. Characteristics of the toddler

- The second year of life is characterized by increasing physical and intellectual development.
- With increasing control over his or her actions at about age 2, "**the terrible twos**," the child becomes increasingly autonomous; the **favorite word** is "**no**."
- **Toilet training** often occurs at about age 2 and can be a source of parent-child conflict.
- **Core gender identity**, an individual's sense of being male or female, is established between 18–30 months of age.

C. Developmental theorists

1. Erikson

- This age (15 months to 2½ years) is Erikson's stage of **autonomy versus shame and doubt**: the child resolves its internal desires for independence with parental control.
- The term autonomy is used when the child has command of his impulses and has achieved separateness from the mother.
- If autonomy is not achieved because of excessive parental control, the child will feel that the outside world looks down on him or her (shame).

2. Freud

- The **anal stage** of development, as described by Freud, occurs during the toddler years.

V. The Preschool Child: 2½ to 6 Years

A. Characteristics

- The child reaches half of adult height between 2 and 3 years of age.
- The child's **vocabulary increases** rapidly.

– The birth of a sibling is likely to occur in the preschool years; although the child may learn cooperation and sharing with a new sibling, **sibling rivalry** may also occur.

B. Fears

– The child can distinguish fantasy from reality, although the line between them may still not be drawn sharply.
– Sleep disturbances such as **nightmares** are common at this age.
– The child may also develop **transient phobias** such as fears of robbers or monsters.
– Preschool children may become overly concerned about illness and may point out every injury (**the "Band-Aid" phase**).

C. Sexuality

1. Children 2½–6 years of age are very interested in physical sex differences; children act out fantasies about sex differences in **games of "doctor."**

2. Freud called this period of development the **phallic** or **oedipal stage**.
   – The genitals become a focus of pleasure.
   – The **oedipal conflict** arises and involves strong feelings of rivalry with the same-sex parent and love for the parent of the opposite sex.
   – This stage is resolved when the child begins to identify with the same-sex parent.

D. Formation of the conscience

– By the end of the preschool years, the child's **conscience** (the **superego** of Freud) begins to form.
– With the development of the conscience, the child learns how he is allowed to behave.
– The child also learns that aggressive impulses can be used in acceptable ways such as playing competitive games.

1. Erikson

– Erikson termed this period the stage of **initiative versus guilt**; the child begins to take risks, although there may be fear of punishment and a sense of guilt.
– If the stage of initiative is resolved successfully, the child is more likely to become a dependable, self-disciplined, and responsible adult.

2. Piaget

– Piaget considered this stage to be the beginning of the **preoperational phase** (ages 2–7 years), the period when the child begins to think in symbolic terms.
– Laurence Kohlberg described the development of **morality** in children based on Piaget's cognitive stages.

E. Play in the preschool child

– **Role playing** is important to children of this age.
– While 2-year-old children play alongside each other in **parallel play**, by age 4, they begin to play cooperatively with others.
– Among children 3–10 years of age, almost half have **imaginary companions** which help to decrease loneliness and anxiety.

VI. Latency or School Age: 7 to 11 Years (Puberty)

A. Characteristics

- The child develops the ability to perform complex motor tasks and activities.
- Formation of the **conscience** is completed.
- The child acquires the capacity for logical thought (Piaget's **stage of concrete operations**).
- The demands for **success in school** are important to further personality development.
- The child acquires a sense of whether he is competent or not competent in interactions with the world (Erikson's stage of **industry versus inferiority**).

B. The family and the outside world

- The child makes new identifications with teachers and group leaders.
- Family becomes less important and the outside world, including **peers, becomes more important**.

C. Sexuality

- Psychosexual issues are not of primary importance during latency.
- The child identifies with the same-sex parent and no longer wants the opposite-sex parent as a love object.
- Latency-age children prefer to **play with children of the same sex**.

VII. Adolescence: 11 to 20 Years

A. Characteristics

- Adolescence is distinguished biologically by **puberty**, a process marked by **menarche** in girls, the **first ejaculation** in boys, development of secondary sex characteristics, and acceleration in skeletal growth.
- Psychologically, adolescence is identified by cognitive growth and **formation of the personality**; socially, adolescence is a time of preparation for entering the adult world and accepting adult responsibilities.
- Adolescence is Erikson's stage of **identity consolidation versus role confusion**, in which a sense of an independent self is developed.
- Strong sexual impulses and attempts at independence occur.

B. Phases of adolescence

1. Early adolescence (11–14 years)

- Dramatic **endocrine changes** occur; girls mature at about 12 years of age, two years before boys.
- Early adolescents are very sensitive to the opinions of peers.
- Any **alteration in expected patterns** of development, such as acne, obesity, or late breast development, may lead to psychological problems.
- Sex drives are released by **masturbation** and **physical activity**.

2. Middle adolescence (14–17 years)

- Male-female roles, body image, and popularity often preoccupy the adolescent.
- At this stage, boys equal and exceed girls in height and weight.
- Most girls have reached menarche.
- Heterosexual **crushes** commonly occur.
- **Homosexual experiences** may occur.

3. **Late adolescence (17–20 years)**
   – In most individuals, moral and ethical sense and control of one's behavior develop by late adolescence.
   a. According to Piaget, by late adolescence many individuals have developed the ability for abstract reasoning (**stage of formal operations**).
      – Most adults function between Piaget's stages of concrete operations and formal operations.
   b. Concern with **humanitarian issues, ethics,** and world problems occurs in late adolescence.
   c. Normally, an **identity crisis** develops during late adolescence; if this stage is not handled successfully, the adolescent does not have a strong identity and suffers from **identity diffusion** or **role confusion.**
      – With role confusion, an individual does not have a sense of himself and does not know where he belongs in the world.
      – Behavioral abnormalities such as **criminality** may occur; the adolescent may also manifest interest in **cults**.

VIII. Illness and Death in Childhood
   – A child's reaction to illness is closely associated with the developmental stage.

A. Toddlers and preschoolers
   – During the **toddler years,** hospitalized children **fear separation** from the parent more than they fear bodily harm, death, or pain.
   – During the **preschool years** (Freud's phallic stage), the child becomes more **fearful of bodily harm** (such as castration).
   – The preschool-age child may not fully understand the meaning of death and may expect that a dead friend or relative will come back to life.

B. School-age children and adolescents
   – **School-age children** are often aware when they have a life-threatening illness.
      – Because school-age children cope with hospitalization relatively well, this is the **best age to perform elective surgery.**
   – **Adolescents** may challenge the authority of doctors and nurses and **not comply with medical advice.**

IX. Child Abuse

A. Incidence and characteristics (Table 4-2)
   – Child abuse includes **physical and sexual abuse** as well as **emotional neglect** such as harsh rejection and severe withholding of parental love and attention.
   – Reported child abuse is increasing in the United States.
   – Parents typically perceive the children they abuse as slow, different, bad, or difficult to control.

B. Evidence of physical abuse
   – Specific evidence of child abuse includes **belt marks,** old **healed fractures, cigarette burns, bruises on buttocks or lower back,** and **subdural hematomas.**

C. Sexual abuse
   – Sexual abuse of children, both male and female, has become more common (see Table 4-2).

Table 4-2. Characteristics of Physical and Sexual Child Abuse

Characteristics	Physical Abuse	Sexual Abuse
Incidence per year	1,000,000; 2000–4000 deaths	200,000
Abuser	Usually female	Usually male and known to the victim (father, stepfather, other relatives, friends); less commonly strangers
Age of child	32% under age 5 years 27% age 5–9 years 27% age 10–14 years 14% age 15–18 years	Highest incidence at 9–12 years 25% under age 8
High risk factors	Poverty Social isolation Substance abuse Parents abused as children Prematurity, low birth weight Hyperactivity	Single-parent home Marital problems Substance abuse Sick mother Crowded living conditions

- Evidence of sexual abuse includes **genital or anal trauma, sexually transmitted disease,** and **urinary tract infection**.
- Although the individual may not remember that the abuse took place, sexual abuse predisposes the child to later anxiety, phobias, depression, and an inability to deal with his own and others' aggression.

D. Physician's role in child abuse cases
- When child neglect or abuse is suspected, the **physician should intervene,** report the case to the appropriate agency, admit the child to the hospital when necessary, confer with members of the child abuse committee, and arrange for follow-up by social service agencies.

Review Test

Directions: Each of the numbered items or incomplete statements in this section is followed by answers or by completions of the statement. Select the **one** lettered answer or completion that is **best** in each case.

1. Which of the following developmental signposts normally appears first in the infant?

(A) Stranger anxiety
(B) Social smile
(C) Rapprochement
(D) Core gender identity
(E) Phobias

2. The infant mortality rate in 1990 in the United States was about

(A) 1 per 1000 live births
(B) 5 per 1000 live births
(C) 9 per 1000 live births
(D) 21 per 1000 live births
(E) 40 per 1000 live births

3. A physician evaluates a mother who has not bonded properly with her 18-month-old child. All of the following factors are likely to cause this problem EXCEPT

(A) separation of mother and child after delivery
(B) problems in the mother-father relationship
(C) a pregnancy that is longer than the expected term
(D) low-birth weight
(E) illness in the child

4. The principal psychological task of infancy is the

(A) formation of an intimate attachment to the mother
(B) development of speech
(C) development of stranger anxiety
(D) development of a conscience
(E) ability for logical thought

5. A 10-year-old girl is least likely to show which of the following characteristics?

(A) Formation of her conscience is complete
(B) Capacity for logical thought
(C) Identification with her mother
(D) Her family, rather than friends, is more important to her
(E) She plays mainly with other girls

6. Which of the following characteristics of adolescence is true?

(A) The sense of an independent self develops
(B) The end of adolescence is marked by puberty
(C) Crushes are uncommon
(D) It is Erikson's stage of industry versus inferiority
(E) Identity crises frequently develop at its start

7. Women preparing for childbirth with a formal training regimen typically experience

(A) more medical complications
(B) longer labors
(C) better initial relationships with their infants
(D) more need for medication

8. A new mother develops a mildly depressed mood 2 days following the birth of her child. All of the following factors are involved in the development of this condition EXCEPT

(A) changes in hormone levels
(B) breast feeding
(C) awareness of increased responsibility
(D) stress of childbirth
(E) fatigue

9. Which of the following statements about postpartum reaction is true?

(A) Postpartum blues occurs in about 10% of women
(B) Major depression occurs in about 25% of women after childbirth
(C) Postpartum psychosis occurs in about 8% of women
(D) Lack of social support is common in postpartum reactions
(E) Experience in child care is not related to the occurrence of postpartum reactions

10. A 10-month-old child is separated from his mother for a period of 2 months. Which of the following responses is the child least likely to manifest at this time?

(A) Loud protests at the loss
(B) Lack of responsiveness to others
(C) Physical illness
(D) Anaclitic depression
(E) Developmental retardation

11. Which of the following statements about illness in childhood is true?

(A) Toddlers frequently fear bodily harm more than they fear separation from parents
(B) Preschool children usually understand the meaning of death
(C) Preschool children frequently believe that a dead person will come back to life
(D) Older children are rarely aware that they have a life-threatening illness
(E) School age is a poor time for performing elective surgery

12. Which of the following statements about stranger anxiety is true?

(A) It develops at 1–2 months of age
(B) It reaches a peak at 3–4 months of age
(C) It indicates that the child is emotionally disturbed
(D) It is more likely to occur in infants exposed to multiple caregivers
(E) It occurs in normal infants

13. A 2-year-old girl is likely to show all of the following attributes EXCEPT

(A) she is in Erikson's stage of industry versus inferiority
(B) she shows increasing motor development
(C) toilet training usually takes place
(D) core gender identity is established
(E) the favorite word is "no"

14. Which of the following developments is characteristic of a child 4 years of age?

(A) Fantasy cannot be distinguished from reality
(B) Nightmares rarely occur
(C) The child begins to think abstractly
(D) Imaginary companions are common
(E) The child is not aware of physical sex differences

15. The physician discovers that a 15-year-old patient is pregnant. All of the following risk factors are likely to be characteristic of this patient EXCEPT

(A) depression
(B) low academic goals
(C) living in a rural area
(D) parents are divorced
(E) poor planning for the future

16. All of the following are risk factors for the physical abuse of children EXCEPT

(A) parents have been abused as children
(B) being the oldest child in the family
(C) poverty
(D) the child was premature at birth
(E) social isolation

17. A 23-year-old woman reveals that she was sexually abused by her stepfather at the age of 8. All of the following problems are likely to characterize this young woman as an adult EXCEPT

(A) depression
(B) anxiety
(C) phobias
(D) inability to deal with the aggression of others
(E) clear memories of the abuse

Directions: Each group of items in this section consists of lettered options followed by a set of numbered items. For each item, select the **one** lettered option that is most closely associated with it. Each lettered option may be selected once, more than once, or not at all.

Questions 18–27

Match the phrase with the developmental theorist with which it is most closely associated.

(A) Freud
(B) Erikson
(C) Piaget
(D) Mahler

18. Separation-individuation

19. Trust versus mistrust

20. Assimilation and accommodation

21. Stage of symbiotic development

22. Oral phase

23. Period of differentiation

24. Practicing phase

25. Sensorimotor stage

26. Normal autistic phase

27. Object permanence

Questions 28–31

Match the developmental milestone with the age at which it commonly first appears.

(A) 0–3 months
(B) 5–7 months
(C) 8–12 months
(D) 12–18 months
(E) 18–24 months

28. Sitting unassisted

29. Stranger anxiety

30. Visual tracking

31. The social smile

Answers and Explanations

1–B. The social smile is the first developmental milestone to appear in the infant.

2–C. In 1990, the infant mortality rate in the United States was about 9 per 1000 live births.

3–C. The initial bonding between mother and child can be adversely affected by illness of the child, low birth weight, separation of mother and child, and problems in the mother-father relationship. There is no evidence that a pregnancy that is longer than term adversely affects bonding.

4–A. The principal psychological task of infancy is the formation of an intimate attachment to the mother.

5–D. During latency, peers become more important to the child and the family becomes less important.

6–A. In adolescence, the sense of an independent self develops. Identity crises frequently develop during late, not early, adolescence.

7–C. Women preparing for childbirth with a formal training regimen typically experience shorter labors, fewer medical complications, better immediate relations with their infants, and less need for medication.

8–B. Breast feeding usually is not a contributing factor in developing a mildly depressed mood after childbirth. Changes in hormone levels, fatigue, stress of childbirth, and awareness of increased responsibility do contribute to the development of a mildly depressed mood, otherwise known as the "baby blues."

9–D. Lack of social support is common in postpartum reactions. Although postpartum blues may occur in one-third to one-half of women, postpartum psychosis is rare and occurs in less than 1% of women after childbirth. *30 to 50%*   *< 1%*

10–A. Loud protests occur initially when the mother leaves the child. With her continued absence of over 2 months, the child suffers more serious consequences.

11–C. Preschool children cannot usually comprehend the meaning of death and may believe that the dead person will come back to life. Older children frequently are aware when they have a life-threatening illness.

12–E. Stranger anxiety develops in normal infants at 7–9 months of age and is seen less frequently in children exposed to multiple caregivers.

13–A. The toddler years are Erikson's stage of autonomy versus shame and doubt.

14–D. In the preschool child fantasy can be distinguished from reality, although the line between them may not be sharply drawn. Imaginary companions are quite common at this stage.

15–C. Teenagers who become pregnant frequently are from homes where the parents are divorced, are depressed, show poor planning for the future, and have low academic goals. Studies have not indicated that living in a rural area is related to teenage pregnancy.

16–B. Social isolation, parents abused as children, poverty, and prematurity are high risk factors in people who physically abuse their children. Being the oldest child in the family is not relevant to child abuse.

17–E. Depression, anxiety, phobias, and an inability to deal with aggression both in others and oneself are characteristics of adults who have been sexually abused as children.

18–D. The stage of separation-individuation, as described by Margaret Mahler, occurs during infancy and follows the symbiotic phase.

19–B. Erik Erikson noted that children establish a sense of trust or mistrust by the end of the first year of life.

20–C. During Piaget's sensorimotor stage, mastery of the child's environment is achieved through assimilation and accommodation.

21–D. Mahler's symbiotic stage occurs from 1–5 months of age.

22–A. According to Freud, the oral phase occurs during the first year of life.

23–D. According to Mahler, the first phase of separation-individuation is the period of differentiation.

24–D. According to Mahler, the second phase of separation-individuation is the practicing phase.

25–C. Piaget described the period from 0–2 years of age as the sensorimotor stage.

26–D. Mahler described the period from 0–1 month of age as the normal autistic phase.

27–C. According to Piaget, object permanence develops at 18 months to 2 years of age. *12" " 24 months*

28–B. Infants can usually sit unassisted at about 6 months of age.

29–C. Stranger anxiety begins at about 8 months of age.

30–A. Infants can visually track a human face from birth.

31–A. The social smile first appears at 5–7 weeks of age.

5

Adulthood, Aging, and Death

I. Early Adulthood: 20 to 40 Years

A. Characteristics

- In early adulthood, one's role in society is defined, biologic development reaches its peak, and the independent self develops.
- At about **age 30**, there is a **period of reappraisal** of one's life. According to Daniel Levinson, this is an age of transition.

B. Responsibilities and relationships

- Responsibilities of early adulthood include **development of an intimate relationship** with another person.
- According to **Erikson**, this is the stage of **intimacy versus isolation**; if the individual does not develop the ability to nurture an intimate relationship, he or she suffers emotional isolation.
- By age 30, most people are married and have children.
- During their middle thirties, many women alter their lifestyles by returning to work or school or by resuming their careers.

II. Middle Adulthood: 40 to 65 Years

A. Characteristics

- Erikson noted that the individual either maintains a continued sense of productivity or develops a sense of emptiness and stagnation (**generativity versus stagnation**).
- People of this age group generally are the members of society who possess **power** and **authority**.
- For many people, middle adulthood is a time of great satisfaction.
- George Vaillant noted that happiness at age 65 was related to having a **happy childhood** and the use of **mature defense mechanisms** (see Chapter 6).

B. Midlife crisis

- According to Daniel Levinson, **age 50–55** is another period of transition; a crisis may occur if the person is unable to change a life pattern that he finds unendurable.

1. As many as 70%–80% of men in their middle forties or early fifties show a moderate to significant change in **work** or **marital relationships**.
   - These changes include changing professions, infidelity, severe depression, increased use of alcohol or drugs, or a change in lifestyle.
   - Although studies are not as complete, they do indicate that women may also experience a midlife crisis.
2. The midlife crisis is associated with an **awareness of one's own aging and death**.
3. **Severe or unexpected changes in one's life** at this time (such as the death of a spouse, job loss, or serious illness) predispose an individual toward a midlife crisis.
4. Characteristics of men or women likely to have a midlife crisis include problems between their own parents, anxiety, impulsiveness, and withdrawal of the same-sex parent during the individual's adolescence.

C. **Climacterium and menopause**
   - The **climacterium** is the diminution in physiologic function that occurs during midlife in men and women.
1. For men, the climacterium is mainly psychological rather than physical, although decreases in muscle strength, endurance, and sexual performance occur.
2. For women, **menopause** is the climacterium and usually occurs gradually during the **late forties or early fifties**.
   - Menopause is characterized by the **cessation** of **menstruation** as a result of lack of ovarian estrogen production.
   - Although some women experience severe psychological symptoms, such as anxiety and depression, **most go through menopause with relatively few problems**.
   - A common physical problem related to menopause is vasomotor instability, or **hot flashes**, which may continue over a number of years.

III. Late Adulthood: 65 Years and Older

A. Demographics
   - In the United States, 80% of people reach 60 years of age.
   - In 1993, 12% of the U.S. population was over 65 years of age; by 2020, this number will exceed 20%.
   - Gerontology, the study of aging, and geriatrics, the care of aging people, have become important new medical disciplines.
   - The life expectancy for **women** is **8 years longer than for men**; because men are often older at marriage, most married women can expect to be widows for about 10 years.

B. Characteristics of aging
   - **Strength and physical health gradually decline.** This decline shows great variability, but aging people typically show impaired immune responses, visual and hearing impairment, decreased muscle mass, increased fat deposits, osteoporosis, decreased blood flow to the gastrointestinal tract, and changes in the brain including decreased weight and enlarged ventricles and sulci.

- Although **intelligence remains approximately the same**, learning in the elderly may be impaired as a result of the effects of physical disease.
- The individual recognizes that all life options are no longer available.
- Loss of friends and family in late adulthood gives the realization of one's finite life span.
- Erikson said of late adulthood that there is a either a sense of ego integrity and satisfaction and pride in one's past accomplishment or a sense of despair and worthlessness (**ego integrity versus despair**). Many elderly people achieve ego integrity.

C. **Depression in aging people**
- **Depression is the most common psychiatric disorder in the elderly**; it occurs to some extent in about 15% of persons age 65 years or older; 3% of these suffer from major depression.
- Depression is not a natural condition of aging.
- Factors associated with depression in the elderly are **loss of spouse, family members, and friends, loss of prestige, and loss of health**.
- **Suicide is twice as common** in the elderly as in the general population.
- Depression in the elderly can be treated successfully with psychotherapy, pharmacotherapy, and electroconvulsive therapy (ECT).

D. **Alzheimer's disease**
- Alzheimer's disease or dementia of the Alzheimer's type causes **severe memory loss, personality changes**, and **cognitive deficits** resulting in overall apathy, cessation of normal functioning, and death.
- Since depression in the elderly is often associated with memory loss, it may mimic Alzheimer's disease (**pseudodementia**).
- Unlike depression, Alzheimer's disease cannot be cured with psychotherapy or pharmacotherapy.

E. **Other disorders of aging**
- Physical illnesses characteristic of aging include **hypertension, heart disease**, and **kidney dysfunction**.
- Elderly people often report **changes in sleep patterns** resulting in poor sleep.
- **Anxiety** related to insecurity and anxiety-producing situations can arise easily in the elderly.
- Psychoactive drugs and other agents often produce different effects in the elderly than in younger patients.

F. **Longevity**
- Longevity has been correlated with numerous factors, including a family history of longevity, work involving physical activity, sleeping about 6–9 hours nightly, advanced education, and suburban (rather than urban) living.
- Longevity is also associated with **marriage**, the availability of strong social support systems, a **calm personality**, and the retention of **occupational activity**.

IV. Death and Dying
- **Thanatology** is the study of death, dying, grief, bereavement, and mourning.

A. **Stages of dying**
- According to **Elizabeth Kübler-Ross**, the process of dying involves five stages.
- The stages may be present simultaneously or may appear in any order.
- Similar stages occur following other losses, such as the loss of a body part.

1. **Denial**: The patient refuses to believe that he or she is dying.

2. **Anger**: The patient may become angry at the physician and hospital staff.

3. **Bargaining**: The patient may try to strike a bargain with God (e.g., "I promise to go to church every day if only I can get rid of this disease").

4. **Depression**: The patient becomes preoccupied with death and may be emotionally detached.

5. **Acceptance**: The patient is calm and accepting of his fate.

B. **Characteristics of grief**

1. Grief is characterized initially by **shock and denial**.

2. In normal grief or bereavement, the bereaved may have a sense that the deceased person is physically present, which may be strong enough to be considered an **illusion** or hallucination.

3. Normal grief generally **subsides after 1–2 years**, although some symptoms may continue longer.
   - **Mild sedatives** to aid in sleeping may be useful for the bereaved, but antidepressant or antianxiety drugs are rarely necessary.
   - Heavy doses of sedative drugs may interfere with the normal grieving process.

4. **Physical expressions** of grief are similar to those of depression and include crying, weakness, decreased appetite, weight loss, difficulty concentrating, and sleep disturbances.
   - Although similar in symptoms, there are differences between normal grief and depression. In grief, guilt and concern about not having done enough for the dead person occur; in depression, feelings of worthlessness and hopelessness predominate.
   - **Suicide** is more common among depressed people than among grieving people.

5. The **mortality rate** is high for close relatives (especially **widowed men**) in the first year of bereavement.

C. **Physician's response to death**
   - The major **responsibility of the physician** is to provide continuing **support** to the dying patient and the patient's family.
   - There is a trend in hospitals to make patient, family, and staff completely aware of the diagnosis and prognosis.
   - Physicians often feel a **sense of failure** at not conquering death, which is often perceived as the enemy. They often become **emotionally detached** in order to deal with the death of patients.

Review Test

Directions: Each of the numbered items or incomplete statements in this section is followed by answers or by completions of the statement. Select the **one** lettered answer or completion that is **best** in each case.

1. A 79-year-old man is brought to a clinic by his wife who complains that he has become forgetful since his best friend died 1 month previously. Which of the following statements best describes this patient?

(A) He probably has Alzheimer's disease
(B) He is probably suffering from depression
(C) He is at decreased risk of suicide when compared with a younger man with the same situation
(D) He cannot be treated effectively with psychoactive drugs
(E) He probably has a decreased IQ

2. A terminally ill patient using statements such as, "It is the doctor's fault that I became ill; she didn't take my blood pressure when I came for my last office visit," is most likely in which stage of dying?

(A) Denial
(B) Anger
(C) Acceptance
(D) Depression
(E) Bargaining

3. Which of the following developmental signposts characterize middle adulthood?

(A) Peak biologic development
(B) Stage of intimacy versus isolation
(C) Stage of ego integrity versus despair
(D) Drastic changes in work relationships in men

4. Men and women at greatest risk of a midlife crisis are most likely raised in families exhibiting all of the following characteristics EXCEPT

(A) impulsiveness
(B) withdrawal of the same-sex parent
(C) anxiety
(D) low socioeconomic status
(E) parental discord

5. Which of the following characteristics of menopause is true?

(A) It occurs suddenly
(B) It is characterized by cessation of menstruation
(C) Severe depression is common
(D) Severe anxiety is common
(E) It usually occurs in the early forties

6. Which of the following statements about the elderly is true?

(A) Suicide is rarer than in the general population
(B) Anxiety due to insecurity is rare
(C) Most of the elderly have a sense of despair or worthlessness
(D) Sleep disturbances are more common than in the general population
(E) Depression is less common in the elderly than in younger people

7. Which of the following responses is characteristic of normal bereavement?

(A) Initial loss of appetite
(B) Feelings of worthlessness
(C) Threats of suicide
(D) Grief lasting 3–4 years after the death of a close friend
(E) Feelings of hopelessness

8. All of the following statements about death and responsibilities and reaction of the physician are true EXCEPT

(A) there is a trend to make patients aware of a diagnosis of terminal illness
(B) the physician is responsible for classifying the cause of death
(C) a role of the physician is to provide strong sedation for close family members until the initial shock wears off
(D) physicians often feel a sense of failure when a patient dies
(E) physicians often become emotionally detached in order to deal with the death of a patient

9. Which of the following statistics regarding late adulthood in the United States is true?

(A) Life expectancy for women is 12 years longer than for men
(B) Most women can expect to be widows for 14 years
(C) Fifty percent of people reach 60 years of age
(D) Approximately 5% of the population is over age 65
(E) By the year 2020, 20% of the population will be over age 65

Answers and Explanations

1–B. Depression is commonly seen in elderly patients and, because of memory loss, this may mimic Alzheimer's disease. The sudden onset of the condition and the concurrent loss of an important friend indicate that the patient is likely to be suffering from depression.

2–B. During the anger stage of dying, the patient is likely to blame the physician.

3–D. Drastic changes in work relationships in men characterize middle adulthood.

4–D. Low socioeconomic status is not related to midlife crisis. However, characteristics of the families of people likely to have a midlife crisis include parental discord, anxiety, impulsiveness, and withdrawal of the same-sex parent during the individual's adolescence.

5–B. Menopause is characterized by cessation of menstruation. Most women go through menopause gradually at about age 50 and with relatively few problems.

6–D. Sleep disturbances commonly occur in the elderly. Suicide is more common in the elderly than in the general population. Anxiety may arise easily due to insecurity. Many elderly people have a sense of satisfaction and pride in their accomplishments.

7–A. Feelings of worthlessness, threats of suicide, and an extended period of grief characterize depression rather than normal bereavement.

8–C. Heavy sedation is rarely indicated as treatment for the bereaved because it may interfere with the grieving process.

9–E. By the year 2020, 20% of the population of the United States will be over age 65.

6
Psychoanalytic Theory

I. Overview

– Classic psychoanalytic theory originated with **Sigmund Freud** in the late 1800s and early 1900s.
– Psychoanalytic theory is based on the concept that forces motivating behavior derive from **unconscious mental processes**.
– Other key concepts of psychoanalytic theory include **repression, the force that keeps unconscious processes out of consciousness**, and the belief that **sexual** (libido) and **aggressive drives** motivate the activities of the mind

II. Topographic Theory of the Mind

A. The unconscious mind

1. The unconscious mind contains **repressed thoughts and feelings** that are not available to consciousness.

2. The unconscious mind is associated with a type of thinking called **primary process**.

   – Primary process thinking is common in young children and involves primitive drives, wish fulfillment, and **pleasure**.
   – Logic is disregarded, and the concept of time is absent.

B. The preconscious mind

– The preconscious mind evolves during childhood and is available to both the unconscious and conscious minds.
– Memories, which can be brought to mind easily, are examples of preconscious thought.
– The preconscious mind uses **secondary process** thinking, which is logical and associated with reality.

C. The conscious mind

– The conscious mind operates in close conjunction with the preconscious mind but does not have access to the unconscious mind.
– By using the process of attention, an individual becomes aware of stimuli from the external world.

III. Dreams

- Freud believed that dreams represented gratification of unconscious instinctual impulses and wish fulfillment.
- The **manifest dream** (which an individual may or may not remember) involves the actual contents of the dream, including events that happened during the preceding day (the **day residue**).
- **Latent dream** content involves the unconscious thoughts and desires represented in the dream.
- **Dream work** is the means by which latent dream content is changed into the manifest dream.

IV. Structural Theory of the Mind

- Freud's structural theory, which he developed later in his career, divides the mind into the **id, ego,** and **superego**. All three of these structures operate primarily on an **unconscious level**.

A. Id

- The id represents instinctive **sexual and aggressive drives**.
- The id is controlled by primary process thinking, acts in concert with the pleasure principle, and is not influenced by external reality.

B. Ego

- The ego controls the expression of instinctual drives in order to adapt to the requirements of external reality.
- The major function of the ego is to **maintain a relationship to the outside world** and to be flexible to life's frustrations.
- The ego also maintains a sense of reality about the body and about the external world through constant evaluation of what is valid (**reality testing**) and then adapting to that reality.
- The ego also maintains **object relationships** and is responsible for sustaining satisfying interpersonal relationships.

C. Superego

- Id impulses are also controlled by the superego, which represents **moral values** and **conscience**.

V. Defense Mechanisms

- Defense mechanisms are **unconscious mental techniques** used by the ego to keep conflicts out of consciousness, thereby decreasing anxiety and maintaining an individual's sense of safety, equilibrium, and self-esteem.
- **George Vaillant** classified each defense mechanism as mature or less mature according to its adaptive value (Table 6-1).

VI. Psychoanalysis

A. Characteristics

- Psychoanalysis is a **psychotherapeutic treatment** technique based on Freud's theories about the unconscious mind and defense mechanisms.
- The purpose of psychoanalysis is to recover and integrate experiences repressed in the unconscious mind into the individual's personality.
- Treatment is usually conducted 4–5 times weekly for 3–4 years.

Table 6-1. Defense Mechanisms

Classification	Definition
Less mature	
Acting out	Unacceptable feelings are expressed in actions
Denial	Disbelief of intolerable facts about external reality such as of serious illness or death
Displacement	Emotions are transferred from an unacceptable to an acceptable idea, person, or object
Dissociation	Separation of function of some mental processes, as seen in multiple personality disorder
Identification	A person's behavior is patterned after that of another
Intellectualization	The mind is used to explain away frightening feelings or conflicts
Isolation of affect	Strong feelings are separated from the stressful events that provoked them
Projection	Unacceptable impulses are attributed to others
Rationalization	An irrational feeling or behavior is made to appear reasonable
Reaction formation	Unconscious feelings are denied and opposite attitudes and behaviors are adopted
Regression	Childlike patterns of behavior reappear under stress such as physical illness or hospitalization
Repression	Unacceptable feelings are prevented from reaching awareness
Splitting	People or events are seen as being totally bad or totally good
Mature	
Altruism	An individual unselfishly assists others
Humor	Reduces anxiety
Sublimation	An unacceptable instinctual drive is rerouted to a socially acceptable action
Suppression	Unwanted feelings are consciously put aside but are not repressed

[handwritten margin note: try to deal in intellectually c conflicts or frightening feelings.]

B. Free association

- The major technique used in psychoanalysis is free association—the patient says whatever comes to mind.
- Inhibition of free association is called **resistance**; unconscious thoughts are stopped from reaching awareness because they are not acceptable to the patient's conscious mind.
- In psychoanalysis, the role of the therapist is to interpret the material produced by the patient during free association.

C. Transference and countertransference

- In **transference**, the patient's unconscious feelings from the past about the parents are experienced in the present relationship with the therapist.
- In **countertransference**, the analyst unconsciously reexperiences feelings about his or her own parents with the patient.

D. Psychoanalytic psychotherapy

- Psychoanalytic psychotherapy is a form of psychotherapy that is based theoretically on psychoanalysis.
- Rather than using free association and analysis of transference reactions, discussions with the patient are used to identify the underlying unconscious basis for current conflicts and behavior.

Review Test

Directions: Each of the numbered items or incomplete statements in this section is followed by answers or by completions of the statement. Select the **one** lettered answer or completion that is **best** in each case.

1. The major method used to investigate the unconscious mental processes of a patient in psychoanalysis is

(A) symbolism
(B) repression
(C) free association
(D) primary process
(E) examination of the preconscious

2. All of the following statements about defense mechanisms are true EXCEPT

(A) they are used to keep conflicts out of consciousness
(B) they are unconscious mental techniques
(C) they decrease anxiety
(D) they are always manifestations of immature functioning
(E) they help maintain an individual's sense of self-esteem

3. Which of the following defense mechanisms is seen in a patient who exhibits multiple personalities?

(A) Repression
(B) Displacement
(C) Dissociation
(D) Isolation of affect
(E) Intellectualization

4. A physician who has been given a diagnosis of terminal pancreatic cancer constantly discusses the technical aspects of his case with many of the other physicians in the hospital. This is an example of which one of the following defense mechanisms?

(A) Repression
(B) Displacement
(C) Dissociation
(D) Regression
(E) Intellectualization

5. The defense mechanism used when unacceptable feelings are prevented from reaching awareness is known as

(A) repression
(B) regression
(C) displacement
(D) rationalization
(E) isolation of affect

6. Which of the following defense mechanisms is classified as the most mature?

(A) Sublimation
(B) Repression
(C) Rationalization
(D) Projection
(E) Regression

7. A previously toilet-trained child is hospitalized and begins wetting the bed again. This is an example of

(A) isolation of affect
(B) displacement
(C) projection
(D) regression
(E) denial

8. All of the following statements concerning psychoanalysis are true EXCEPT

(A) the therapist plays an active role
(B) treatment is usually conducted 4 times/week
(C) treatment is usually conducted for 3–4 years
(D) inhibition of free association is called resistance
(E) resistance blocks unconscious ideas that are unacceptable to the conscious mind

9. A patient's reexperiencing of feelings about the parent with the therapist during psychoanalysis is known as

(A) interference
(B) resistance
(C) association
(D) transference
(E) cognitive dissonance

10. Which of the following is a characteristic of primary process thinking?

(A) Disregards logic
(B) Closely attuned to time
(C) Associated with reality
(D) Accessible to the conscious mind
(E) Logical

11. About 1 week after the Gross Anatomy practical examination, the names of the cranial nerves are most likely to reside in

(A) the unconscious mind
(B) the preconscious mind
(C) the conscious mind
(D) the superego
(E) the id

12. Which of the following statements correctly describes aspects of Freud's structural theory of the mind?

(A) The id is conscious
(B) The mind is divided into the preconscious and conscious
(C) The superego is unconscious
(D) The id is closely associated with reality
(E) The ego is under the domination of primary process thinking

13. Which of the following is a function of the superego?

(A) Maintaining relationships to the outside world
(B) Reality testing
(C) Maintaining object relationships
(D) Controlling secondary process thinking
(E) Controlling id impulses

Directions: Each group of items in this section consists of lettered options followed by a set of numbered items. For each item, select the **one** lettered option that is most closely associated with it. Each lettered option may be selected once, more than once, or not at all.

Questions 14–19

Match each clinical profile with the defense mechanism that is most closely associated with it.

(A) Regression   (F) Dissociation
(B) Acting out   (G) Reaction formation
(C) Denial   (H) Intellectualization
(D) Splitting   (I) Sublimation
(E) Projection   (J) Displacement

14. A man who is angry at his supervisor kicks his dog

15. A depressed teenager steals a car

16. A person who has unconscious violent feelings becomes a surgeon

17. A husband who is attracted to another woman accuses his wife of cheating

18. A hospitalized patient who has just received a diagnosis of breast cancer checks out of the hospital against the advice of her physician

19. A man who is afraid of flying states his love of airplanes

Questions 20–22

A nurse (in uniform) gives a child an injection in the arm. That night the child dreams that Casper the Friendly Ghost hit her in the arm and that she killed Casper. Match the events in the dream with the dream elements.

(A) Day residue
(B) Manifest dream
(C) Latent dream
(D) Dream work
(E) Dream censor

20. Desire to kill the nurse

21. Killing Casper

22. Getting an injection in the arm

Answers and Explanations

1–C. The technique of free association is used to investigate unconscious mental processes in psychoanalysis.

2–D. Defense mechanisms are not always manifestations of immature functioning; they help individuals to maintain a sense of equilibrium and self-esteem.

3–C. Dissociation is the defense mechanism seen in individuals with multiple personality disorders.

4–E. Intellectualization is the defense mechanism used to explain away frightening feelings or conflicts.

5–A. Repression is the defense mechanism in use when unacceptable feelings are prevented from reaching awareness.

6–A. Sublimation is classified as the most mature defense mechanism. Repression, rationalization, projection, and regression are all classified as less mature defense mechanisms.

7–D. Regression is the defense mechanism used by the previously toilet-trained child who begins bed-wetting when under stress.

8–A. In psychoanalysis, the role of the therapist is to interpret the material produced by the patient during free association.

9–D. Reexperiencing feelings about the parent with the therapist during psychoanalysis is known as transference.

10–A. Primary process thinking disregards logic, has no concept of time, and is not accessible to the conscious mind. Secondary process thinking is logical and is associated with reality.

11–B. Memory of the names of the cranial nerves, while no longer in the forefront of the mind, hopefully can be recalled relatively easily. This memory therefore resides in the preconscious mind.

12–C. Based on Freud's structural theory, the mind is divided into the id, ego, and superego. The id is under the domination of primary process thinking and has no regard for reality. The id, ego, and superego all operate primarily on an unconscious level.

13–E. The superego controls impulses of the id.

14–J. In displacement, the man's unacceptable angry feelings toward his supervisor are taken out on his dog.

15–B. By acting out, the teenager's unacceptable depressed feelings are expressed in actions (stealing a car).

16–I. In sublimation, the surgeon reroutes his unacceptable wish for violence to a socially acceptable route (cutting people during surgery).

17–E. Using projection, the husband attributes his unacceptable sexual feelings toward another woman to his wife.

18–C. By using denial, intolerable facts about the reality of having breast cancer are not believed.

19–G. In reaction formation, the man denies his unconscious fear of flying and embraces the opposite idea by stating that he loves airplanes.

20–C. In the latent dream, the unconscious wish to kill the nurse is expressed.

21–B. The manifest dream includes the actual subject matter of the dream.

22–A. The day residue includes events that actually took place on that day.

7

Learning Theory and Behavioral Medicine

I. Classical Conditioning

– Learning is the acquisition of behavior patterns. One method of learning is through classical conditioning.

A. Principles

– The principles of classical conditioning were formulated by **Ivan Pavlov**.
  – In classical conditioning, a **natural** or **reflexive behavior** is elicited in response to a stimulus.
  – A **stimulus** is a cue from an internal or external event.
  – A **response** is a behavior that is provoked by a stimulus.

B. Unconditioned and conditioned stimuli and responses

– Something that naturally or automatically produces a response is an **unconditioned stimulus**, such as salivation in response to the odor of food.
– The behavior produced (salivation) is known as an **unconditioned response** because it does not have to be learned.
– A **conditioned response** is one that is learned, such as salivation in response to the sound of a bell that, in the past, has been rung in conjunction with the presentation of food.

C. Response acquisition and extinction

– In the **acquisition phase**, the conditioned response (such as salivation in response to a bell) is learned.
– In the **extinction phase**, the conditioned response decreases when the conditioned stimulus (the bell) is never followed by the unconditioned stimulus (food).
– **Spontaneous recovery** occurs after extinction when the conditioned response (salivation in response to a bell) reappears.
– In **stimulus generalization**, a new stimulus (such as the noise of a buzzer) that resembles the conditioned stimulus (the noise of a bell) also results in the conditioned response (salivation).

Table 7-1. Schedules of Reinforcement

Schedule	Example
Continuous	Payment for each shirt sewn
Fixed ratio	Payment for every tenth shirt sewn
Fixed interval	Payment every Friday, no matter how many shirts are sewn
Variable ratio	Payment, in no predictable pattern, for every second, fifth, or tenth shirt sewn
Variable interval	Payment daily, weekly, monthly, or whenever the supervisor can afford to pay, no matter how many shirts are sewn

D. **Aversive conditioning**

- Classical conditioning to an aversive stimulus (also called aversive conditioning) **pairs an unwanted behavior**, such as sexual interest in children, with a painful or aversive stimulus, such as **electric shock**.
- Aversive conditioning also shows acquisition, extinction, and spontaneous recovery.

II. Operant Conditioning

A. **Principles**

- Operant conditioning is primarily associated with the work of **B. F. Skinner**.
- Skinner's theories relate to the concept of **reinforcement**: Behavior is determined by its consequences for the individual. The **consequence**, or **reinforcement**, follows **immediately** after a behavior.
- In operant conditioning, a behavior that is **not part of the organism's natural repertoire** can be learned through reward or punishment.
- The focus of operant conditioning is an observable behavior; the organism's history is not important.

B. **Reinforcement**

- Reinforcement establishes a connection between a stimulus and a response and can be **positive** or **negative**.
- Reinforcement is **positive** (reward) if the **introduction** of a pleasant or positive stimulus **increases the rate** at which the behavior occurs (e.g., giving a child money results in increased time devoted to studying).
- Reinforcement is **negative** if the **removal** of an aversive or negative stimulus **increases the rate** of behavior (e.g., to avoid a shock, a rat presses a bar more frequently).
- Positive or negative reinforcement can be used to **increase a desired behavior**. A reward can be tangible (e.g., candy) or intangible (e.g., attention from a teacher).
- **Extinction** is the disappearance of a learned behavior when the reward is withheld.

C. **Patterns of reinforcement** (Table 7-1)

- When and in what pattern reinforcement is presented determines the rate of the response or behavior.

1. **Continuous reinforcement** is presented after every response and is the pattern of reinforcement in which the desired behavior is initially learned most quickly and in which the behavior disappears most quickly when reinforcement is not presented (least resistant to extinction).

2. **Fixed reinforcement** is presented after a set number of responses.

3. **Variable reinforcement** occurs after a random and unpredictable number of responses and is very resistant to extinction. Because every desirable response rarely can be rewarded, variable reinforcement is the type of reinforcement that occurs most often in daily life. ↳ *Variable interval*
   - Payoffs on slot machines demonstrate **variable ratio** reinforcement.
   - Fishing demonstrates **variable interval** reinforcement.

D. Punishment
   - Punishment is an aversive stimulus aimed at **reducing an unwanted behavior**.
   - Ignoring a child who misbehaves (extinction) rather than hitting him (punishment) is more likely to result in long-lasting disappearance of the unacceptable behavior.

E. Shaping and modeling
   - **Shaping** involves rewarding closer and closer approximations of the wanted behavior until the correct behavior is achieved.
   - **Modeling** is a type of observational learning (e.g., an individual adopts the behavior of someone who is admired).

III. Applications of Behavioral Techniques

   - Behavioral techniques have been used to eliminate **unwanted habits**, such as smoking. They are also used to treat medical conditions such as obesity and cardiovascular disease.

A. Systematic desensitization
   - Systematic desensitization is a behavioral technique based on classical conditioning. It is used to **eliminate phobias** (irrational fears).

1. An individual is exposed to the frightening stimulus in increasing doses in conjunction with relaxation procedures.

2. Since relaxation is incompatible with fear, the relaxed patient is less likely to be anxious or fearful when the frightening stimulus is presented.

B. Token economy
   - Token economy, a behavioral technique that uses positive reinforcement, based on operant conditioning. It has been used in **mental hospital** wards and in working with the **mentally retarded**.
   - Each desired behavior is rewarded with a token reinforcer. Tokens are later exchanged for desired objects such as candy or dessert.

C. Cognitive therapy
   - Cognitive therapy is a method of **short-term psychotherapy** (up to 25 weeks) that deals specifically with **depression** and **anxiety**.
   - A patient's distorted, negative way of **thinking is reorganized** and substituted with **self-enhancing thoughts**.

– Behavioral techniques used in conjunction with cognitive therapy help patients structure their time and gain a sense of mastery and accomplishment in their daily activities.

D. Biofeedback

1. Principles

– Biofeedback involves learning to gain control over physiologic parameters. It is based on three fundamental principles of operant conditioning.

a. The physiologic parameter must be **measurable**.

b. The patient must receive **continuous information** about the physiologic parameter.

c. The patient must have a high degree of **motivation** to learn because it requires a great deal of **practice**.

2. Therapeutic uses

– Biofeedback training for voluntary control of the autonomic system has been used to treat **hypertension**, peptic ulcer disease, and asthma.
– Biofeedback-based control of peripheral **temperature regulation** has been useful in the treatment of **migraine headache**.
– Biofeedback training involving relaxation of skeletal muscles has been used to treat **tension headache** and generalized anxiety disorders.

Review Test

Directions: Each of the numbered items or incomplete statements in this section is followed by answers or by completions of the statement. Select the **one** lettered answer or completion that is **best** in each case.

1. All of the following elements of classical conditioning must be learned EXCEPT

(A) the conditioned response
(B) the unconditioned response
(C) the conditioned stimulus
(D) the acquisition phase
(E) stimulus generalization

2. Which of the following schedules of reinforcement is most resistant to extinction?

(A) Continuous
(B) Fixed ratio
(C) Fixed interval
(D) Variable ratio
(E) Discontinued

3. A child who likes and looks up to her physician states that she wants to become a doctor when she grows up. This behavior is an example of

(A) stimulus generalization
(B) modeling
(C) shaping
(D) positive reinforcement
(E) variable reinforcement

4. Teaching a patient to relax her skeletal muscles through biofeedback is particularly important in the treatment of

(A) hypertension
(B) peptic ulcer disease
(C) asthma
(D) tension headache
(E) obesity

5. All of the following statements about learning are true EXCEPT

(A) learning involves the acquisition of behavior patterns
(B) classical conditioning is a method of learning
(C) operant conditioning is a method of learning
(D) history of the individual is important in all forms of learning
(E) stimuli may be internal or external to the individual

Questions 6 and 7

6. A patient who has undergone three sessions of chemotherapy becomes nauseous when she enters the hospital for her fourth session. This is an example of which type of learning?

(A) Operant conditioning
(B) Classical conditioning
(C) Modeling
(D) Shaping

7. The patient becomes nauseous when she drives by the hospital 6 months after her chemotherapy sessions have been completed. This response has which of the following characteristics?

(A) It diminishes when the conditioned stimulus is not followed by the unconditioned stimulus
(B) It occurs when the conditioned response reappears after extinction
(C) It occurs after an aversive stimulus
(D) It occurs before extinction
(E) It occurs when a related stimulus produces a conditioned response

8. A 2-year-old child is afraid of nurses in white uniforms. When his grandmother comes to visit him wearing a white jacket, he begins to cry. The best explanation for this phenomenon is

(A) stimulus generalization
(B) habit
(C) instrumental conditioning
(D) learning by trial and error
(E) an emitted operant

9. Which of the following statements about reinforcement in operant conditioning is true?

(A) It establishes a connection between a stimulus and a response
(B) It can only be positive
(C) It decreases the rate at which a behavior occurs
(D) It precedes a behavior
(E) It was first described by the work of Pavlov

10. All of the following statements about biofeedback are true EXCEPT

(A) it is based on classical conditioning
(B) it has been used in the treatment of generalized anxiety disorder
(C) control over physiologic activity is learned
(D) it can be used to control autonomic activity
(E) relaxation of striated muscle can be achieved

11. All of the following factors are important in the successful use of biofeedback EXCEPT

(A) the patient must receive continuous information about the physical parameter
(B) the physical parameter must be detectable and measurable
(C) the patient's motivation is important
(D) it is used to gain control over the central nervous system
(E) a large amount of practice is required

12. A patient with diabetes increases her time spent exercising in order to reduce the number of insulin injections she must receive. The exercising behavior is an example of

(A) positive reinforcement
(B) negative reinforcement
(C) extinction
(D) stimulus generalization
(E) punishment

13. Although a mother slaps a child on the hand every time she touches a stove, the child begins to touch the stove more frequently. This is an example of

(A) punishment
(B) negative reinforcement
(C) positive reinforcement
(D) aversive conditioning
(E) classical conditioning

Directions: The group of items in this section consists of lettered options followed by a set of numbered items. For each item, select the **one** lettered option that is most closely associated with it. Each lettered option may be selected once, more than once, or not at all.

Questions 14–17

A child comes to the hospital laboratory to have a blood sample drawn for the first time and has a painful experience. The next time the child returns for this procedure, she begins to cry when she smells the odor of antiseptic in the hospital hallway. For each clinical scenario, select the definition that best describes it.

(A) Unconditioned stimulus
(B) Unconditioned response
(C) Conditioned stimulus
(D) Conditioned response

14. Painful blood withdrawal procedure

15. Hospital odors

16. Crying upon the smell of antiseptic

17. Crying when the blood sample is drawn

Answers and Explanations

1–B. The unconditioned stimulus produces an unconditioned response that does not have to be learned.

2–D. Variable ratio reinforcement is most resistant to extinction.

3–B. This behavior is an example of modeling; the child wants to become like someone she admires.

4–D. In treating tension headache with biofeedback, the patient is trained to relax skeletal muscles.

5–D. In learning by operant conditioning, history of the individual is not important.

6–B. In this example of classical conditioning, the hospital where the treatments took place (the conditioned stimulus) has become paired with chemotherapy (the unconditioned stimulus), which elicited nausea.

7–B. This response, spontaneous recovery, occurs after extinction when the conditioned response reappears.

8–A. Stimulus generalization occurs when a new conditioned stimulus (the grandmother's white jacket) that resembles the original conditioned stimulus (the nurse's white uniform) results in the conditioned response (crying when he sees his grandmother).

9–A. Reinforcement establishes a connection between a stimulus and a response.

10–A. Biofeedback is based on operant conditioning.

11–D. Biofeedback is used to gain control over the autonomic nervous system.

12–B. Increasing behavior (e.g., increasing exercise) to avoid a negative stimulus (injection) is an example of negative reinforcement.

13–C. Because the behavior increases, this child has received positive reinforcement, probably increased attention from her mother.

14–A. The painful blood withdrawal procedure is the unconditioned stimulus.

15–C. The antiseptic odor in the hospital has become associated with the painful procedure and is therefore the conditioned stimulus.

16–D. The conditioned response, which is crying in response to the smell of the antiseptic, has been learned.

17–B. Crying in response to the pain of an injection does not have to be learned and is the unconditioned response.

8

Psychoactive Substance Dependence and Abuse

I. Overview

A. Definitions and demographics of substance abuse

- The *DSM-IV* uses the term **psychoactive substance use disorder** to identify a pattern of abnormal drug use leading to impairment of social, physical, or occupational functioning. Categories of psychoactive substance use disorder are shown in Table 8-1.
- The use of illegal drugs is more common among individuals age 18–25 years and is three times more common in males.
- Dependence on drugs has biologic, psychologic, and social causes; abstinence from drugs frequently leads to **withdrawal symptoms** (Table 8-2).

B. Tolerance and dependence (Table 8-3)

- **Tolerance** is the need for increased amounts of the drug to gain the same effect.
- **Cross-tolerance** occurs when tolerance develops to one drug as the result of use of another drug.

II. Caffeine

A. Demographics

- Caffeine, used by three-fourths of the adult population in the United States, is found in many things, including coffee (125 mg/cup), tea (65 mg/cup), cola (40 mg/cup), nonprescription stimulants, and nonprescription diet drugs.

B. Physical effects

- Caffeine use results in alertness, diuresis, central nervous system (CNS) and cardiac stimulation, and increased peristalsis, secretion of gastric acid, and blood pressure.

III. Nicotine

A. Demographics

- About one-third of all adults in the United States smoke cigarettes.
- Although the total number of people who smoke appears to have declined in recent years, the proportion of teenage, black, and female smokers has increased.
- Psychiatric patients smoke at a higher rate than the general population.

Table 8-1. *DSM-IV* Categories and Characteristics of Substance Use

Category	Characteristics
Psychoactive substance dependence	Intoxication, tolerance, withdrawal symptoms; symptoms continue for at least 1 month or intermittently over an extended time
Psychoactive substance abuse	Psychoactive substance use for at least 1 month or intermittently over an extended period; most common in people just starting to use drugs and with use of drugs that do not have severe withdrawal symptoms
Polysubstance dependence	Repeated use of at least three types of psychoactive drugs for at least 6 months

B. Physical effects
  – Nicotine is a toxic substance that causes increased peristalsis and catecholamine release, vasoconstriction of peripheral blood vessels, changes in sleep patterns, tremor, and low-birth weight in infants of mothers who smoke.

C. Withdrawal and relapse
  – Up to 80% of people who stop smoking relapse within the first 2 years.
  – Factors associated with successful abstinence from smoking include encouragement from a spouse or child, fear of ill effects, membership in a support group of people who have previously smoked, and counseling by a physician who does not smoke.

IV. Alcohol
A. Demographics
  – Alcohol has been used at some time by most of the adult population in the United States.
  – Approximately 13% of all adults abuse alcohol or become alcohol-dependent during their lives.
  – Alcohol use is highest in the 21–34-year-old age group.
  #### 1. Gender
    – Fewer women than men use alcohol, although alcohol use is increasing among women.

Table 8-2. Withdrawal Symptoms of Substance Use

Substance	Withdrawal Symptoms
Alcohol	Tremor, tachycardia, hypertension, malaise, nausea, seizure, delirium tremens ("DTs")
Amphetamines	Post-use "crash," including anxiety, lethargy, headache, stomach cramps, hunger, and severe depression
Barbiturates	Anxiety, seizures, delirium, life-threatening cardiovascular collapse
Benzodiazepines	Long-lasting anxiety, convulsions, tremor, insomnia
Caffeine	Headache, lethargy, depression, weight gain
Cocaine	Hypersomnolence, fatigue, depression, malaise, severe craving (peaking 2–4 days after last dose)
Nicotine	Irritability, headache, anxiety, weight gain
Opioids	Anxiety, insomnia, anorexia, sweating, fever, rhinorrhea, piloerection, nausea, stomach cramps

Table 8-3. Effects of Psychoactive Substance Use

Substance	Withdrawal Symptoms	Tolerance	Adverse Effects
Alcohol	Yes	Yes	Liver dysfunction, hallucinations, Korsakoff's and Wernicke's syndromes
Amphetamines	Yes	Yes	Cardiac symptoms, hypertension, delusions
Barbiturates	Yes	Yes	Low safety margin
Benzodiazepines	Yes	Yes	Alcohol interactions, amnesia
Caffeine	Yes	Yes	Agitation, insomnia, cardiac arrhythmia
Cocaine	Yes	Yes	Psychosis, nasal problems, hypertension, cardiac arrhythmias, sudden death
LSD	No	Yes	"Bad trips," flashbacks, *diaphoresis (profuse*
Marijuana	Occasionally	No	Hallucinations, amotivational syndrome *possibilities*
Nicotine	Yes	Yes	Cancer (lung, pharynx, bladder), cardiac and circulatory disease
Opioids	Yes	Yes	Overdose is life-threatening
PCP	No	No	Psychotic symptoms, violence *(in contrast to LSD)*

(PCP Psychosis)

- The onset of alcoholism occurs at a later age in women than in men.
- Because of possible gender differences in alcohol metabolism, women may suffer more serious health effects with lower alcohol doses than men.
- Alcohol abuse may be more difficult to detect in women because they may be more secretive about their drinking habits.

2. **Regional and socioeconomic factors**
   - In the United States, alcohol use is lowest in the southern states and highest in the northeastern states.
   - Blacks in urban ghettos, American Indians, and Eskimos have high rates of alcoholism.
   - Jews, Asians, and conservative Protestants use alcohol less than liberal Protestants and Catholics.

3. **Physical and behavioral factors**
   - A childhood history of problems such as attention-deficit hyperactivity disorder and conduct disorder correlate with alcoholism.

B. **Effects of alcohol use**
   - Half of all traffic fatalities and homicides and one-quarter of all suicides are correlated with the use of alcohol.
   - The life expectancy of persons with a history of alcohol abuse is 10 years less than that of non-alcoholics.
   - Family, work, and legal problems are common in patients who chronically abuse alcohol.
   - **Fetal alcohol syndrome** (including facial abnormalities, reduced height and weight, and mental retardation) occurs in the children of mothers who use alcohol during pregnancy.

C. **Intoxication**
   - Alcohol depresses the CNS, probably through the γ-aminobutyric acid (GABA) system.
   - Legal intoxication is defined as **0.08%–0.15% blood alcohol concentration**, depending on individual state laws.
   - Coma occurs at a blood alcohol concentration of 0.40%–0.50% in nonalcoholics.

D. Treatment of alcoholism

– **Disulfiram** [Antabuse] is a drug given to help recovery in patients with a history of alcohol abuse.
– Taken regularly, disulfiram causes a toxic reaction when the patient subsequently drinks alcohol.
– The toxic reaction, a result of **acetaldehyde accumulation** in the blood, causes intense nausea, headache, and flushing.
– The anxiety and hyperactivity of the sympathetic nervous system accompanying alcohol withdrawal can be reduced with **antianxiety drugs**.
– Psychotherapy may be useful for treating patients with alcoholism, particularly if the spouse participates.
– **Alcoholics Anonymous** (AA) and other voluntary peer support groups are the most successful means of controlling problem drinking.

V. Opioid Drugs

– Opioid drugs include morphine, heroin, methadone, and codeine.

A. Physical effects and withdrawal

– Opioids induce euphoria and sedation, are analgesic, and depress the respiratory system.
– The intravenous method of drug use employed by many addicts (sharing of contaminated needles) contributes to AIDS and hepatitis B infection.
– While overdose may be fatal, death from withdrawal of opioids is rare unless a serious physical illness is present.
– Because of cross-dependence, opioids such as methadone can be substituted for illegal opioids such as heroin to prevent withdrawal.
– Regular use of **opioid antagonists** such as **naloxone** can be used to maintain abstinence in opioid abusers.

B. Heroin

– In the United States, heroin is a frequently abused opioid.
– About 50% of all heroin addicts in the United States live in New York City.
– There are three male addicts to every female addict; most are in their early thirties.
– When compared to morphine, heroin is more potent, crosses the blood–brain barrier more quickly, and has a faster onset of action and more euphoric action.
– **Clonidine**, an adrenergic agonist, can block heroin withdrawal syndrome.

C. Methadone

– Methadone is a **synthetic opioid** dispensed by federal health authorities to treat heroin addiction.
– Although methadone also causes physical dependence and tolerance, it has advantages over heroin for the addict: Methadone is legal, **can be taken orally**, suppresses heroin withdrawal symptoms, has a longer duration of action, and causes less euphoria, drowsiness, and depression.
– Individuals taking methadone can maintain work status and avoid the criminal activity that is necessary to maintain a costly heroin habit.

VI. Sedatives

A. Barbiturates

- Barbiturates are used as **sleeping pills,** sedatives, tranquilizers, anticonvulsants, and anesthetics.
- Frequently used and abused barbiturates include amobarbital, pentobarbital, and secobarbital.
- Barbiturates **depress the respiratory system** and therefore are the drugs most commonly taken to commit suicide.
- Because withdrawal from barbiturates is more dangerous than withdrawal from any other drug, it must be accomplished gradually.
- Gradual reduction in dosage of the abused drug and the substitution of long-acting barbiturates (such as phenobarbital) for the more commonly abused short-acting types are used during withdrawal.

B. Benzodiazepines

- Benzodiazepines are used as **tranquilizers,** sedatives, muscle relaxants, anticonvulsants, and anesthetics. Benzodiazepines are also used to treat alcohol withdrawal.
- Unlike barbiturates, benzodiazepines produce only minor respiratory depression; however, such depression can be life-threatening if alcohol is used concurrently.

VII. Amphetamines

- Amphetamines, a group of frequently abused **stimulant drugs,** include dextroamphetamine [Dexedrine], methamphetamine [Desoxyn], and methylphenidate [Ritalin].
- Amphetamines release catecholamines from presynaptic terminals.
- Current indications for amphetamines include attention-deficit hyperactivity disorder (ADHD) in children, narcolepsy, and the short-term treatment of obesity refractory to other treatments. It may also be prescribed for mild depression.
- **"Ice,"** a street form of methamphetamine that is injected or smoked, has relatively long-lasting effects when compared with crack cocaine.
- Amphetamines act rapidly, have euphoric action, reduce fatigue, increase performance, elevate pain threshold, reduce appetite, and may increase libido.
- **Overdose** can result in cardiovascular problems, fever, and psychotic symptoms that resemble those of schizophrenia.

VIII. Cocaine

- Although cocaine (especially in its cheap, smokable **"crack"** form) is more available now, cocaine use has declined since its peak in 1985.
- Cocaine blocks the reuptake of dopamine and serotonin at the synapse.
- Cocaine produces **intense euphoria** that lasts up to 1 hour; this is often **followed by acute depression** ("the crash").
- Cocaine **intoxication** is marked by aggressiveness, agitation, hypersexuality, irritability, impaired judgment, and combativeness.
- Cocaine psychosis can occur with high doses.
- **Hyperactivity** and **growth retardation** are seen in **newborns** of mothers who used cocaine during pregnancy.

IX. Marijuana

– Of illegal drugs, marijuana is the most frequently used drug in the United States.
– **Hashish** is a concentrated form of compressed marijuana resins.

A. Physical effects

– **Tetrahydrocannabinol (THC)** is the primary active compound found in **cannabis** (marijuana).
– Physiologic effects of THC include orthostatic hypotension and tachycardia.

B. Psychological effects

– Psychological effects of THC include euphoria, relaxation, and sleepiness; these begin soon after smoking marijuana and continue for a few hours.
– In low doses, marijuana impairs memory and complex motor activity, alters sensory and time perception, causes conjunctival reddening, and may increase appetite and sexual desire.
– With high doses, marijuana may cause delusions, hallucinations, paranoia, and anxiety, and may decrease sexual functioning.
– Chronic users experience lung problems associated with smoking and a decrease in motivation ("**the amotivational syndrome**") characterized by lack of desire to work and increased apathy.

X. Hallucinogens

A. Psychological effects

– Hallucinogens alter perception and emotional states shortly after administration.
– "**Bad trips**" (panic reactions that may include psychotic symptoms) may occur.
– **Flashbacks** (a reexperience of the sensations associated with use of a hallucinogen in the absence of the drug) can occur months after the last dose.
– In susceptible individuals, psychiatric problems and long-term cognitive impairment may occur.

B. Lysergic acid diethylamide (LSD)

– LSD is the most commonly known hallucinogen and acts primarily through the serotonergic system.
– The effects of LSD usually last between 8–12 hours.
– Physical effects of LSD use include diaphoresis (profuse perspiration), blurred vision, mydriasis (pupil dilation), tachycardia, tremor, and palpitations.
– Physical withdrawal symptoms and tolerance are rare.

C. Phencyclidine piperidine (PCP)

– PCP, also known as **angel dust**, is an illegal drug that is typically smoked in a marijuana or other cigarette.
– The effects of PCP are similar to those of LSD and include **fantasies and euphoria**; in contrast to LSD, **episodes of violent behavior** occur with PCP use.
– Auditory and visual hallucinations, as well as alterations of body image and distortions of time and space (PCP psychosis), may occur.
– Emergency room findings include hypertension, hyperthermia, and nystagmus (abnormal eye movements).

– Consumption of more than 20 mg of PCP may cause convulsions, coma, and death.
– The effects of PCP may last several days; PCP may be detectable in the blood for over 1 week.
– **Long-term effects** of PCP use include **memory loss, lethargy, and reduced attention span**.

Review Test

Directions: Each of the numbered items or incomplete statements in this section is followed by answers or by completions of the statement. Select the **one** lettered answer or completion that is **best** in each case.

1. Physical effects of caffeine use include all of the following EXCEPT

(A) blood pressure reduction
(B) CNS stimulation
(C) cardiac stimulation
(D) increased gastric acid secretion
(E) diuresis

2. All of the following statements concerning PCP are true EXCEPT

(A) its effects may last for several days
(B) it may be detected in the blood for more than 1 week
(C) psychosis may occur with long-term use
(D) violent behavior occurs
(E) it has few long-term effects

3. Which of the following effects commonly occurs following withdrawal from nicotine?

(A) Weight gain
(B) Euphoria
(C) Excitability
(D) Delirium tremens
(E) Long-term abstinence

4. Which of the following drugs is most frequently abused in the United States?

(A) Marijuana
(B) Cocaine
(C) Speed
(D) LSD
(E) Heroin

5. All of the following are common effects of marijuana use EXCEPT

(A) impaired memory
(B) alteration in time perception
(C) decreased appetite
(D) conjunctival reddening
(E) increased sexual desire

6. The amotivational syndrome is characteristic of chronic use of

(A) PCP
(B) LSD
(C) marijuana
(D) cocaine
(E) heroin

7. Which of the following statements about LSD is true?

(A) The effects commonly last 1–2 hours
(B) It is a hallucinogen
(C) The effects have a slow onset
(D) Physical dependence is common
(E) Withdrawal symptoms are common

8. Which of the following is an effect of amphetamines?

(A) Increased fatigue
(B) Reduced pain threshold
(C) Reduced appetite
(D) Slow onset of action
(E) Reduced libido

9. Benzodiazepines are prescribed for all of the following uses EXCEPT

(A) sedatives
(B) muscle relaxants
(C) anesthetics
(D) antihistamines
(E) tranquilizers

10. All of the following effects are commonly seen as a result of opiate use EXCEPT

(A) sedation
(B) analgesia
(C) decreased respiratory drive
(D) euphoria
(E) hyperactivity

11. Which of the following statements is true concerning heroin addiction?

(A) Most addicts are in their late teenage years
(B) Addicts are more likely to be female than male
(C) Ten percent of heroin addicts live in New York City
(D) Death from withdrawal of heroin is rare
(E) Amphetamines can block the heroin withdrawal syndrome

12. Legal intoxication is defined by which of the following blood alcohol concentrations?

(A) 0.05%–0.09%
(B) 0.08%–0.15%
(C) 0.40%–0.50%
(D) 1.5%–2.0%
(E) 2.5%–3.0%

13. The age group in which illegal drug use is most common is

(A) 10–15 years
(B) 15–18 years
(C) 18–25 years
(D) 25–35 years
(E) 35–45 years

14. Abuse of which of the following drugs is least likely to result in physical dependence?

(A) Alcohol
(B) Amphetamines
(C) Benzodiazepines
(D) PCP
(E) Opiates

15. Withdrawal from which of the following drugs is most likely to cause life-threatening symptoms?

(A) PCP
(B) LSD
(C) Heroin
(D) Secobarbital
(E) Alcohol

16. Korsakoff's syndrome is associated with long-term use of

(A) amphetamines
(B) alcohol
(C) barbiturates
(D) cocaine
(E) LSD

17. In which of the following age groups is the prevalence of alcohol use highest?

(A) 15–19 years
(B) 21–34 years
(C) 35–44 years
(D) 45–60 years
(E) 65–75 years

18. Which of the following groups has the lowest rate of alcoholism?

(A) Eskimos
(B) Native Americans
(C) Blacks in urban ghettos
(D) Catholics in urban ghettos
(E) Jews in urban ghettos

19. Which of the following statements about alcoholism is true?

(A) Alcohol excites the CNS
(B) Life expectancy is reduced by approximately 4 years
(C) It is more common in Asian Americans than in white Americans
(D) Women are more secretive about use of alcohol than men
(E) It is associated with about 20% of traffic fatalities

20. Which of the following statements about heroin is true?

(A) It is a barbiturate
(B) It has a faster onset of action than morphine
(C) It is less potent than morphine
(D) It has half as much euphoric action as morphine
(E) It crosses the blood–brain barrier more slowly than morphine

21. All of the following symptoms occur with heroin withdrawal EXCEPT

(A) lacrimation
(B) nausea
(C) sedation
(D) sweating
(E) vomiting

22. Amphetamines have been used to treat all of the following disorders EXCEPT

(A) attention-deficit hyperactivity disorder
(B) narcolepsy
(C) mild depression
(D) anorexia nervosa
(E) obesity

23. Which of the following statements about methadone is true?

(A) It does not cause physical dependence
(B) It shows no cross-dependence with heroin
(C) Its use does not result in tolerance
(D) It is given out by federal health authorities
(E) It is taken by injection

24. Which of the following is a common physical symptom of LSD use?

(A) Sedation
(B) Bradycardia
(C) Fever
(D) Constricted pupils
(E) Blurred vision

25. Which of the following statements about cocaine use is true?

(A) There are usually severe physiologic signs of withdrawal
(B) Severe craving for cocaine often peaks 2–4 days after the previous dose
(C) The euphoria produced by cocaine lasts 3–4 days
(D) Propranolol is useful as a treatment for withdrawal symptoms
(E) Cocaine intoxication is characterized by sedation

26. All of the following statements about amphetamines are true EXCEPT

(A) overdose results in cardiovascular problems
(B) overdose results in subnormal body temperature
(C) overdose can result in psychotic symptoms
(D) withdrawal can result in depression
(E) withdrawal can result in fatigue

27. Which of the following is a physical effect of nicotine?

(A) Decreased catecholamine release
(B) Decreased peristalsis
(C) Weight gain
(D) Tremor
(E) Dilation of peripheral blood vessels

28. Which of the following symptoms occurs with withdrawal from benzodiazepines?

(A) Hypersomnia
(B) Tremor
(C) Lethargy
(D) Respiratory depression
(E) Sedation

29. All of the following statements about smoking are true EXCEPT

(A) about 10% of the adults in the United States smoke cigarettes
(B) nicotine is a toxic drug
(C) psychiatric patients smoke more than the general population
(D) the relapse rate for smokers who attempt to quit is as high as 80% within the first 2 years
(E) withdrawal from nicotine may result in headache

30. Which of the following conditions is commonly associated with caffeine withdrawal?

(A) Excitement
(B) Euphoria
(C) Headache
(D) Decreased appetite
(E) Mydriasis

31. All of the following statements about PCP are true EXCEPT

(A) it is usually injected
(B) it is also known as angel dust
(C) its effects are similar to those of LSD
(D) overdose may result in coma and death
(E) it may remain in the blood for over 1 week

Directions: The group of items in this section consists of lettered options followed by a set of numbered items. For each item, select the **one** lettered option that is most closely associated with it. Each lettered option may be selected once, more than once, or not at all.

Questions 32–35

For each patient, select the drug most likely responsible for the symptom listed.

(A) Alcohol
(B) Secobarbital
(C) Cocaine
(D) Methylphenidate
(E) Caffeine
(F) Diazepam
(G) Heroin
(H) Marijuana
(I) Nicotine
(J) PCP

32. A 40-year-old man with a history of depression and insomnia is brought to the emergency department with signs of severe respiratory depression.

33. The police bring a 25-year-old man to the hospital in a coma. His girlfriend tells the physician that prior to having a convulsion and fainting, he said that he felt his body expanding and floating up to the ceiling.

34. A 22-year-old woman is brought to the hospital highly agitated and aggressive and demonstrating paranoid ideation. Physician examination reveals tachycardia, hypertension, and nasal inflammation.

35. A 32-year-old man is brought to a New York City hospital. He appears sedated, but euphoric. A blood test reveals the presence of HIV.

Answers and Explanations

1–A. Caffeine tends to increase blood pressure.

2–E. Psychosis and long-term effects may occur with PCP use.

3–A. Weight gain commonly occurs following nicotine withdrawal.

4–A. Marijuana is the most frequently abused illegal drug in the United States.

5–C. Appetite may increase with marijuana use.

6–C. The amotivational syndrome is characteristic of chronic users of marijuana.

7–B. The effects of LSD, a hallucinogen, commonly last 8–12 hours and have a rapid onset. Physical withdrawal symptoms and tolerance are rare.

8–C. Amphetamines reduce appetite and have been used as diet pills.

9–D. Benzodiazepines are used as sedatives, muscle relaxants, anesthetics, and tranquilizers; they are not used as antihistamines.

10–E. Sedation, analgesia, decreased respiratory drive, and euphoria may result from opiate use. Hyperactivity does not usually result from opiate use.

11–D. Death from withdrawal of opioids is rare unless a serious physical illness is present.

12–B. Legal intoxication is defined by blood alcohol concentrations of 0.08%–0.15%, depending on individual state law.

13–C. Illegal drug use is most common in people ages 18–25.

14–D. Use of PCP generally is not linked to physical dependence.

15–D. The most severe symptoms of drug withdrawal are associated with barbiturates such as secobarbital.

16–B. Korsakoff's syndrome is associated with long-term use of alcohol.

17–B. The prevalence of alcohol use is highest at ages 21–34 years.

18–E. In general, Jews have a lower rate of alcoholism than other groups.

19–D. Women are often more secretive about their use of alcohol than men.

20–B. Heroin has a faster onset of action, is more potent, has more euphoric action, and crosses the blood–brain barrier more quickly than morphine.

21–C. Lacrimation, nausea, sweating, and vomiting are associated with heroin withdrawal.

22–D. Use of amphetamines is associated with anorexia (loss of appetite).

23–D. Methadone is given out by federal health authorities. It is taken orally, not given by injection; it shows cross-dependence with heroin and causes both physical dependence and tolerance.

24–E. Tachycardia, diaphoresis, mydriasis, and blurred vision are physical symptoms that occur with the use of LSD.

25–B. The intense euphoria produced by cocaine lasts up to 1 hour. Severe craving for the drug peaks 2–4 days after the previous dose, although there may be few physiologic signs of withdrawal. Propranolol is not used as a treatment for cocaine withdrawal. Cocaine intoxication is characterized by agitation and irritability.

26–B. Overdose of amphetamines can result in cardiovascular problems, fever, and psychotic symptoms; depression and fatigue result from withdrawal.

27–D. Increased peristalsis and vasoconstriction of peripheral blood vessels are physical effects of nicotine. Tremor, sleep changes, and increased catecholamine release also occur.

28–B. Withdrawal from benzodiazepines is associated with insomnia, tremor, and anxiety.

29–A. Approximately one-third of adults in the United States smoke cigarettes.

30–C. Caffeine withdrawal is associated with headache, lethargy and depression, and weight gain.

31–A. PCP, or angel dust, is usually smoked. Many of its psychotropic effects are similar to those of LSD. PCP may remain in the blood for over 1 week; overdose can result in death.

32–B. The history of insomnia indicates that this patient may have been given a prescription for secobarbital [Seconal]. His depression may have resulted from using this drug in a suicide attempt.

33–J. PCP use, like other hallucinogens, results in feelings of altered body state.

34–C. Paranoia, agitation and aggressiveness, tachycardia, hypertension, and nasal inflammation all indicate that this patient was using cocaine.

35–G. The presence of HIV as well as signs of sedation and euphoria indicate that this patient is an intravenous heroin abuser.

9
Sleep

I. Normal Sleep

A. Stages of sleep

- The electroencephalogram (**EEG**) of a relaxed, awake individual with eyes closed, recorded over the occipital and parietal lobes, is characterized by **alpha waves**.
- **Beta waves** over the frontal lobes are commonly seen with **active mental concentration**.
- In sleep, brain waves show distinctive changes that are classified as stages 1, 2, 3, and 4 and rapid eye movement (REM).

1. **Non-rapid eye movement (non REM) sleep** (Table 9-1)
   - Stages 1, 2, 3, and 4 are classified as non-REM sleep, which is characterized by peacefulness, slowed pulse and respiration, decreased blood pressure, and episodic body movements.
   - Slow wave sleep (stages 3 and 4 of non-REM sleep), or **delta sleep,** is the deepest, most relaxed part of sleep.
   - Slow wave sleep is associated with **enuresis** (bed-wetting), **somnambulism** (sleepwalking), and **night terrors**.

2. **Rapid eye movement (REM) sleep**
   - In addition to rapid eye movements, REM sleep is characterized by **increased pulse, respiration, blood pressure**, and **brain oxygen use**.
   - REM sleep is also characterized by **penile and clitoral erection**, paralysis of skeletal muscles, and dreaming.
   - The onset of REM sleep (REM latency) occurs about 90 minutes after falling asleep.
   - An REM period occurs about every **90 minutes** during the night; the majority of REM sleep occurs in the last third of the night.
   - Newborn infants and animals demonstrate REM sleep.

B. Neurotransmitters involved in sleep

1. **Serotonin** is involved in producing sleep.
   - Increase in serotonergic activity by ingestion of L-**tryptophan** has been used to improve sleep quality; however, L-tryptophan has recently been removed from the market because of product contamination.

Table 9-1. Stages in Sleep

Sleep Stage	Cycles/Second on EEG	Characteristics	Sleep in Young Adults (% of total sleep time)
Stage 1	3–7	Alpha waves disappear; theta waves; low-voltage, regular activity; lightest stage of sleep	5
Stage 2	12–14	Sleep spindles and K-complexes	45
Stages 3 and 4	0.5–2.5	Slow wave sleep (SWS), delta waves, high-voltage activity, night terrors, sleepwalking *enuresis*	25
REM		Low-voltage, sawtooth waves; dreaming	25

2. **Norepinephrine** is also involved in sleep.

   – Drugs that increase the activity of noradrenergic neurons **reduce REM sleep**.

3. **Acetylcholine (ACh)** is associated primarily with increased REM sleep.

   – Sleep changes associated with **major depression** (shortened REM latency, more time spent in REM sleep, and a shift in REM sleep from the end of the sleep cycle to the beginning of the night) are associated with **increased central cholinergic activity**.
   – Patients with **Alzheimer's disease** have **reduced slow wave and REM sleep**, which is most likely due to decreased cholinergic neurons in the basal forebrain.

4. Drugs that block **dopamine**, such as antipsychotics, **increase time spent sleeping**; increasing dopamine results in wakefulness.

II. Sleep Disorders

A. Physical causes of sleep problems

   – Frequently, medical conditions such as pain and endocrine and metabolic diseases are associated with sleep problems.
   – Withdrawal of alcohol, benzodiazepines, phenothiazines, marijuana, or opiates is associated with insomnia.
   – The use of central nervous system (CNS) stimulants such as caffeine is associated with insomnia; withdrawal of CNS stimulants is associated with hypersomnolence.

B. Psychological causes of sleep problems

   – In severe **unipolar depression**, sleep is characterized by normal sleep onset, repeated nighttime awakenings, and **waking too early in the morning**. Reduced slow wave sleep, long first REM period, and short REM latency may occur.
   – Depression in **bipolar disorder** may be associated with the sleep problems seen in unipolar depression as well as those observed in hypersomnia.

– In mania and hypomania, patients may have trouble falling asleep and appear to need less sleep.
– Sleep in the elderly is characterized by decreased REM and slow wave sleep and increased sleep latency.

C. Classification of sleep problems

– The *DSM-IV* classifies sleep disorders into two major categories: **dyssomnias** (insomnia, hypersomnia, and sleep-wake schedule disorders) and **parasomnias** (sleepwalking, sleeptalking, night terrors, and dream anxiety disorder or nightmares).

D. Insomnia

– Insomnia occurs in 30% of people and is defined as having a problem falling asleep or staying asleep that occurs 3 times per week for at least 1 month and leads to sleepiness during the day or results in problems fulfilling social or occupational obligations.
– Behavioral techniques such as relaxation may be used to treat insomnia.
– Insomnia is associated with **anxiety** and may be the early sign of the onset of a severe depressive or psychotic episode.

E. Hypersomnia

– Hypersomnia includes sleeping too much as well as feeling sleepy during the daytime (**somnolence**).
– Hypersomnolence is associated with **sleep apnea** and **narcolepsy**.
– Other conditions that produce hypersomnolence include Kleine-Levin syndrome (recurrent periods of hypersomnia and hyperphagia), menstrual-associated syndrome (hypersomnia in the premenstrual period), and sleep drunkenness (difficulty coming fully awake after sleep).

1. Narcolepsy

– Narcolepsy occurs in about 4 of every 10,000 people, most frequently is seen in adolescents or young adults, may have a genetic component, and involves sleep attacks in which the **patient falls asleep suddenly**.
– Narcolepsy may include **hypnagogic or hypnopompic hallucinations** (hallucinations that occur just as one falls asleep or wakes up, respectively) and is characterized by the appearance of REM sleep within a few minutes of falling asleep.
– **Cataplexy**, when an individual suddenly collapses because of loss of all muscle tone, occurs in about half of all patients with narcolepsy.
– **Stimulant drugs** are the primary treatment used in narcolepsy.

2. Sleep apnea

– In sleep apnea, seen more frequently in the **elderly** and the **obese (pickwickian syndrome)**, the person **stops breathing** for a brief period of time.
– In **central sleep apnea**, there is no respiratory effort.
– In **obstructive sleep apnea**, respiratory effort is present but an airway obstruction prevents air from reaching the lungs.
– A mixture of central and obstructive sleep apnea also occurs.
– People with sleep apnea cannot sleep deeply because anoxia awakens them during the night; these individuals may become **chronically tired**.
– Sleep apnea may be the cause of **sudden death** during sleep in the elderly and in infants.

F. Night terrors
  – Night terrors are an extreme form of fright in which a person, usually a child, awakens in terror.
  – In contrast to nightmares, which occur during REM sleep, night terrors **occur during slow wave sleep**.
  – Generally, there is no memory of the arousal or of a dream.
  – Night terrors may develop into sleepwalking (somnambulistic) episodes.
  – Night terrors may be an early sign of temporal lobe epilepsy.

Review Test

Directions: Each of the numbered items or incomplete statements in this section is followed by answers or by completions of the statement. Select the **one** lettered answer or completion that is **best** in each case.

1. Which of the following statements concerning narcolepsy is true?

(A) The REM sleep of a narcoleptic person is abnormal
(B) Narcolepsy occurs in approximately 50 out of every 10,000 persons
(C) Narcolepsy occurs most frequently in the elderly
(D) Sedatives are used to treat narcolepsy
(E) Cataplexy rarely occurs

2. Which neurotransmitter is particularly involved in increasing of REM sleep?

(A) Serotonin
(B) Norepinephrine
(C) Acetylcholine (ACh)
(D) Dopamine
(E) Histamine

3. Which of the following is characteristic of a patient in REM sleep?

(A) Hyperactivity of skeletal muscles
(B) Decreased blood pressure
(C) Penile and clitoral erection
(D) Decreased brain oxygen use
(E) Decreased pulse

4. Which of the following signs is characteristic of a patient in non-REM sleep?

(A) Paralysis of skeletal muscles
(B) Decreased blood pressure
(C) Increased pulse
(D) Increased respiration
(E) Agitation

5. A patient who is suffering from major depression has sleep problems. Which of the following is likely to be found in this patient?

(A) Increased slow wave sleep
(B) Lengthened REM latency
(C) Reduced percentage of REM sleep
(D) Shift in REM from last to first part of the night
(E) Short first REM period

6. All of the following statements about hypersomnia are true EXCEPT

(A) it is associated with narcolepsy
(B) it is associated with sleep apnea
(C) it is associated with withdrawal of CNS stimulants
(D) it is seen frequently in patients with mania
(E) it includes complaints about somnolence

7. Slow wave sleep is characterized by

(A) penile erection
(B) dreaming
(C) night terrors
(D) total recall of the arousal
(E) increased brain oxygen use

8. Which of the following statements about sleep is true?

(A) Patients with Alzheimer's disease have increased slow wave sleep
(B) Drugs that decrease brain dopamine produce wakefulness
(C) Patients with Alzheimer's disease have reduced REM sleep
(D) Dopamine blockers decrease sleep time
(E) Increased noradrenergic activity is associated with increased REM sleep

9. Which of the following statements about patients with insomnia is most likely to be true?

(A) It occurs in less than 5% of the population
(B) It has little effect on daytime functioning
(C) It is rarely associated with anxiety
(D) It may be an early sign of severe depression
(E) It must occur daily for at least 6 months to be diagnosed as insomnia

10. Which of the following is characteristic of sleep in a person age 79?

(A) Increased total sleep time
(B) Decreased REM sleep
(C) Decreased sleep latency
(D) Increased stage 3 sleep
(E) Increased stage 4 sleep

Directions: The group of items in this section consists of lettered options followed by a set of numbered items. For each item, select the **one** lettered option that is most closely associated with it. Each lettered option may be selected once, more than once, or not at all.

Questions 11–16

Match the sleep characteristic with its appropriate sleep stage.

(A) Stage 1
(B) Stage 2
(C) Stages 3 and 4
(D) REM sleep

11. Sleep spindles

12. K-complexes

13. Theta waves

14. Sawtooth waves

15. Slow wave sleep

16. Amounts to 45% of sleep time

Answers and Explanations

1–A. Shortening of REM latency is seen in narcolepsy; it also occurs in depression.

2–C. ACh is involved in increasing REM sleep.

3–C. REM sleep is characterized by penile and clitoral erection.

4–B. Non-REM sleep is associated with decreases in blood pressure, pulse, and respiration, and with calmness and episodic body movements.

5–D. Major depression is associated with reduced slow wave sleep, shortened REM latency, greater percentage of REM, shift in REM from the last to the first part of the night, and long first REM period.

6–D. Patients with mania frequently have a reduced need for sleep rather than hypersomnolence.

7–C. Slow wave sleep is associated with enuresis, somnambulism, night terrors, and no memory of the arousal.

8–C. Drugs that increase brain dopamine produce wakefulness; dopamine blockers tend to increase sleep time. Patients with Alzheimer's disease have reduced slow wave sleep and REM sleep.

9–D. Insomnia occurs in up to 30% of the population, may be associated with anxiety, and may also be an early sign of severe depression.

10–B. Sleep in the elderly is characterized by decreased REM sleep, decreased slow wave sleep (stages 3 and 4), and increased sleep latency.

11–B. Sleep spindles are seen in stage 2 sleep.

12–B. K-complexes are seen in stage 2 sleep.

13–A. Theta waves are seen in stage 1 sleep.

14–D. Sawtooth waves are seen in REM sleep.

15–C. Slow waves are characteristic of sleep stages 3 and 4.

16–B. Forty-five percent of sleep time is spent in stage 2 sleep.

10
Schizophrenia

I. Overview

A. History

- In the early 1900s, Eugene Bleuler first used the term **schizophrenia** and described the four "A's" that characterize this illness: **autism** (self-preoccupation and lack of communication), **affect** (blunted), **associations** (loosened), and **ambivalence** (uncertainty).

B. Epidemiology

- There is no significant gender difference in the prevalence of schizophrenia. Most men who develop the disease are between the **ages of 15 and 25 years**; **women** typically develop schizophrenia between the **ages of 25 and 35 years**.
- High population density is correlated with increased rates of schizophrenia.
- Schizophrenia **occurs in all countries and cultures** that have been studied. Less developed countries may tolerate the individual with schizophrenia better than more highly industrialized countries.
- The **season of birth** is related to the incidence of schizophrenia. More individuals with schizophrenia are **born during cold weather months**— January through April in the northern hemisphere and July through September in the southern hemisphere.

C. Downward drift

- Schizophrenia is diagnosed more often in populations of low socioeconomic status. This increased incidence may be caused by "downward drift" as people with schizophrenia move into lower socioeconomic classes because of their handicap.

II. Etiology

A. Psychological etiology

- In psychoanalytic theory, a disruption in organization of the ego alters how reality is interpreted and how aggressive and sexual desires are controlled.
- Another psychodynamic factor thought to be involved in the development of schizophrenia is the **double bind family situation**. In this situation, the parent constantly gives the child contradictory messages that force the child to make impossible choices.

– In the **stress-diathesis model** of schizophrenia, biologic vulnerability (diathesis) permits schizophrenic symptoms to emerge when the individual is stressed by internal or external environmental factors.

B. Biologic etiology

1. Neurotransmitter systems

– The **dopamine hypothesis** asserts that the dopaminergic system in the brains of schizophrenics is hyperactive (see Chapter 2).
  – Decreased γ-aminobutyric acid (GABA) activity can lead to increased dopaminergic activity.
– Norepinephrine activity also may be elevated, particularly in paranoid schizophrenia.

2. Anatomic and other changes

– Computed tomographic studies of patients with schizophrenia show **enlargement of the lateral and third ventricles** as well as cortical atrophy.
– Abnormalities of the **frontal lobes, limbic system, and basal ganglia** (because of the prevalence of movement disorders) have been implicated in the development of schizophrenia.
– **Abnormal eye movements** and excessive blinking are often seen in people with schizophrenia.
– **Viral infection, immunologic abnormalities, and psychoneuroendocrine abnormalities** have been proposed as factors in the etiology of schizophrenia.

III. Clinical Signs and Symptoms

A. The premorbid personality

– Typically, the premorbid personality of the patient with schizophrenia as a child is **quiet, obedient, passive**, and does not form friendships.
– As an adolescent, the premorbid personality is introverted, daydreams, and **avoids social activities**.
– **Somatic complaints** such as back pain, headache, digestive problems, or anxiety may coincide with the onset of illness. Also, at the onset of illness, the patient may begin to show an **interest in philosophy, religion, or the occult**.
– Other prodromal signs include abnormal mood changes and strange perceptions and behavior.

B. Characteristics of schizophrenia

– Evidence of a disorder in thinking that includes **hallucinations, bizarre behavior, and delusions** indicates schizophrenia.
– Most commonly, individuals with schizophrenia show **flat or blunted affect**; their emotions may also be extreme or inappropriate.
– The patient may report feelings of power, fear, or isolation.
– Although **auditory hallucinations** are most common, other types such as cenesthetic hallucinations (altered sensations of body organs) may also occur.
– The patient is usually **oriented to person, place, and time**.
– **Memory is intact**; if not, an organic brain syndrome should be suspected.
– Tests of neuropsychological performance in schizophrenia often suggest temporal and frontal lobe dysfunction.
– Intelligence quotient (**IQ) scores tend to decline** over the course of the disease.

Table 10-1. Hallucinations, Delusions, and Illusions

Symptom	Definition	Example
Illusion	Misperception of real external stimuli	Interpreting the appearance of a coat in a dark closet as a man
Hallucination	False sensory perception	Hearing voices when alone in a room
Delusion	False belief not shared by others	The feeling of being followed by the FBI

C. Thought disorders of schizophrenia

1. **Disorders of content of thought** are exemplified by the **delusion**.

   – Typical delusions of schizophrenia include the feeling that someone is controlling one's thoughts.
   – An **idea of reference** is a notion, less strongly held than a delusion, in which the patient believes that other people or the media are talking about him or her.
   – For accurate diagnosis, a distinction must be made between hallucinations, delusions, and illusions (Table 10-1).

2. **Disorders of form of thought** include incoherence, word salad, loose associations, neologisms, mutism, and echolalia.

   – In **word salad**, the patient produces an incoherent, unrelated combination of words and phrases.
   – **Loose associations** (ideas shift from one subject to another in an unrelated fashion) are also seen in mania.
   – **Neologisms** (making up new words) and **echolalia** (repeating a word over and over) are also seen.

3. **Disorders of thought processes** include flight of ideas, illogical ideas, thought blocking (an abrupt halt in the train of thinking), short attention span, deficiencies in thought and content of speech, impaired memory and abstraction abilities, and clang associations (speaking in rhyming words or phrases).

D. Negative (deficit) and positive (productive) symptoms

– **Negative symptoms** include flattening of affect, thought blocking, deficiencies in speech content, cognitive disturbances, poor grooming, lack of motivation, and social withdrawal.
– **Positive symptoms** include loose associations, strange behavior, hallucinations, and talkativeness.

E. Suicide in patients with schizophrenia

– Suicide is common in patients with schizophrenia; over 50% attempt suicide and 10% of those die in the attempt.
– **Risk factors that predict suicide** in schizophrenia are male sex, college education, youth, many relapses, depressed mood, high ambitions, and living alone.

F. Prognosis

– Certain factors are useful in predicting the prognosis of schizophrenia (Table 10-2).

Table 10-2. Factors in the Prognosis of Schizophrenia

Poor Prognosis	Better Prognosis
Uncommunicative and withdrawn	Depressed or manic
Young age at onset	Older age at onset
Slow onset	Rapid onset
No immediate life stressors	Immediate life stressors
Poor employment history	Good employment history
Unmarried	Married
Neurologic problems	No neurologic problems
Few or no friends	Strong relationship with friends
Family history of schizophrenia	Family history of mood disorder
Negative symptoms	Positive symptoms
Frequent relapses	Few relapses

IV. Subtypes of Schizophrenia

- The **differential diagnoses** of schizophrenia include **brief reactive psychosis, manic-depressive illness, schizoaffective illness, and organic delirium**.
- The *DSM-IV* lists five types of schizophrenia: disorganized (hebephrenic), catatonic, paranoid, undifferentiated, and residual (Table 10-3).

V. Treatment

A. **Antipsychotic drugs** are the major treatment for schizophrenia (see Chapter 3). Various antipsychotics show almost equal efficacy.

- If adequate doses are used, the **minimum trial period** of an antipsychotic agent is **4–6 weeks**.
- Relapse occurs most often because patients fail to take neuroleptic medications, often because of adverse effects.
- When antipsychotic drug treatment is discontinued, about two-thirds of patients show symptoms within 18 months; **most relapse within 6 months**.
- Psychosocial interventions such as behavioral, family, group, and individual therapy can increase the clinical improvement induced by neuroleptic drugs in schizophrenia.

B. **Extrapyramidal neurologic signs**

- The most common adverse effects seen with the use of neuroleptic medications include weight gain, extrapyramidal neurologic signs, and impotence.

Table 10-3. *DSM-IV* Subtypes of Schizophrenia

Subtype	Characteristics
Disorganized	Disinhibited, disorganized, poor personal appearance, inappropriate emotional responses; onset before age 25
Catatonic	Stupor, bizarre posturing (waxy flexibility); rare since introduction of antipsychotic agents
Paranoid	Delusions of persecution or grandeur; better social functioning and older age at onset than other subtypes
Undifferentiated	Has characteristics of more than one subtype
Residual	Patient experiences one schizophrenic episode and subsequently shows flat affect, illogical thinking, odd behavior, and social withdrawal, but no severe psychotic symptoms

- Extrapyramidal neurologic signs include **tremor, akinesia** (slowing of body movements), **rigidity, akathisia** (motor restlessness), and **acute dystonias** (muscle spasms).
- These signs are **seen more frequently in men** than in women; they also occur **more frequently in younger patients** than in older patients.
- Extrapyramidal neurologic signs can be treated with anticholinergic drugs.

C. Tardive dyskinesia and neuroleptic malignant syndrome

- Tardive dyskinesia and neuroleptic malignant syndrome are serious adverse effects that occur from the use of neuroleptic medications.
- **Clozapine** is not associated with extrapyramidal neurologic signs, tardive dyskinesia, or neuroleptic malignant syndrome.

1. **Tardive dyskinesia** involves uncontrollable writhing and jerking movements, often of the mouth and tongue, which may be irreversible. This condition **occurs most commonly in women and in older patients**.

2. **Neuroleptic malignant syndrome**, which **occurs more commonly in men**, has a mortality rate of about 20%. Symptoms include fever, sweating, increased pulse and blood pressure, muscular rigidity, dystonia, akinesia, and agitation.

Review Test

Directions: Each of the numbered items or incomplete statements in this section is followed by answers or by completions of the statement. Select the **one** lettered answer or completion that is **best** in each case.

1. Bleuler's four "A's" that characterize schizophrenia include all of the following EXCEPT

(A) anhedonia
(B) autism
(C) affect
(D) association
(E) ambivalence

2. Which of the following is thought to be the major neurotransmitter involved in the development of schizophrenia?

(A) Norepinephrine
(B) GABA
(C) Dopamine
(D) Acetylcholine
(E) Enkephalin

Questions 3 and 4

3. A 16-year-old male who will have his first schizophrenic episode in 6 months is least likely to show

(A) abnormal mood changes
(B) strange behavior
(C) strange perceptions
(D) excessive spending
(E) somatic complaints

4. The patient is most likely to show which type of hallucination during his first schizophrenic episode?

(A) Kinesthetic
(B) Auditory
(C) Cenesthetic
(D) Visual
(E) Olfactory

5. Which of the following is a disorder of content of thought in schizophrenia?

(A) Flight of ideas
(B) Delusions
(C) Short attention span
(D) Thought blocking
(E) Clang associations

6. Which of the following is a positive symptom of schizophrenia?

(A) Hallucinations
(B) Flattening of affect
(C) Deficiencies in speech content
(D) Thought blocking
(E) Social withdrawal

7. The percentage of patients with schizophrenia who attempt suicide is approximately

(A) 10%
(B) 20%
(C) 35%
(D) 50%
(E) 75%

8. All of the following are risk factors for suicide in patients with schizophrenia EXCEPT

(A) college education
(B) female
(C) depression
(D) high ambitions
(E) living alone

9. All of the following statements about the use of antipsychotic drugs are true EXCEPT

(A) most patients relapse within 6 months when medication is discontinued
(B) antipsychotics show about equal efficacy
(C) failure to take neuroleptic medication is a major reason for patient relapse
(D) adverse effects of neuroleptic medications are a common reason for noncompliance
(E) the minimum trial period of an antipsychotic is 2–3 weeks

10. A patient on antipsychotic medication *(neuroleptic drug)* begins to show extrapyramidal symptoms. Which of the following statements about these symptoms is true?

(A) They cannot be treated effectively with anticholinergic drugs
(B) They are more common in women than in men
(C) They are an uncommon adverse effect of the neuroleptics
(D) They are more common in older people than in younger people
(E) They are likely to include tremor

11. All of the following statements about schizophrenia are true EXCEPT

(A) peak age of onset is different for men than for women
(B) it is more prevalent in low socioeconomic populations
(C) increased rates correlate with high population density
(D) more schizophrenics are born during warm weather months
(E) it is seen in all countries and cultures

12. Which of the following behaviors is least likely to characterize the premorbid personality of the patient with schizophrenia?

(A) Passivity
(B) Obedience
(C) Failure to form friendships
(D) Introversion
(E) Acting out

13. Which of the following statements best describes a patient with schizophrenia?

(A) Memory is impaired
(B) The patient is not oriented to person
(C) The IQ score will remain stable over the course of the disease
(D) Tests of neuropsychologic performance often suggest frontal lobe dysfunction
(E) The patient is not oriented to place

14. Which of the following is a characteristic of tardive dyskinesia?

(A) It is more common in men than in women
(B) It is a serious adverse effect of the use of neuroleptic drugs
(C) It is more common in younger patients than in older patients
(D) It is easily reversible
(E) It is characterized primarily by rigidity

15. Which of the following disorders is least likely to be included in the differential diagnosis of schizophrenia?

(A) Organic delirium
(B) Schizoaffective illness
(C) Manic-depressive illness
(D) Brief reactive psychosis
(E) Anxiety

16. A patient reports that someone is controlling her thoughts. This feeling is an example of

(A) an illusion
(B) a disorder of form of thought
(C) a disorder of content of thought
(D) a hallucination
(E) an idea of reference

17. Negative symptoms of schizophrenia include

(A) hallucinations
(B) cognitive deficits
(C) loose associations
(D) strange behavior
(E) talkativeness

Answers and Explanations

1–A. Bleuler's four "A's" of schizophrenia are autism, affect, association, and ambivalence. Anhedonia was not a characteristic noted by Bleuler.

2–C. Dopamine is the major neurotransmitter believed to be involved in the development of schizophrenia.

3–D. Prodromal signs of schizophrenia include somatic complaints such as headache, anxiety, abnormal affect, and strange behavior and perceptual experiences.

4–B. Auditory hallucinations are the most common type of hallucination seen in schizophrenia.

5–B. Disorders of content of thought include delusions. Disorders of thought processes in schizophrenia include flight of ideas, thought blocking, short attention span, and clang associations.

6–A. Flattening of affect, deficiencies in speech content, thought blocking, and social withdrawal are negative symptoms of schizophrenia; hallucinations are positive symptoms.

7–D. Approximately 50% of patients with schizophrenia attempt suicide.

8–B. Risk factors for suicide in schizophrenics are male sex, college education, many relapses, depression, high ambitions, living alone, and young age.

9–E. The minimum trial period of an antipsychotic agent is 4–6 weeks.

10–E. Extrapyramidal neurologic signs, including tremor, dystonias, akinesia, and akathisia, are common adverse effects of neuroleptic drugs. These symptoms respond to anticholinergic drugs and are more common in men than in women and in younger rather than in older people.

11–D. More schizophrenics are born in the cold weather months than in the warm weather months.

12–E. Passivity, obedience, introversion, and failure to form friendships characterize the premorbid personality of the patient with schizophrenia. Acting out does not characterize the premorbid personality of the schizophrenic patient.

13–D. In schizophrenia, memory is intact although the IQ score tends to decline over the course of the disease. The patient usually is oriented to person, time, and place.

14–B. Tardive dyskinesia is a serious adverse effect associated with the use of neuroleptic drugs; it is frequently irreversible. It involves uncontrollable movements, is seen more often in women than in men, and occurs more often in older patients than younger patients.

15–E. Anxiety is least likely to be included in the differential diagnosis of schizophrenia.

16–C. The feeling that someone is controlling one's thoughts is a delusion. A delusion is an example of a disorder of content of thought seen in schizophrenia.

17–B. Hallucinations, talkativeness, loose associations, and strange behavior are positive symptoms of schizophrenia. Cognitive deficits are negative symptoms of schizophrenia.

11

Mood Disorders

I. Overview

A. Mood and affect

- **Mood** is defined as an internal emotional condition.
- **Affect** refers to how that emotional condition is expressed.
- **Mood disorders** are abnormalities of mood and affect.

B. Mania and depression

Elevation of mood, or **mania**, is associated with rapid, excited speech, decreased need for sleep, and feelings of self importance (grandiosity).
- **Depression of mood** is associated with decreased energy, difficulty in concentrating and in sleeping, guilt, reduction in appetite, and suicidal thoughts.

C. Categories of mood disorder

1. In **major depressive disorder** (unipolar depression or major depression), patients have only depression.

2. Patients with **bipolar** (manic-depressive) **disorder** have both mania and depression; about 15% of patients exhibit only mania.

3. Other categories of mood disorder are **hypomanic episode** (an episode of manic symptoms that does not meet all of the criteria for a manic episode) and **cyclothymic and dysthymic disorders** (mild forms of bipolar disorder and major depressive disorder, respectively).

II. Epidemiology

- Demographic characteristics and comparison of major depressive disorder and bipolar disorder are shown in Table 11-1.
- There are **no racial differences** in the occurrence of mood disorders. Because of limited access to health care, mood disorders in poor black and Hispanic patients may progress to a point where they are misdiagnosed as schizophrenic.
- Mood disorders occur **more frequently in single, divorced, and separated people** than in married people.

Table 11-1. Comparison of Major Depressive Disorder and Bipolar Disorder

Major Depressive Disorder UNIPOLAR	Bipolar Disorder MANIA
Mean age of onset 40 years	Mean age of onset 30 years
Occurs twice as often in women than in men	Occurs equally in women and men
No correlation with social class	Higher incidence in upper socioeconomic groups
Some evidence of genetic etiology	Strong evidence of genetic etiology

III. Etiology

A. Biologic factors

1. Neurotransmitters and mood disorders

  – The activity of **norepinephrine and serotonin**, the primary neurotransmitters associated with mood disorders, is altered in patients with mood disorders.

  – **Dopamine activity** may be decreased during depressive episodes and increased during manic episodes. Psychosis, Schizophrenia

  – Abnormal levels of the norepinephrine metabolites 3-methoxy-4-hydroxyphenylglycol (**MHPG**) and vanillylmandelic acid (**VMA**), of the serotonin metabolite 5-hydroxyindoleacetic acid (**5-HIAA**), and of the dopamine metabolite homovanillic acid (**HVA**) occur in the urine, blood, and cerebrospinal fluid (CSF) of many patients with mood disorders (see Chapter 2).

  – **Acetylcholine** (ACh) levels may also be abnormal in mood disorders.

  – Decreased levels of **platelet monoamine oxidase (MAO) activity** are seen in depression.

2. The neuroendocrine system and mood disorders

  – Abnormalities of the limbic-hypothalamic-pituitary-adrenal axis are seen in patients with mood disorders (see Chapter 17).

  – The **dexamethasone suppression test (DST)**, which measures the regulation of cortisol production, has been used in the diagnosis of depression but with limited clinical usefulness (see Chapter 17).

3. Other biologic factors

  – Immune system function and sleep patterns (see Chapter 9) may be abnormal in persons with mood disorders.

  – Evidence of abnormalities can be seen in the basal ganglia, limbic system, and hypothalamus in mood disorders.

B. Psychosocial factors

  – Life stressors are probably related to the development of depression.

    – The **loss of a parent** in the first decade of life and **loss of a spouse** correlate with major depression.

    – **Misinterpretation of life events, low self-esteem, and loss of hope** are involved in cognitive theories about the development of depression. Cognitive therapy is particularly useful in treating these emotional problems.

IV. Clinical Signs and Symptoms of Mood Disorders (Table 11-2)

A. Depression

1. Signs and symptoms

  – With depression, the depressed mood often is very different from sadness. Unlike patients who are sad, patients with depression may report that they are unable to cry.

Table 11-2. Symptoms of Mood Disorder

Symptom	Occurrence (%, if known)
Depression	
Depressed mood	Hallmark; may be denied in 50%
Diminished interest or pleasure in activities	Common
Reduced energy	Common
Decreased motivation	Common
Sleep problems, insomnia	80%
Suicidal ideation	66%
Suicide	10%–15%
Decreased or increased appetite	Common
Weight loss	May occur
Decreased interest in sex	May occur
Diurnal variation in symptoms (worse in the morning)	50%
Inability to concentrate	Common
Impaired thinking	50%–75%
Psychomotor retardation	Common (particularly in the elderly)
Delusions	May occur
Mania *spends money*	
Elevated, expansive, or irritable mood	Hallmark
Grandiosity	Common
Disinhibition	Common
Impulsivity	Common
Distractibility	Common
Talkativeness	Common
Flight of ideas	Common
Assaultiveness	75%
Impaired judgment	Common
Delusions	75%

- Some patients seem unaware of or may deny depression (i.e., **"masked" depression**) even though symptoms are present.
- Both **psychomotor agitation and retardation** are seen in patients with depression.
- Patients who experience delusions or hallucinations while depressed have **depression with psychotic features**.
- Symptoms of depression in both major depressive disorder and bipolar disorder are similar.
- Objective rating scales of depression include the **Hamilton, Raskin, and Zung scales**.

2. **Delusions in depression**

- **Mood congruent delusions** (those appropriate to a depressed mood) include feelings of guilt, worthlessness, failure, evil-mindedness, persecution, and terminal illness. They are more common than mood incongruent delusions.
- **Mood incongruent delusions** (those inappropriate to a depressed mood) include feelings of power and importance.
- Although hallucinations sometimes occur, they are not common in major depression.
- **Orientation** with respect to person, place, and time **is usually intact** in patients with depression.
- Cognitive impairment, the impaired concentration and memory loss that frequently occurs in depression, is also known as **pseudodementia**.

3. **Suicide**
   - Frequently, patients with severe depression do not have the energy to commit suicide.
   - The risk of suicide increases as depression lifts and energy returns.

B. **Mania**
   - Although patients may be euphoric, excitable, and hyperactive, those experiencing a manic episode can also be irritable, angry, and hostile.
   - In mania, mood congruent delusions include those of strength, exceptional abilities, and financial power.
   - **Disorders of form and process of thought** such as those seen in schizophrenia (including loosening of associations, flight of ideas, word salad, and neologisms) may occur in a manic episode.
   - As a manic episode proceeds, speech becomes difficult to follow and comprehend.
   - **Judgment is impaired** during a manic episode; laws are often broken.

V. Course of Mood Disorders

A. **Major depressive disorder**
   - One-half to three-fourths of patients with major depression have a second depressive episode.
     - Patients usually are mentally healthy between episodes of major depression.
     - Among patients with major depression, an average of five or six depressive episodes commonly occur over a twenty-year-period.
   - Premorbid problems rarely occur in patients with major depressive disorder.
   - If **untreated**, depression lasts from **6–12 months**; **with treatment,** an episode resolves in about **3 months**.
   - Frequency and length of depressive episodes often increase with age.

B. **Bipolar disorder**
   - In three-fourths of female patients and two-thirds of male patients, bipolar disorder begins with depression.
   - The first manic episode often occurs after about three episodes of depression.
   - The characteristics of depression in people who later have a manic episode include psychotic behavior, psychomotor retardation, family history of bipolar disorder, history of hypomania following antidepressant drug therapy, and postpartum depression.
   - **Manic episodes** usually have a **rapid onset** and when **untreated last about 3 months**.
   - The period of time between manic episodes becomes shorter as bipolar illness progresses.
     - The period between episodes in bipolar illness is generally 6–9 months; 40% of patients have more than 10 episodes of mania.

VI. Prognosis of Mood Disorders

A. **Major depressive disorder**
   - Indicators of recurrence include alcohol and drug abuse, anxiety, dysthymia, and a history of multiple depressive episodes.
   - Chronic problems, which occur in about 20% of patients, are more common in men.

Table 11-3. Nonpsychiatric Causes of Depressive Symptoms

Category	Cause
Medical	Pancreatic and other cancers, renal and cardiopulmonary disease
Endocrine	Thyroid, adrenal, or parathyroid dysfunction
Infectious	Pneumonia, mononucleosis, AIDS
Inflammatory	Systemic lupus erythematosus, rheumatoid arthritis
Neurologic	Epilepsy, multiple sclerosis, Parkinson's disease, stroke, brain trauma
Nutritional	Nutritional deficiencies
Prescription drugs	Reserpine, propranolol, steroids, methyldopa, oral contraceptives
Drugs of abuse	Alcohol, marijuana, hallucinogens, amphetamine withdrawal

B. Bipolar disorder

- The prognosis for bipolar disorder is not as favorable as that for major depressive disorder.
- Patients who show only manic symptoms have a better prognosis than those with both depression and mania.
- Chronic problems are present in about 30% of patients with bipolar disorder.

VII. Differential Diagnosis

A. Psychiatric disorders

- Psychiatric disorders that have depressive features include alcohol and drug abuse, anorexia nervosa, anxiety disorders, schizophrenia, and somatization disorders.

B. Nonpsychiatric disorders

- A number of medical diseases, neurologic disorders, and drugs are associated with depression (Table 11-3).

VIII. Treatment of Mood Disorders

A. Overview

- **Depression** is a **self-limiting** disorder that is successfully treated in about 75% of patients.
- About 25% of patients with major depression receive treatment for the disorder.

B. Pharmacologic treatment and electroconvulsive therapy (ECT)

1. Major depressive disorder

- A **4–6 week trial** of a **heterocyclic antidepressant** agent is usually the initial treatment for major depressive disorder.
- Antidepressant agents often take 3–4 weeks to show an effect.
- If heterocyclic antidepressants fail, antidepressants such as fluoxetine [Prozac] or a monoamine oxidase (MAO) inhibitor can be introduced.
- **Fluoxetine** is now often used as a first-line drug because it has limited adverse effects.

- Combinations of heterocyclic antidepressant agents with either MAO inhibitors or lithium can be used with extreme caution. Antipsychotic and antidepressant drugs may be used in patients who have depression with psychotic features.
- **ECT works more quickly** than pharmacotherapy and is useful in patients who are refractory to or who suffer uncomfortable adverse effects from antidepressant medications.

2. **Bipolar disorder**
   - **Lithium** is the drug of choice for patients with **mania**; carbamazepine may be used if lithium is ineffective.
   - Lithium is often used in a maintenance regimen in patients with bipolar disorder.

C. **Psychological treatment**
   - **Psychological treatment used in conjunction with drug treatment** has been found to be more beneficial than either treatment alone.
   - Psychological treatment can increase compliance with drug treatment in mood disorders.
   - Types of psychological treatment used in mood disorders include interpersonal, family, behavioral, cognitive, and psychoanalytic therapy.

Review Test

Directions: Each of the numbered items or incomplete statements in this section is followed by answers or by completions of the statement. Select the **one** lettered answer or completion that is **best** in each case.

1. All of the following statements about bipolar disorder are true EXCEPT

(A) about 1% of men and women will develop the disorder
(B) it is more common in lower socioeconomic groups
(C) it has a genetic component
(D) differential diagnoses include schizophrenia
(E) differential diagnoses include drug abuse

2. Which of the following statements is most likely to be true about major depressive disorder in a 30-year-old patient?

(A) Frequency of episodes will decrease with age
(B) Length of episodes will decrease with age
(C) Premorbid problems occurred
(D) The patient shows serious behavioral abnormalities between episodes of depression
(E) Treated episodes last for about 3 months

3. Which of the following statements is most likely to be true about a patient with bipolar disorder?

(A) Illness began with a manic episode
(B) Untreated manic episode will last about 3 months
(C) Manic episodes typically emerge slowly
(D) Period between episodes is about 2 years
(E) Amount of time between episodes increases as the illness progresses

4. Which of the following is a mood congruent delusion in mania?

(A) Guilt
(B) Terminal illness
(C) Failure
(D) Importance
(E) Persecution

5. All of the following statements about depression are true EXCEPT

(A) it correlates with the loss of a parent in the first decade of life
(B) the depressed mood is basically a severe form of sadness
(C) depressed patients are often unable to cry
(D) stressful life events are related to clinical depression
(E) it is related to loss of a spouse

6. Which of the following statements is characteristic of major depressive disorder?

(A) Severely depressed patients often do not have the energy to commit suicide
(B) As severe depression lifts, the risk of suicide decreases
(C) Orientation with respect to person, place, and time is usually impaired
(D) Presence of delusions indicates that the patient is schizophrenic, not depressed
(E) Psychomotor retardation is seen mainly in depressed teenagers

7. Which of the following symptoms is least likely to occur in a patient experiencing a manic episode?

(A) Loose associations
(B) Flight of ideas
(C) Word salad
(D) Neologisms
(E) Lack of energy

8. Which of the following statements about bipolar disorder is true?

(A) Patients with mania usually have a poor memory
(B) The judgment of patients with mania is rarely impaired
(C) Patients with mania are rarely assaultive
(D) The symptoms of depression in unipolar depression and bipolar disorder are similar
(E) Patients with mania usually have poor orientation

9. All of the following are characteristics of depression in people who later have a manic episode EXCEPT

(A) psychomotor retardation
(B) postpartum depression
(C) psychotic symptoms
(D) family history of bipolar disorder
(E) agitated depression

10. Which of the following statements about bipolar disorder is true?

(A) It has a better prognosis than major depressive disorder
(B) Patients with both depression and mania have better prognoses than those with only manic symptoms
(C) Chronic problems are present in most patients
(D) Forty percent of bipolar patients will have more than 10 manic episodes
(E) White patients are more likely to suffer from bipolar disorder than black patients

11. Which of the following statements about the treatment of mood disorders is true?

(A) Antidepressants usually work within 1 week
(B) Depression is treatable in approximately 20% of patients
(C) Combinations of heterocyclic and MAO inhibitors cannot be used to treat depression
(D) Heterocyclic antidepressants are usually the first choice of treatment for major depression
(E) Lithium is used in manic patients only when carbamazepine is ineffective

12. Which of the following prescription drugs is least likely to cause depressive symptoms?

(A) Methyldopa
(B) Oral contraceptives
(C) Steroids
(D) Propranolol
(E) Amitriptyline

13. All of the following statements about the treatment of mood disorders are true EXCEPT

(A) psychological treatment in conjunction with drug treatment is more beneficial than either treatment alone
(B) psychological treatment can increase compliance with treatment in mood disorders
(C) lithium is often used in a maintenance regimen in patients with bipolar disorder
(D) carbamazepine is the drug of choice for patients with mania
(E) antidepressants often take 3–4 weeks to become effective

Answers and Explanations

1–B. Bipolar disorder is more common in higher (not lower) socioeconomic groups.

2–E. Treated episodes of major depression last for about 3 months; untreated episodes last from 6–12 months.

3–B. Each untreated manic episode lasts about 3 months.

4–D. Mood congruent delusions consistent with mania include power and importance.

5–B. In depression, the mood has a different quality than that of sadness. Although biologic factors are involved, stressful life events are also related to clinical depression.

6–A. In major depressive disorder, orientation with respect to persons, place, and time is usually normal. Although severely depressed patients may not have enough energy to commit suicide, as the depression lifts the risk of suicide increases. Psychomotor retardation is seen in depressed elderly patients.

7–E. Excessive energy and hyperactivity characterize manic episodes.

8–D. Patients with mania usually show intact memory and orientation but may be assaultive and show poor judgement. The symptoms of depression are similar in unipolar depression and bipolar disorder.

9–E. Psychomotor retardation, postpartum depression, psychotic symptoms, and family history of bipolar disorder characterize patients with depression who later have a manic episode.

10–D. Forty percent of patients with bipolar disorder have more than 10 manic episodes. Bipolar disorder has a poorer prognosis than major depressive disorder. There are no racial differences in the occurrence of mood disorders. Patients with bipolar disorder who experience only manic symptoms have a better prognosis than those with both depression and mania. Chronic impairment is present in only about 10% of patients with bipolar disorder.

11–D. Heterocyclic antidepressants can be used in conjunction with MAO inhibitors. Depression is a treatable disorder in about 75% of patients. Antidepressants frequently require a 4–6 week trial.

12–E. Amitriptyline is an antidepressant. Use of methyldopa, propranolol, steroids, or oral contraceptives may be associated with symptoms of depression.

13–D. Lithium is the drug of choice for patients with mania; carbamazepine may be used if lithium is ineffective.

12

Anxiety Disorders

I. Overview

A. Fear and anxiety

- **Fear** is a normal reaction to a known, environmental source of danger. In **anxiety**, the individual experiences apprehension but the source of the danger is unknown or unrecognized.
- Physical manifestations of anxiety are similar to those of fear and include restlessness, dizziness, palpitations, mydriasis (pupil dilation), syncope, tingling in the extremities, tachycardia, tremor, gastrointestinal disturbances, diarrhea, and urinary urgency and frequency.
- The *DSM-IV* classification of anxiety disorders includes panic disorder, phobias, obsessive-compulsive disorder, post-traumatic stress disorder, and generalized anxiety disorder.

B. Neurotransmitters and anxiety

- The major neurotransmitters involved in the development of anxiety are **γ-aminobutyric acid (GABA), norepinephrine, and serotonin** (see Chapter 2).
- Other neurotransmitters that have been associated with anxiety are histamine, acetylcholine (**ACh**), and endogenous opioids.

C. Anatomy

- The **locus ceruleus and raphe nuclei** are areas of the brain likely to be involved in anxiety disorders.
  - The **limbic system**, which receives information from these areas of the brain, has many benzodiazepine receptor–binding sites.
- The temporal and frontal cerebral cortex are associated with anxiety.
- Organic causes of symptoms of anxiety include vitamin B_{12} deficiency, hypothyroidism and hyperthyroidism, hypoglycemia, hypoparathyroidism, cardiac arrhythmias, mitral valve prolapse, and pheochromocytoma (adrenal tumor).

II. Panic Disorder

A. Characteristics

- Panic disorder is identified by **episodic periods of intense anxiety** that occur suddenly and usually last about 30 minutes.
  - Symptoms include dyspnea, sweating, fainting, chest pain, and the feeling that one is about to die.

99

– **Mitral valve prolapse** is seen in up to 50% of all patients with this disorder.
– Panic attacks can be induced in susceptible people by an infusion of **sodium lactate** (see Chapter 17).
– Panic attacks commonly occur twice weekly, and they are **often associated with agoraphobia** (panic disorder with agoraphobia). They appear mainly in young adults and occur twice as often in women as in men.
– Panic disorder has a **strong genetic component**; the concordance rate is about 85% in monozygotic twins and only about 12% in dizygotic twins.

B. Treatment

– **Antidepressant drugs**, primarily imipramine, are the major pharmacologic treatment for panic disorder; alprazolam has also proven useful.
– The efficacy of antidepressant drugs in panic disorder may be mediated through the serotonergic system.
– **Systematic desensitization and cognitive therapy** are useful adjuncts to pharmacotherapy in panic disorder.

III. Phobias

A. Characteristics

– Phobias are **irrational fears** of objects or social or environmental situations; because of the fear, the object or situation is avoided.
  – Anxiety is seen with exposure to the feared object or place.
  – **Agoraphobia** (fear of open areas) and **claustrophobia** (fear of closed areas) are examples of phobic disorders. In agoraphobia, an individual may feel intense anxiety accompanied by physical symptoms such as palpitations when outdoors.

B. Treatment

– Behavioral therapy that includes **systematic desensitization** is the most effective treatment for phobias; family therapy and psychotherapy are also useful.
– Antidepressants, primarily the monoamine oxidase (MAO) inhibitors, and β-adrenergic antagonists, such as propranolol, are helpful adjuncts to psychotherapeutic treatment of phobias.

IV. Obsessive-Compulsive Disorder

A. Characteristics

– Obsessive-compulsive disorder is characterized by obsessions (**recurrent thoughts,** feelings, and images) and compulsions (**repetitive actions**).
  – Patients with this disorder frequently show electroencephalographic (EEG) abnormalities.
  – Sleep and neuroendocrine studies show abnormalities similar to those seen in patients with depression.

B. Treatment

– **Clomipramine,** a tricyclic antidepressant, is the most effective drug used to treat obsessive-compulsive disorder; other tricyclics as well as trazodone and fluoxetine also have proven useful.
– **Behavioral therapy and insight-oriented psychotherapy** are useful in many patients.

V. Post-traumatic Stress Disorder

A. Characteristics

- People who have had a severe **physiological or psychological trauma** are at risk for post-traumatic stress disorder.
- One-half to three-fourths of survivors of severe natural disasters may develop post-traumatic stress disorder.

B. Treatment

- Short-term psychotherapy, group therapy, tricyclic antidepressants, and MAO inhibitors are used in the treatment of post-traumatic stress disorder.

VI. Generalized Anxiety Disorder

A. Characteristics

- Generalized anxiety disorder is characterized by **persistent anxiety** lasting at least 6 months with tension, sympathetic and parasympathetic symptoms, and insomnia.
  - Symptoms of anxiety cannot be related to a specific person or situation.
- Generalized anxiety disorder develops more frequently in women than in men and commonly starts during the third decade of life.

B. Treatment

- Treatment of generalized anxiety disorder includes **relaxation therapy and antianxiety agents**, including benzodiazepines and buspirone.

Review Test

Directions: Each of the numbered items or incomplete statements in this section is followed by answers or by completions of the statement. Select the **one** lettered answer or completion that is **best** in each case.

1. Which of the following is a physical manifestation of anxiety?

(A) Flight of ideas
(B) Depression
(C) Tingling in the extremities
(D) Ideas of reference
(E) Neologisms

2. Which of the following findings best describes a 55-year-old female patient experiencing panic attacks?

(A) Symptoms include dizziness, sweating, and fainting
(B) Attacks commonly occur once a month
(C) Intense periods of anxiety usually last 3–4 hours
(D) Attacks first appeared at age 45
(E) Chlorpromazine is the primary pharmacologic treatment

3. Which of the following statements about obsessive-compulsive disorder is true?

(A) EEG abnormalities are rare
(B) It is characterized by recurrent thoughts or feelings
(C) The most effective drug treatment is diazepam
(D) Antipsychotic drugs are the primary treatment
(E) Associated sleep disorders are similar to those that occur in mania

4. Which of the following statements about generalized anxiety disorder is true?

(A) It occurs more frequently in men than in women
(B) It is characterized by a chronic, persistent thought disorder
(C) Parasympathetic symptoms rarely occur
(D) The symptoms usually can be related to a single cause
(E) It commonly develops about age 25

5. Which of the following regions of the brain is least likely to be implicated in anxiety disorders?

(A) Cerebellum
(B) Locus ceruleus
(C) Raphe nuclei
(D) Limbic system
(E) Temporal cerebral cortex

6. Which of the following is least likely to be used in the treatment of phobias?

(A) β-adrenergic antagonists
(B) Electroconvulsive therapy (ECT)
(C) Antidepressant drugs
(D) Psychotherapy
(E) Systematic desensitization

Directions: The group of items in this section consists of lettered options followed by a set of numbered items. For each item, select the **one** lettered option that is most closely associated with it. Each lettered option may be selected once, more than once, or not at all.

Questions 7–9

Match the clinical profile with the disorder that best describes it.

(A) Post-traumatic stress disorder
(B) Generalized anxiety disorder
(C) Obsessive-compulsive disorder
(D) Panic disorder
(E) Phobias

7. A lawyer who works in the World Trade Center has recurrent flashbacks of his experiences after the center is bombed

8. A patient checks five times to be sure that her front door is locked every time she leaves home

9. A 40-year-old woman has palpitations and feels tense most of the time

Generalised anxiety

Answers and Explanations

1–C. Tingling in the extremities is a physical manifestation of anxiety.

2–A. Symptoms of panic attacks include dizziness, sweating, and fainting, which commonly occur twice weekly and last about 30 minutes. Panic attacks are most common in young women and are effectively treated with antidepressant medication.

3–B. Obsessive-compulsive disorder is characterized by recurrent feelings and repetitive actions; clomipramine is the most effective treatment.

4–E. Generalized anxiety disorder commonly develops in the third decade of life.

5–A. The cerebellum is not implicated in anxiety disorders. However, the locus ceruleus, raphe nuclei, limbic system, and temporal cerebral cortex are areas of the brain involved in anxiety disorders.

6–B. Common treatments for phobias include antidepressant drugs such as imipramine and β-adrenergic antagonists as well as psychotherapy and systematic desensitization.

7–A. Flashbacks that occur after a very stressful life event indicate post-traumatic stress disorder.

8–C. Repetitive actions or compulsions such as checking locks indicate that this patient is suffering from obsessive-compulsive disorder.

9–B. Chronic feelings of anxiety with no specific cause indicate generalized anxiety disorder.

13

Cognitive Disorders

I. Overview

A. Etiology

- **Cognitive disorders** (formerly called organic mental syndromes) are caused primarily by abnormalities in brain chemistry, structure, or physiology.
- The underlying problem may originate in the brain or it may be secondary to physical illness.

B. Characteristics

- The hallmarks of cognitive disorders are **cognitive problems** such as deficits in memory, orientation, judgment, or mental function.
- Mood changes, anxiety, irritability, paranoia, and psychosis, if present, are secondary to the cognitive loss.

II. Delirium

A. Characteristics

- **Delirium** is impaired cognitive functioning caused by central nervous system (CNS) dysfunction. It is characterized by **clouding of consciousness.**
  - Cognitive impairment shows **diurnal variability** and is worse at night and in the early morning hours. Patients experiencing this pattern of impairment are referred to as **"sundowners."**
- Orientation to time and place is abnormal; orientation to person is usually normal.
- **Illusions and hallucinations**, often **visual**, occur. The hallucinations associated with delirium are less organized than those associated with schizophrenia.
- The patient is either hypoactive or hyperactive.
- Autonomic dysfunction, fear, and anxiety occur.

B. Occurrence

- Delirium is the **most common psychiatric syndrome** seen in patients who are admitted to medical and surgical **hospital units.**
  - Delirium has many causes and may occur in up to one-third of patients in surgical and coronary intensive care units (Table 13-1).
- Delirium is **more common in the elderly and in children**.
- A history of delirium increases the chances of recurrence.

105

Table 13-1. Causes of Delirium

Cerebral	Somatic	External or Pharmacologic
Brain trauma	Arrhythmias	Alcohol
Encephalitis	Carbon monoxide narcosis	Anticholinergics
Epilepsy	Cardiac failure	Anticonvulsants
Meningitis	Electrolyte imbalance	Antihypertensives
Subarachnoid hemorrhage	Endocrine dysfunctions	Antiparkinson drugs
	Hepatic encephalopathy	Carbon monoxide
	Hypotension	Cimetidine
	Hypoxia	Disulfiram
	Normal pressure hydrocephalus	Hypnotics
	Postoperative states	Insulin
	Systemic infections	Opiates
	Thiamine deficiency	Phencyclidine (PCP)
	Uremic encephalopathy	Poisons
		Sedatives
		Steroids
		Tranquilizers

C. Treatment

– If the underlying cause is treated and removed, the delirium will resolve. Untreated delirium can advance to dementia.

III. Dementia

A. Characteristics

– Dementia involves a general **loss of intellectual abilities** and **impaired functioning**.
– **Memory loss** is an early symptom of dementia; in contrast to delirium, the level of consciousness remains normal.
– In subcortical dementias (seen in Huntington's disease, Parkinson's disease, and in HIV encephalopathy), **movement disorders** are seen.
– Inability to control impulses, lack of judgment, and mood changes are often found, particularly with involvement of the frontal lobes.
– Symptoms that develop later include confusion and psychosis progressing to coma and death.

B. Occurrence

– Dementia **most commonly occurs in the elderly.**
  – In the United States, approximately 15% of individuals over age 65 suffer from dementia.
  – Because the incidence of dementia increases with age, it is seen more frequently as people live longer.
– In about two-thirds of cases, the disorder is **dementia of Alzheimer type**; other types include Pick's disease (5% of dementias), multi-infarct dementia (10% of dementias), and Korsakoff's syndrome (relatively rare).
  – When compared with patients with Alzheimer's disease, personality is more affected and cognitive function is less affected in patients with **Pick's disease**. Both illnesses are similar in clinical course and age of onset.

Table 13-2. Causes of Dementia

Nervous System	Somatic	Infections
Alzheimer's disease	Cardiovascular disease	AIDS
Brain trauma	Cyanocobalamin deficiency	Creutzfeldt-Jakob disease
Cerebral hypoxia	Endocrine disorders	Cryptococcal meningitis
Huntington's disease	Folic acid deficiency	Fungal meningitis
Intracranial tumors	Liver disease	Neurosyphilis
Korsakoff's syndrome	Normal pressure hydrocephalus	Tuberculosis
Multi-infarct dementia	Renal disease	Viral encephalitis
Multiple sclerosis	Respiratory disease	
Pick's disease	Sarcoidosis	

C. **Causes of dementia**
  – Although the etiology of dementia is unknown, a **reduction in brain levels of choline acetyltransferase** (needed to synthesize acetylcholine [ACh]) and aluminum toxicity, as well as genetic factors (see Chapter 1), have been implicated in Alzheimer's disease.
  – Long-term alcohol abuse results in **Korsakoff's syndrome, or alcohol amnestic disorder,** a form of dementia caused in part by thiamine deficiency.
    – Retrograde and anterograde amnesia and confabulation (untruths told to cover up memory loss) occur in Korsakoff's syndrome.
  – Although normal aging is associated with reduction in the ability to learn new things quickly and a general slowing of mental processes, in contrast dementia changes with normal aging do not interfere with normal life.
  – Various factors, including exposure to drugs and toxins, can result in dementia (Table 13-2).

D. **Pseudodementia**
  – Pseudodementia, which occurs in elderly patients, may mimic dementia. It is characterized by loss of memory and other cognitive problems resulting from **depression**.
  – The distinction between dementia and both delirium and pseudodementia is important because the latter two conditions are highly treatable (Table 13-3).

E. **Treatment**
  – Dementia is reversible in about 15% of cases; in most cases, treatment is symptomatic.
  – **Pharmacotherapy** is used to treat the associated symptoms of anxiety, depression, and psychosis; psychotherapy is used mainly for support of the patient and family.
  – The lives of individuals with dementia can be improved by providing a structured environment, nutritious diet, exercise, and recreational therapy.

Table 13-3. Comparison of Dementia and Delirium

Dementia (Hallmark: Memory Loss)	Delirium (Hallmark: Impaired Consciousness)
Consciousness not impaired	Consciousness impaired
Normal level of arousal	Stupor or agitation
Develops slowly and insidiously	Develops quickly
Often irreversible	Frequently reversible

IV. Dementia Due to HIV Infection and AIDS-Related Complex

A. Incidence and causes

- At least two-thirds of patients with HIV infection eventually develop some level of dementia.
- Symptoms of HIV dementia include memory loss, confusion, delusions, agitation, and depression progressing to psychosis and coma.
- The brains of patients with HIV dementia typically show cortical atrophy, inflammation and demyelination (**AIDS dementia complex or HIV encephalopathy**), as well as **cerebral lymphomas and opportunistic infections.**
- The **basal ganglia and white matter** are areas of the brain most affected in HIV dementia.

B. AIDS-Related Complex (ARC)

- ARC is comprised of physical symptoms of HIV infection that have not yet qualified as a diagnosis of AIDS. It is often associated with psychiatric problems that result from the physical symptoms of fatigue and general malaise characteristic of the disease.
- Fear, anxiety, and depression are common in patients with ARC.
- Antidepressant and antipsychotic agents and psychotherapy are used to treat the psychiatric symptoms of AIDS and ARC.

Review Test

Directions: Each of the numbered items or incomplete statements in this section is followed by answers or by completions of the statement. Select the **one** lettered answer or completion that is **best** in each case.

1. All of the following are common causes of delirium EXCEPT

(A) brain trauma
(B) encephalitis
(C) meningitis
(D) epilepsy
(E) Alzheimer's disease

2. Which of the following statements about dementia is true?

(A) About 35% of Americans over age 65 suffer from dementia
(B) The incidence of dementia decreases with age
(C) The most common type of dementia is multi-infarct dementia
(D) The quality of life of a patient with dementia cannot be improved
(E) Dementia is reversible in about 15% of patients

3. Which of the following statements about the psychiatric dimensions of AIDS is true?

(A) HIV dementia is seen in about 10% of AIDS patients
(B) Antidepressant agents are of no value in treating the depression associated with AIDS
(C) Brain abnormalities are rarely seen in patients with AIDS
(D) Psychiatric symptoms associated with AIDS include psychosis
(E) The gray matter of the brain is more likely to be involved than the white matter in patients with AIDS

4. All of the following statements about delirium are true EXCEPT

(A) cognitive impairment is worse at night than during the day
(B) it usually resolves without treatment
(C) the patient may be hyperactive
(D) autonomic dysfunction may occur
(E) illusions may occur

5. Which of the following conditions is associated with normal aging?

(A) Impaired consciousness
(B) Abnormal level of arousal
(C) Reduced speed of new learning
(D) Psychosis
(E) Depression

6. Which of the following statements about pseudodementia is true?

(A) It is rarely treatable
(B) It is characterized by mania
(C) Memory loss frequently occurs
(D) It is common in young adults
(E) It results in Alzheimer's disease

Answers and Explanations

1–E. Alzheimer's disease is a common cause of dementia. Brain trauma, encephalitis, meningitis, and epilepsy are common causes of delirium.

2–E. Dementia is reversible in only about 15% percent of patients.

3–D. The psychiatric symptoms associated with HIV dementia include psychosis and depression. Antipsychotic and antidepressant agents may be useful in treating psychosis and depression associated with HIV dementia.

4–B. If the underlying cause of delirium is treated and removed, the condition will usually resolve. If untreated, delirium can advance to dementia.

5–C. In normal aging, while there may be a reduction in how fast new material is learned, level of consciousness, memory, and mood are normal.

6–C. Pseudodementia includes cognitive problems such as memory loss, occurs in elderly patients, and may mimic dementia. It is characterized by depression and is treatable.

14

Other Psychiatric Disorders in Adults and Children

I. Somatoform and Related Disorders

A. Characteristics and classification

- Somatoform disorders consist of **physical symptoms without organic pathology.**
- The *DSM-IV* categories of somatoform disorders and their characteristics are listed in Table 14-1.

B. Treatment

- Treatment of somatoform disorders includes **individual and group psychotherapy.**
- **Anxiolytic drugs, hypnosis, and behavioral relaxation therapy** may also be used, particularly in the treatment of conversion disorder.

C. Factitious disorders

- While individuals with somatoform disorders truly believe that they are ill, patients with factitious and related disorders **fake illness** for psychological or tangible gain (Table 14-2).

II. Personality Disorders

A. Characteristics

- Individuals with personality disorders often show long-standing rigid, **unsuitable patterns of relating to others** and to the world around them.
- They generally are not aware of their problems, do not seek psychiatric help, and do not have empathy with others.

B. Classification

- Personality disorders are categorized by the *DSM-IV* into **three clusters—A, B, and C**—each with its own hallmark characteristics (Table 14-3).
- Schizoid, paranoid, antisocial, and obsessive-compulsive personality disorders are seen more often in males; histrionic, borderline, avoidant, and dependent personality disorders are seen more often in females.

C. Treatment

- Treatment of personality disorders involves **individual and group psychotherapy** as well as self-help groups.

Table 14-1. *DSM-IV* Classification of Somatoform Disorders

Classification	Characteristics
Somatization disorder (Briquet's syndrome)	Multiple physical complaints; seeks medical help; more common in women and in low socioeconomic groups; genetic influences
Conversion disorder	Loss of sensory or motor function; more common in adolescent and young adult women; patients appear relatively unconcerned—"la belle indifference"
Hypochondriasis	Exaggerated concern with one's health and illness; no gender or age differences
Body dysmorphic disorder	Normal-appearing patient believes he or she is physically abnormal
Pain disorder associated with psychological factors	Intense, prolonged pain without physical disease
Undifferentiated somatoform disorder	Multiple physical symptoms lasting more than 6 months

- **Pharmacotherapy** can also be used to treat symptoms such as depression and anxiety that may be associated with the personality disorders.

III. Dissociative Disorders

A. Characteristics
- The dissociative disorders are rare, dramatic disorders characterized by abrupt but temporary **loss of memory or identity** due to psychological factors.

B. Classification
- The *DSM-IV* categories of dissociative disorders are listed in Table 14-4.

C. Amnesia
- Besides psychogenic amnesia, other causes of amnesia include head injury, electroconvulsive therapy (ECT), or anesthesia.
  - In **psychogenic amnesia**, the **amnesia** is usually **retrograde** (unable to recall past events).
  - In **head trauma**, the **amnesia** is usually **anterograde** (unable to learn new material) as well as retrograde.

D. Treatment
- Treatment of the dissociative disorders includes **hypnosis** and **amobarbital sodium interviews** (see Chapter 17) as well as long-term **psychotherapy**.

IV. Eating Disorders

- The eating disorders include obesity, anorexia nervosa, and bulimia nervosa, all of which **occur more often in women** than in men.

Table 14-2. *DSM-IV* Factitious Disorder and Related Conditions

Classification	Characteristics
Factitious disorder (Munchausen syndrome)	Simulation of a physical or psychiatric illness in order to receive attention from medical personnel
Munchausen syndrome by proxy	Simulation of an illness in another person, typically in a child by a parent
Malingering	Simulation of a physical illness for financial or other obvious gain

Table 14-3. *DSM-IV* Types and Characteristics of Personality Disorders

Type	Characteristics
Cluster A (Hallmarks: eccentric, strange, fear of social relationships)	
Paranoid	Suspiciousness, mistrust, responsibility for problems attributed to others
Schizoid	Lifelong pattern of social withdrawal without psychosis
Schizotypal	Peculiar appearance, odd thought patterns, behavior without psychosis
Cluster B (Hallmarks: emotional, dramatic, erratic)	
Histrionic	Dramatic, extroverted behavior; cannot maintain intimate relationships; occurs more often in females; associated with somatization disorder and alcoholism
Narcissistic	Grandiosity, sense of entitlement, lack of empathy, envy
Antisocial	Inability to conform to social norms, criminality; bedwetting, setting fires, and torturing animals are seen in childhood; EEG abnormal
Borderline	Unstable affect, mood, and behavior; suicide attempts; impulsiveness
Cluster C (Hallmarks: fearful, anxious)	
Avoidant	Sensitive to rejection, socially withdrawn, shy; inferiority complex; may be related to timidity in infancy
Obsessive-compulsive	Orderliness, stubborn, indecisive; perfectionist
Dependent	Lack of self-confidence; lets others assume responsibilities
Personality disorder not otherwise specified	
Passive-aggressive	Procrastination, stubborn, inefficient

A. Obesity

1. Overview

- Obesity is defined as being **more than 20%** over ideal weight based on common height and weight charts.
- About 25% of adults in the United States are obese.
- **Genetic factors are important** in obesity; adult weight is closer to that of biologic rather than of adoptive parents.
- Obesity is more common in **lower socioeconomic groups** and is associated with increased risk for heart problems, hypertension, diabetes mellitus, and gallbladder disease.

Table 14-4. *DSM-IV* Classification and Characteristics of Dissociative Disorders

Classification	Characteristics
Dissociative amnesia	Failure to remember important information about oneself
Dissociative fugue	Amnesia combined with sudden wandering from home
Dissociative identity disorder (multiple personality disorder)	At least two distinct personalities in an individual
Depersonalization disorder	Feelings of detachment from one's own body or the social situation
Dissociative disorder not otherwise specified: derealization (a variant of depersonalization disorder)	Feeling that the environment and objects within it are unreal

2. Treatment

- Most weight loss achieved using commercial dieting-weight loss programs is regained within a 5-year-period.
- Gastric stapling and other surgical techniques are initially effective but are of little value in maintaining long-term weight loss.

B. Anorexia nervosa

1. Overview

- Anorexia nervosa is characterized by excessive dieting and **weight loss** (15% or more of body weight), and by abnormal behavior in dealing with food, disturbance of body image, conflicts about sexuality, excessive exercising, abuse of laxatives and diuretics, and overwhelming fear of becoming obese.
- Anorexia is more common during **late adolescence**, in high academic achievers, and in **higher socioeconomic groups**; it occurs in up to 1% of teenage girls.
- **Amenorrhea** may occur.
- Early age of onset and few or no previous hospitalizations are predictors of a positive outcome.

2. Treatment

- Because anorexia can result in death, initial treatment is directed at **reinstating the nutritional condition** of the patient.
- Psychoactive drugs such as amitriptyline and cyproheptadine [Periactin] have been used in the treatment of anorexia.
- Family therapy has proven to be the most useful form of psychotherapy.

C. Bulimia nervosa

1. Overview

- Bulimia nervosa is characterized by **binge eating followed by purging** with vomiting, laxatives, or diuretics.
- Like anorexia, bulimia usually begins during **adolescence.**
- In contrast to anorexics, most bulimics are at or near their normal weight, rarely have amenorrhea, and are sexually active.

2. Treatment

- Treatment of bulimia includes **psychotherapy and behavioral therapy.**
- Antidepressants, including heterocyclic drugs, monoamine oxidase (MAO) inhibitors, and fluoxetine, may be useful in the treatment of bulimia.

V. Infantile Autism

A. Characteristics

- Autistic disorder, or infantile autism, is a severe, pervasive developmental disorder of childhood.
  - Autistic disorder becomes apparent in infancy or childhood and is characterized by **deficits in the ability to interact and communicate.**
  - Some autistic children may show unusual abilities, such as exceptional memories or calculational abilities (idiot savants), but they usually have subnormal intelligence.

B. Occurrence

- Autistic disorder occurs in about 5 children per 10,000, begins before 3 years of age, and is much **more common in boys** than in girls.

– When present in girls, autistic disorder is more severe and is associated with a family history of other cognitive disorders.

C. Etiology

– Recent studies suggest that **neurologic abnormalities** such as seizures and other evidence of cerebral dysfunction are associated with autistic disorder. **Perinatal complications** are frequently found in the history of autistic children.

– As in some children with severe mental retardation, **increased serum serotonin levels** are present in about 35% of autistic children.

– A concordance rate for autism in monozygotic twins of 35% and a lack of concordance in dizygotic twins suggest a **genetic component**.

D. Treatment

– Treatment of autistic children involves intensive work with the child with aims of increasing social and communicative skills, decreasing behavioral problems, improving self-care skills, and providing support and counseling to the parents.

E. Prognosis

– Most autistic children continue to be severely impaired in adulthood; only about 2% are able to work and live independently.

VI. Attention-Deficit Hyperactivity Disorder (ADHD)

A. Characteristics

– Major characteristics of children with ADHD include **hyperactivity, limited attention span,** propensity for accidents, impulsiveness, emotional lability, and irritability; intelligence is normal.

– Although some children with ADHD were placid as infants, more commonly children with ADHD cried excessively, showed **high sensitivity to stimuli,** and did not sleep well.

– Differential diagnoses of ADHD include major depression, anxiety disorder, an early form of bipolar disorder, and conduct disturbances.

B. Occurrence

– In the United States, the incidence of ADHD is about 3%–5% of children ages 5–12.

– ADHD is up to five times **more common in boys**, particularly firstborn boys.

C. Etiology

– **Genetic factors** may be involved in the etiology of ADHD.
  – Siblings of children with ADHD (particularly monozygotic twins) have a higher incidence of the disorder than children in the general population.
  – Parents of children with ADHD have a higher incidence of antisocial personality disorder, somatization disorder, and alcoholism.

– Although evidence of serious structural problems in the brain is not present, children with ADHD may have **minor brain damage.**

D. Treatment

– Pharmacologic treatment for ADHD consists of use of **amphetamines**, including methylphenidate [Ritalin, Methidate], dextroamphetamine sulfate, and pemoline [Cylert].

- CNS stimulants may lower activity level and increase attention span and the ability to concentrate in children with ADHD; antidepressants such as imipramine are also useful.
- Adverse effects of use of CNS stimulants include inhibition of growth and weight gain; both usually return to normal once the child stops taking the medication.

E. Prognosis

- Most patients retain characteristics of ADHD, such as impulsivity, into adulthood and **remain at risk** for mood and personality disorders.
- Some patients show complete remission during adolescence with few long-term negative effects.

VII. Tourette's Syndrome

A. Characteristics

- Tourette's syndrome is characterized by **motor and vocal tics**; the involuntary use of profanity often occurs.
- The disease begins before age 21, usually between the ages of 7 and 8.

B. Etiology

- **Dysfunctional regulation of dopamine** is probably involved in the etiology of Tourette's syndrome.
- The disease is three times **more common in males** and is concordant in 50% of monozygotic twins and in only 8% of dizygotic twins.
- There is a **genetic relationship** between the disease and both ADHD and obsessive-compulsive disorder.

C. Treatment

- **Haloperidol** is the most effective treatment for Tourette's syndrome.

Review Test

Directions: Each of the numbered items or incomplete statements in this section is followed by answers or by completions of the statement. Select the **one** lettered answer or completion that is **best** in each case.

1. A patient reports that she has no sensation in her left arm. Physical examination fails to reveal evidence of a physiologic problem. The most likely diagnosis for this condition is

(A) hypochondriasis
(B) body dysmorphic disorder
(C) conversion disorder
(D) undifferentiated somatoform disorder
(E) somatoform pain disorder

2. All of the following statements about children with attention-deficit hyperactivity disorder (ADHD) are true EXCEPT

(A) genetic factors are not involved
(B) they are often accident prone
(C) they are often emotionally labile
(D) they are often irritable
(E) emotional difficulties are common

3. Which of the following statements about somatization disorder is true?

(A) It is more common in men than in women
(B) It is more common in higher socioeconomic groups
(C) It has multiple physical complaints with no physical disease
(D) It has similar concordance rates in monozygotic and dizygotic twins
(E) Patients rarely seek medical help

4. Which of the following statements about anorexia nervosa is true?

(A) It is most commonly seen in childhood
(B) It is more common in lower socioeconomic groups
(C) It is seen more often in females than in males
(D) It has few serious medical consequences
(E) Body weight is usually normal

5. All of the following statements about ADHD are true EXCEPT

(A) CNS stimulants are used in treatment of ADHD
(B) differential diagnosis includes depression
(C) differential diagnosis includes anxiety disorder
(D) as infants, children with ADHD often show high sensitivity to stimuli
(E) it is more common in girls

Directions: The group of items in this section consists of lettered options followed by a set of numbered items. For each item, select the **one** lettered option that is most closely associated with it. Each lettered option may be selected once, more than once, or not at all.

Questions 6–10

For each set of clinical manifestations, select the personality disorder that best describes the patient.

(A) Antisocial
(B) Avoidant
(C) Paranoid
(D) Schizotypal
(E) Schizoid

6. A patient who has been passive and withdrawn throughout life but is not psychotic

7. A patient who dresses strangely and behaves oddly but is not psychotic

8. A patient who appears hostile and blames the physician for his illness

9. A patient who is timid, sensitive, and socially withdrawn

10. A patient who has just been released from jail after his third incarceration for armed robbery

Answers and Explanations

1–C. Conversion disorder involves changes in body functions including loss of motor or sensory function with no medical cause.

2–A. There is evidence that genetic factors may be involved in the etiology of ADHD.

3–C. Somatization disorder involves multiple physical complaints with no physical disease. This disorder is more common in women and in lower socioeconomic groups. It has higher concordance rates in monozygotic than dizygotic twins. Although there is no physical disease, patients frequently seek medical help.

4–C. Anorexia nervosa is seen more in females than in males, is more common in late adolescence and in higher socioeconomic groups, and may have very serious medical consequences.

5–E. ADHD is up to five times more common in boys than in girls.

6–E. A lifelong pattern of social withdrawal is seen in schizoid personality disorder.

7–D. Peculiar appearance, thinking, and behavior are seen in schizotypal personality disorder.

8–C. Individuals with paranoid personality disorders show suspiciousness and mistrust.

9–B. The avoidant personality is sensitive to rejection, socially withdrawn, shy and may have an inferiority complex.

10–A. The inability to conform to social norms, as well as criminality, is seen in individuals with antisocial personality disorder.

15

Suicide

I. Overview

- Suicide is the **eighth leading cause of death** in the United States, with only heart disease, cancer, stroke, accidents, pneumonia, diabetes mellitus, and cirrhosis of the liver being more common.
- The suicide rate in the United States is about 12 per 100,000.
- There are about nine times more **suicide attempts** than actual suicides. About 30% of attempted suicides will try again and 10% will succeed in killing themselves; individuals are at highest risk during the three months following the initial suicide attempt.

II. Risk Factors

A. Sex

- **Men successfully commit suicide three times more often than women** even though women attempt suicide four times more often than men.
- Men are generally more successful because they tend to use violent means such as firearms or jumping from heights; women more commonly take drugs or slash their wrists.
- Suicide rates in men **increase after age 45**; in women, most suicides occur after 55 years of age.
- The suicide rate in males aged 15–24 years is increasing significantly; in females, the rate is increasing only slightly.

B. Age-related factors

- The elderly constitute approximately 25% of suicides, although they make up only 10% of the population.
- Suicide is the **second leading cause of death in people aged 15–24 years**; only accidents are responsible for more deaths.
- Suicides among adolescents may run in clusters within communities and may increase after the airing of television programs depicting teenage suicide.
- Although suicide is **rare in children** under the age of 12, about 13% of children have thought about committing suicide.

Table 15-1. Marital Status and Suicide Risk

Marital Status	Approximate Suicide Rate (per 100,000)
Married	11
Divorced women	18
Single, never married	22
Widowed	24
Divorced men	69

C. **Familial factors**
  - Suicide is more common in adolescents with **divorced parents**.
  - Children younger than age 11 at the time of a parent's death are at higher risk for depression and suicide.
  - **Marriage is associated with reduced risk of suicide** (Table 15-1).

D. **Racial and socioeconomic factors**
  - **Whites commit suicide more frequently** than blacks; however, the rate is equivalent among black and white men aged 20–24 years.
  - Suicide rates among Jews and Protestants are higher than the rate among Catholics.
  - Suicide rates increase during economic recessions and economic depressions.

E. **Occupational factors**
  - **Professional women**, particularly physicians, may be at increased risk for suicide.
  - Study sample sizes are small among physicians in general, but psychiatrists appear to be at highest risk.
  - Other professionals at high risk for suicide are dentists, law enforcement officers, lawyers, and musicians.

F. **Physical and psychological factors**
  - Various physical and psychological factors increase the risk of suicide, including (in order of decreasing risk): age over 45 years, alcohol and drug abuse, prior suicide attempts, male sex, serious prior psychiatric illness, recent divorce or death of a spouse, serious medical illness, unemployment, and unmarried status.

III. Suicidal Ideation, Intent, and Plan
  - Clinicians should assess suicide risk during every mental status examination.
  - The majority of patients who eventually kill themselves tell the clinician in some way about their desire to die.
  - **Patients who have a plan** of how they will carry out the suicide are at high risk.
  - Other factors that can help identify patients likely to commit suicide include a **family history of suicide**, possession of a means of suicide, writing a will, and talking about their fears of how suicide may affect family members.

IV. Management of Suicidal Patients
A. **Hospitalization**
  - Indications for hospitalization of a suicidal patient include **impulsiveness, lack of social support**, and presence of a **specific plan** for suicide.
  - Patients may commit suicide even when hospitalized.

B. Recovery
- **Patients recovering from suicidal depression are at increased risk** since they have regained energy and are better able to act on their suicide plans.
- Patients with acute suicidal tendencies have a better prognosis than patients who are chronically suicidal.

Review Test

Directions: Each of the numbered items or incomplete statements in this section is followed by answers or by completions of the statement. Select the **one** lettered answer or completion that is **best** in each case.

1. All of the following are risk factors for suicide EXCEPT

(A) alcoholism
(B) male sex
(C) depression
(D) loss of physical health
(E) Catholic religion

2. Which of the following medical specialists appears to be at highest risk for suicide?

(A) Pediatrician
(B) Obstetrician
(C) Psychiatrist
(D) Radiologist
(E) Urologist

3. Which of the following groups is at the highest risk for suicide?

(A) Married men
(B) Widowed women
(C) Single women
(D) Divorced men
(E) Divorced women

4. Which of the following statements about suicide in children and adolescents is true?

(A) Most children have had serious thoughts of suicide
(B) Suicide is the leading cause of death in adolescents
(C) Suicide is more common in adults whose parents died in the first decade of their lives
(D) Television shows about teenage suicide act as deterrents to suicide in teenagers
(E) Suicide is less common in children with divorced parents

Answers and Explanations

1–E. Catholics have a lower suicide rate than Protestants or Jews.

2–C. Among physicians, psychiatrists appear to be at highest risk for suicide.

3–D. Divorced men are at high risk for suicide.

4–C. Suicide is more common in children whose parents died in the first decade of their lives and in those whose parents were divorced. Suicide is the second leading cause of death in adolescents surpassed only by accidents.

16

Psychological Assessment of Intelligence, Personality, and Achievement

I. Psychological Tests

A. Objective and projective tests

- **Intelligence, personality, achievement, and psychopathology** can be assessed with psychological tests. These tests can be classified by the functional area being addressed or by whether information gathering is achieved objectively or projectively.
- An **objective** test is based on questions that can be easily scored and statistically analyzed.
- A **projective** test requires the subject to interpret the questions. In this type of test, the subject's responses are assumed to be based on motivational state and defense mechanisms.

B. Individual and group testing

- **Individual tests** allow careful observation and evaluation of a particular person; a test battery looks at functioning of an individual in a number of different areas.
- Tests given to a **group of people** have advantages of efficient administration and grading and ease of statistical analysis.
- See Table 16-1 for tests commonly used clinically to evaluate patients.

II. Major Intelligence Tests

A. Intelligence and mental age

- **Intelligence** is an individual's ability to reason, manage abstract concepts, assimilate facts, recall what has been learned, analyze and organize information, and manage the special requirements of a new situation.
- **Mental age**, as defined by Alfred Binet, is the average intellectual level of people of a specific chronological age.
- The **Stanford-Binet scale** is used to test general intellectual ability in individuals 2–18 years of age.

B. Intelligence quotient (IQ)

- On the Stanford-Binet scale, an individual's IQ is the ratio of mental age to chronological age multiplied by 100. When the mental and chronological ages are the same, the person's IQ is 100 (Table 16-2).

Table 16-1. Types of Commonly Used Psychological Assessment Tests

Test Type	Examples
Objective	Minnesota Multiphasic Personality Inventory (MMPI)
Projective	Rorschach Inkblot Test Thematic Apperception Test (TAT) Sentence Completion Test (SCT) Draw-a-Person Test
Individual	Wechsler Adult Intelligence Scale (WAIS) Bender-Gestalt Test
Group	California Achievement Test
Battery	Luria-Nebraska Neuropsychological Battery (LNNB) Halstead-Reitan Battery (HRB)

- Because IQ is relatively **stable throughout life,** the highest chronological age used in determining IQ is 15 years.
- IQ test results are influenced by an individual's culture and early learning; intelligence tests cannot be completely free of cultural influences.

C. **Wechsler intelligence tests**

1. The **Wechsler Adult Intelligence Scale-Revised (WAIS-R)** is the most commonly used intelligence test.
   - Different tables are used to score seven age groups from 16–75 years of age.
   - The WAIS-R consists of 11 subtests (6 verbal and 5 performance) that evaluate information, comprehension, similarities, arithmetic, vocabulary, picture assembly, picture completion, block design, object assembly, digit span, and digit symbol.
   - In addition to heredity, performance on the subtests of the WAIS-R is influenced by **anxiety** (arithmetic, digit span), **level of education** (information and vocabulary), and **psychological problems** (large difference between verbal and performance tests).

2. The **Wechsler Intelligence Scale for Children-Revised (WISC-R)** is used to test children 6–16½ years of age.

3. The **Wechsler Preschool and Primary Scale of Intelligence (WPPSI)** is used to test children 4–6½ years of age.

Table 16-2. IQ and Classification of Intelligence (*DSM-IV* and WAIS-R)

IQ	Classification
<20–25	Profound mental retardation
20–25 to 35–40	Severe mental retardation
35–40 to 50–55	Moderate mental retardation
50–55 to 70	Mild mental retardation
70–79	Borderline
80–89	Low average/dull normal
90–109	Average/normal
110–119	High average/bright normal
120–129	Superior
>130	Very superior

III. Achievement Tests

A. Uses

– Achievement tests evaluate how well an individual has mastered material on which he or she has been instructed. These tests are used in schools and industry for evaluation and career counseling.

B. Specific achievement tests

– The **Wide-Range Achievement Test (WRAT)**, frequently used in medicine, evaluates achievement in arithmetic, reading, and spelling. This test is available for children under age 12 (level 1) and for persons aged 12–75 (level 2).
– Other achievement tests include the California Achievement Tests, the Iowa Test, and the Stanford Achievement Test.

IV. Personality Tests

A. Minnesota Multiphasic Personality Inventory (MMPI)

objective.

– The MMPI is the most **commonly used objective personality test**. This test has 10 clinical scales: hypochondriasis, depression, hysteria, psychopathology, masculinity/femininity, paranoia, psychasthenia (a general measure of anxiety), schizophrenia, hypomania, and social distance.
– The lie scale, frequency scale, and correction scale of the MMPI increase the probability that the test will correctly identify a patient's problems.

projective B. Rorschach test

– The Rorschach test is the **major projective test of personality**. It is used as a diagnostic aid to identify the presence of thought disorders and the nature of a person's defenses.
– The Rorschach test consists of 10 cards, 5 in black and white and 5 in color, each containing a bilaterally symmetrical inkblot design.
– The cards are shown to the individual in a particular order and a record is kept of the patient's reaction time (time to the first response to the card) and the time spent viewing each card.

C. Thematic Apperception Test (TAT)

– The **TAT** requires a patient to make up a story based on the picture presented. The story is then used to evaluate emotions and conflicts that may be out of the individual's awareness.
– The TAT consists of 30 cards depicting persons engaging in activities that are ambiguous and must be interpreted by the patient.
– The TAT is useful for determining what motivates an individual and for identifying possible interpersonal conflicts; it is less useful than the Rorschach test for making diagnoses.

D. Sentence Completion Test (SCT)

– The **SCT** is used to identify a patient's problems by the use of verbal associations (e.g., the patient is asked to complete the sentence, "I am most afraid of....").

V. Neuropsychological Tests

A. Uses

– Neuropsychological tests are designed to assess general intelligence, memory, reasoning, orientation, and perceptuomotor performance.

Table 16-3. Brain Dysfunction and Localization

Dysfunction	Possible Brain Location
Memory and orientation	
Short-term memory (within 5 minutes)	Temporal lobes/frontal lobes (hippocampus)
Recent memory (within a few months)	Temporal lobes (hippocampus, fornix, thalamus)
Long-term memory (within the past few years)	Temporal lobes (hippocampus)
Concentration	Frontal lobes
Global disorientation (memory intact)	Frontal lobes
Language (all in the dominant hemisphere)	
Expressive language (cannot speak fluently—Broca's aphasia)	Frontal lobe (Dominant)
Receptive language (cannot understand speech—Wernicke's aphasia)	Temporal lobe "
Anomia (cannot name objects)	Temporal lobe, angular gyrus "
Transcortical aphasia (impaired speech and comprehension, can repeat phrases)	Temporal-occipital-parietal junction
Alexia (cannot read what one has written)	Occipital lobe, posterior corpus callosum "
Conduction aphasia (cannot repeat phrases)	Parietal lobe "
Global aphasia (absence of any language function)	Frontal, temporal, parietal lobes "
Other functions	
Dyspraxia (patient copies examiner's movements)	Contralateral parietal lobe
Finger agnosia (errors in naming fingers)	Dominant parietal lobe
Dyscalculia (errors in calculating)	Dominant parietal lobe
Dysgraphia (errors in writing)	Dominant parietal lobe
Right/left disorientation	Dominant parietal lobe
Construction apraxia (difficulties copying simple objects)	Nondominant parietal lobe
Identification of camouflaged object	Occipital lobes

- These tests are also used to assess language function, attention, and concentration in patients with neurological problems such as dementia and brain damage.

B. **Specific tests**

1. **The Halstead-Reitan Battery (HRB)** is used mainly to detect the presence of and to localize brain lesions and determine their effects.

2. **The Luria-Nebraska Neuropsychological Battery (LNNB)** is used mainly for determining left or right cerebral dominance and for identifying specific types of brain dysfunction, such as dyslexia.

C. **Performance**

- Other than neuropathology, deviation from normal on neuropsychiatric tests may be due to anxiety, depression, confusion about the directions, language problems, or lack of cooperation.
- Performance of a variety of tasks is associated with problems in specific brain areas (Table 16-3).

Review Test

Directions: Each of the numbered items or incomplete statements in this section is followed by answers or by completions of the statement. Select the **one** lettered answer or completion that is **best** in each case.

1. Which of the following is used to test intelligence in children?

(A) Thematic Apperception Test (TAT)
(B) Minnesota Multiphasic Personality Inventory (MMPI)
(C) Wechsler Intelligence Scale for Children-Revised (WISC R)
(D) Halstead-Reitan Battery (HRB)

2. An individual with a mental age of 8 and a chronological age of 10 has an IQ of

(A) 40
(B) 60
(C) 80
(D) 100
(E) 180

3. An individual with an IQ of 95 is classified as

(A) severely retarded
(B) borderline
(C) dull normal/low average
(D) normal
(E) mildly retarded

4. A large difference in scores between the verbal and performance tests on the WAIS-R is most likely related to the individual's

(A) level of education
(B) anxiety
(C) cultural background
(D) early learning
(E) psychological problems

5. Which of the following is the most commonly used objective personality test?

(A) TAT
(B) SCT
(C) Iowa Test
(D) MMPI
(E) LNNB

6. All of the following are projective tests EXCEPT

(A) TAT
(B) SCT
(C) MMPI
(D) Rorschach test
(E) Draw a Person Test

7. Which of the following statements about IQ is true?

(A) It is usually stable throughout adult life
(B) It is rarely influenced by an individual's culture
(C) It is rarely influenced by an individual's early learning
(D) It is easily increased by formal training in specific subject areas
(E) The highest chronological age used in determining IQ is 25 years

8. Clinical scales of the MMPI evaluate all of the following EXCEPT

(A) depression
(B) hysteria
(C) masculinity and femininity
(D) schizophrenia
(E) intelligence

9. Neuropsychiatric tests are designed to assess all of the following EXCEPT

(A) memory
(B) orientation
(C) problem solving
(D) reasoning
(E) achievement

Directions: The group of items in this section consists of lettered options followed by a set of numbered items. For each item, select the **one** lettered option that is most closely associated with it. Each lettered option may be selected once, more than once, or not at all.

Questions 10–14

For each of the deficits below, choose the part of the brain that is most likely to be affected.

(A) Dominant frontal lobe
(B) Dominant temporal lobe
(C) Hippocampus
(D) Dominant parietal lobe
(E) Thalamus
(F) Nondominant frontal lobe
(G) Nondominant parietal lobe
(H) Dominant occipital lobe

10. The patient has written a sentence correctly but cannot read it

11. The patient understands language but cannot speak

12. The patient cannot understand language

13. The patient cannot copy the outline of a triangle

14. The patient cannot add three single digit numbers

Answers and Explanations

1–C. The WISC-R is used to test intelligence in children aged 6–16½ years.

2–C. Using the formula 8 (mental age) over 10 (chronological age) × 100, the IQ of this individual is 80.

3–D. An individual with an IQ of 95 is classified as normal.

4–E. A large disparity between the verbal and performance test on the WAIS-R may indicate that the person has psychological problems.

5–D. The MMPI is the most widely used objective personality test.

6–C. The MMPI is an example of an objective test.

7–A. IQ is relatively stable throughout adult life, despite increased educational level. The results of an intelligence test can be influenced by an individual's culture and early learning.

8–E. Clinical scales of the MMPI evaluate hypochondriasis, depression, hysteria, psychopathology, masculinity and femininity, paranoia, psychasthenia, schizophrenia, hypomania, and social distance; they do not evaluate intelligence.

9–E. Neuropsychiatric tests are designed to assess general intelligence, reasoning and problem solving, memory, orientation, and perceptuomotor performance.

10–H. Due in part to damage to the dominant occipital lobe, the patient with alexia cannot read what he or she has written.

11–A. The inability to speak although understanding is intact, Broca's aphasia, is associated with damage to the dominant frontal lobe.

12–B. Wernicke's aphasia is associated with damage to the dominant temporal lobe; the patient cannot understand language.

13–G. The inability to copy objects (construction apraxia) is associated with dysfunction of the nondominant parietal lobe.

14–D. Dyscalculia, difficulty doing simple calculations, is associated with dysfunction of the dominant parietal lobe.

17

Psychological and Biological Functioning of the Patient

I. History of the Patient

A. Medical history

- The purpose of obtaining the medical history is to get basic **identifying data** about the patient, to determine the patient's **reliability**, to identify the patient's **chief complaint**, and to establish **rapport** with the patient.
- The medical history is also used to obtain the history of the present illness, the past medical history, and the family medical history.
- During the medical history, a complete **inventory of each symptom** is obtained including onset, location, quality and severity, possible precipitating factors, what increases or decreases the symptoms, changes occurring, and previous treatment.
- Because stress can have a serious impact on health, it is important to identify the **major stressors** in the patient's life by obtaining information on family, home, sexual history, diet, activities, and social life.

B. Psychiatric history

- The patient's psychiatric history is taken as part of the medical history. The psychiatric history addresses the relationship between events in the patient's life and current emotional issues. It includes questioning concerning **previous mental illnesses and drug and alcohol use** in the patient and in his or her family.
- The psychiatric history addresses the patient's current living situation in terms of other people, financial problems, and source of income.
- Questions about events in the patient's history are usually divided into developmental periods: prenatal, early childhood, childhood, adolescence, and adulthood (Table 17-1).
- The **mental status examination** is used to evaluate an individual's current state of mental functioning (Table 17-2).
- Terms used to describe psychophysiologic symptoms and mood in psychiatric illness are listed in Table 17-3.

II. Laboratory Tests of Neuroendocrine Function in Depression

A. Dexamethasone suppression test (DST)

- Dexamethasone is a synthetic glucocorticoid that, when given to a normal patient with a normal hypothalamic-adrenal-pituitary axis, **suppresses the secretion of cortisol**.

131

Table 17-1. The Developmental Psychiatric History

Prenatal
Was the child wanted
Difficulties during pregnancy and delivery

Early Childhood (0–3 years)
Earliest recollections
Early problems with feeding, sleep, toilet training
Sibling relationships
Personality as a child (e.g., shy, outgoing)

Childhood (3–11 years)
Response to first separation from mother
Personality patterns (e.g., assertive, aggressive [a bully], anxious)
Development of reading and motor skills
Peer relationships in school (e.g., follower or leader, popularity)
Fears, setting fires, cruelty to animals, nightmares, bed wetting

Adolescence
Emotional problems (e.g., weight, drug use, running away)
Role models
Relationships with classmates and teachers
Active in sports
Sexuality (e.g., masturbation, crushes, homosexual behavior and fantasies)

Adulthood
Social life and quality of human relationships
Employment history
Sexual interaction

- In about half of patients with depression, this suppression may be absent and the DST may be used as a tool to gather further evidence of mental depression.
- Evidence indicates that patients with a positive DST (reduced suppression of cortisol) will **respond well to treatment** with antidepressant agents or to electroconvulsive therapy (ECT).
- Positive DSTs are also seen in **conditions other than depression**, including pregnancy, anorexia nervosa or severe weight loss, Alzheimer's disease, schizophrenia, obsessive-compulsive personality disorder, endocrine disorders, and with use and abuse of alcohol and antianxiety agents.

B. **Thyroid function**
- Thyroid function tests are used to screen for **hypothyroidism**, which can **mimic depression.**
- A reduced response to a challenge with thyrotropin-releasing hormone (TRH) may occur concurrently with depression.
- Secretion of prolactin in response to administration of tryptophan may be reduced in patients with depression.
- Patients taking lithium can develop hypothyroidism and, occasionally, hyperthyroidism.

C. **Growth hormone, melatonin, and gonadotropin**
- Patients with depression may have abnormal growth hormone regulation and lowered melatonin and gonadotropin levels.
- The response of growth hormone secretion to challenge by clonidine (responsiveness of α_2-adrenergic receptors) is reduced in some patients with depression.

Table 17-2. Variables Evaluated on the Mental Status Examination

Category	Examples
Appearance	Dress, grooming, facial expression, appearance for age
Behavior	Posture, gait, eye contact, mannerisms
Speech	Rate, clarity, vocabulary abnormalities, volume
Emotions	Mood, affect (blunted, labile, appropriate)
Thought content	Preoccupations, delusions, ideas of reference
Perception	Depersonalization, illusions, hallucinations
Cognitive functioning	Level of consciousness, memory, orientation
Intellectual functions	Intelligence, judgment, insight
Attitude toward interviewer	Interested, seductive, defensive, cooperative

III. Measurement of Biogenic Amines and Psychotropic Drugs

A. Biogenic amines

– Abnormalities in catecholamine levels and levels of catecholamine metabolites are found in some psychiatric syndromes (see Table 2-3).

B. Psychoactive drugs

– Measurement of plasma levels of psychotropic drugs may be appropriate for some patients taking certain drugs.
– Plasma levels of antipsychotic drugs do not correlate well with clinical effects but may be used to determine whether the patient is taking the medication.
– Patients taking **carbamazepine** [Tegretol] or **clozapine** [Clozaril] must be monitored for blood abnormalities such as **agranulocytosis** or evidence of bone marrow suppression.
– **Lithium** levels should be monitored regularly because of the drug's **narrow therapeutic range.**
– Measurement of blood levels of **heterocyclic antidepressant agents** to ascertain whether **therapeutic blood levels** of the drug have been attained may be useful in patients medically at risk and in those who have not responded to normal doses of the drug.

IV. Other Laboratory Measurements

A. Electroencephalogram (EEG) and evoked potentials

– EEGs are used primarily to identify **epilepsy** but are also used as an aid in diagnosing **delirium and dementia.**
– **Evoked potentials**, the response of the brain to **touch, sound,** or **visual stimulation** as measured by electrical activity, may be used in psychiatric evaluation.
– Evoked potentials can be used to evaluate the physiology of sensory nerves and can help in the diagnosis of **multiple sclerosis**.
– Evoked potentials may differ between normal patients and patients with schizophrenia.
– **Auditory evoked potentials** are useful because they are **present even in sleep or coma** and can also be used to evaluate loss of vision and hearing in infants.

B. Neuroimaging

1. **Computed tomography (CT) scans** can aid in the diagnosis of anatomically-based organic mental syndromes and may show abnormalities (enlargement of lateral cerebral ventricles) in patients with **schizophrenia.**

134 / *Behavioral Science*

Table 17-3. Psychophysiologic States and Affects

Consciousness and Attention
Distractibility: cannot concentrate on important stimuli
Clouding of consciousness: loss of ability to respond normally to external events
Somnolence: abnormal sleepiness
Delirium: confusion, restlessness, and disorientation associated with anxiety and hallucinations
Stupor: little or no response to environmental stimuli
Coma: total unconsciousness

Affect
Inappropriate affect: discordance between mood and behavior
Restricted affect: decreased display of emotional responses
Blunted affect: strongly decreased display of emotional responses
Flat affect: lack of emotional responsiveness
Labile affect: sudden alterations in emotional responsiveness that do not appear related to environmental events

Mood
Euphoria: strong feelings of elation
Expansive mood: feelings of self-importance
Irritable mood: easily bothered and quick to anger
Euthymic mood: normal mood; no significant depression or elevation of mood
Dysphoric mood: a subjectively unpleasant feeling
Grief: sadness due to a true loss
Depression: sadness not due to a specific loss
Anhedonia: lack of ability to feel pleasure
Mood swings: alternations between euphoric and depressive moods

Other Emotions
Anxiety: apprehension to an imagined danger
Free-floating anxiety: anxiety not connected to a specific cause
Fear: anxiety from a real threat or danger

2. **Nuclear magnetic resonance imaging (MRI)** shows the biochemical condition of neural tissues as well as the anatomy and is particularly useful in identifying **demyelinating diseases** such as multiple sclerosis.

   – In comparison with CT scans, MRI shows greater contrast between normal and abnormal tissue and white and gray matter and does not expose the patient to ionizing radiation.

3. **Positron emission tomography (PET)** can **characterize and measure neurotransmitters and receptors** in neural tissue and localize metabolically active areas of the brain in patients assigned to a specific task. This test is expensive and is used mainly for research.

C. **Amobarbital sodium [Amytal] and sodium lactate administration**

   – Intravenous (IV) administration of amobarbital sodium can relax very anxious patients or mute, psychotic patients so that they can express themselves coherently during an interview (**"the Amytal interview"**).
      – Amytal interviews may also be useful in determining whether organic pathology is responsible for symptomology in patients who exhibit **malingering, amnestic, or conversion disorder.**
   – IV administration of **sodium lactate** (or inhalation of carbon dioxide) **causes panic attacks** in susceptible patients and can thus help to identify individuals with panic disorder.

D. Galvanic skin response
- The **electric resistance of skin,** galvanic skin response, varies in certain psychiatric states.
- Higher sweat gland activity, seen with sympathetic nervous system arousal (e.g., in fear and in sexual activity), results in decreased skin resistance.
- Alterations in galvanic skin response may also be seen in **schizophrenia.**

Review Test

Directions: Each of the numbered items or incomplete statements in this section is followed by answers or by completions of the statement. Select the **one** lettered answer or completion that is **best** in each case.

1. A patient who is confused, disoriented, anxious, and restless is manifesting

(A) stupor
(B) delirium
(C) somnolence
(D) clouding of consciousness
(E) distractibility

2. A patient exhibits abrupt alterations in emotional responses that appear to be unrelated to environmental events. The affect displayed by this patient is

(A) blunted
(B) restricted
(C) flat
(D) labile
(E) inappropriate

3. The inability to feel pleasure is an example of which one of the following psychophysiologic states?

(A) Grief
(B) Anhedonia
(C) Depression
(D) Dysphoria
(E) Euthymia

4. A woman reacts when the plane on which she is riding catches fire. The emotion that she feels is

(A) free-floating anxiety
(B) anxiety
(C) fear
(D) mood swings
(E) dysthymia

5. Which of the following diagnostic techniques is most likely to expose a patient to ionizing radiation?

(A) PET
(B) CT scan
(C) MRI
(D) Visual evoked potentials
(E) Auditory evoked potentials

6. Which of the following laboratory tests is most useful in determining neurotransmitter activity in the brain?

(A) Evoked potentials
(B) Auditory evoked potentials
(C) PET
(D) CT scan
(E) MRI

7. A 40-year-old woman reports that she has no appetite, sleeps poorly, and has lost interest in her normal activities. Which of the following is a likely laboratory finding in this person?

(A) Negative DST
(B) Abnormal growth hormone regulation
(C) Enhanced prolactin response to administration of tryptophan
(D) Increased melatonin levels
(E) Increased gonadotropin levels

8. IV administration of sodium lactate is most useful in the diagnosis of

(A) conversion disorder
(B) cognitive disorder
(C) malingering
(D) panic disorder
(E) major depression

9. Agranulocytosis is most likely to be seen in a patient taking

(A) clonidine
(B) carbamazepine
(C) lithium
(D) alprazolam
(E) chlorpromazine

10. Which of the following statements concerning the dexamethasone suppression test (DST) is true?

(A) It is used frequently in the diagnosis of schizophrenia
(B) It shows abnormalities in at least 95% of depressed patients
(C) It has been used in the diagnosis of depression
(D) It is rarely abnormal in patients with medical conditions
(E) It is affected by decreased melatonin levels

Answers and Explanations

1–B. An individual who is confused, anxious, restless, and disoriented is exhibiting delirium.

2–D. Abrupt alterations in emotionality unrelated to environmental events is an example of labile affect.

3–B. The inability to feel pleasure is known as anhedonia.

4–C. Anxiety caused by real danger such as a fire is likely to elicit the normal reaction of fear.

Computed tomography

5–B. CT scans expose patients to ionizing radiation.

Positron Emission tomography

6–C. PET is most useful in characterizing and measuring neurotransmitter levels in the brain.

7–B. Depressed people, such as this woman, may show abnormal growth hormone regulation, decreased prolactin response to the administration of tryptophan, a positive DST, and lowered melatonin and gonadotropin levels.

8–D. Sodium lactate administration can help identify individuals with panic disorder.

9–B. Agranulocytosis is most likely to be seen in a patient taking carbamazepine [Tegretol].

10–C. The DST has been used in the diagnosis of depression, is abnormal in about half of depressed patients, and may be abnormal in patients with other psychiatric and medical conditions.

18

The Family, Culture, and Illness

I. The Family—Overview

– A group of people related by **blood, adoption,** or **marriage** is a family.
– Intense interpersonal relationships are found in families, and these relationships play an important role in the health of family members.

A. Nuclear and extended families

– The **nuclear family** includes mother, father, and dependent children living together in one household.
– The **extended family** includes family members such as grandparents, aunts, uncles, and cousins who live outside of the household.

B. Phases in the life of the traditional family

1. The first phase begins with **marriage** and continues until the first child is born.

2. The second phase involves **raising children.**

3. The third phase begins when **children leave home** and the parents must reestablish their marital relationship, careers, or interests as well as deal with their own aging and ill parents.

4. The fourth and final phase consists of the physical decline of the parents and the **final distribution** of the goods and money that the family has acquired.

II. Demographics and Current Trends

A. Marriage and children

– Approximately **95%** of people in the United States **marry**.
– Eighty to ninety percent of people in the United States between the ages of 35 and 45 are married.
  – Married people are **mentally and physically healthier** than nonmarried people. A good marriage is a better predictor of health than age, education, race, or socioeconomic status.
– Ten to fifteen percent of married couples have no children; 50% of these are childless by choice.

– Approximately 50% of children live in families with **two working parents;** only 20% of children live in the "traditional family" in which the father works outside the home and the mother remains at home.
  – Having children is expensive. The cost of raising a child to age 17 in the United States in 1992 was $92,000–$180,000. An education at a private college can add more than $80,000 to these figures.

B. Divorce and single-parent families

1. Occurrence of divorce

– During the year 1990, there were about 1.2 million divorces, tripling the rate of the year 1960.
– Approximately **45% of marriages end in divorce.**
  – Factors associated with divorce include short courtship, lack of family support, premarital pregnancy, marriage during teenage years, divorce in the family, differences in religion or socioeconomic background, and serious illness or death of a child.
  – Divorced men are more likely to remarry than are divorced women.

2. Single-parent families

– Approximately 20% of families are headed by a **single parent**; most of these families are headed by a woman; in 14% of cases, they are headed by a man.
– Almost **half of black families** are single-parent households headed by women.
– Single-parent families often have **lower incomes and less social support** and, therefore, face increased chances of physical and mental illness.
– While mothers in low socioeconomic groups are most likely to be unmarried, the number of **educated, professional single women** having children has almost doubled from 1982 to 1992.

3. Child custody

– Types of child custody include joint, split, and sole custody; fathers are increasingly being granted joint or sole custody.

  a. In **joint residential custody**, which has recently become more popular, the child spends equal time with both parents.

  b. In **split custody**, each parent has custody of at least one child.

  c. In **sole custody**, the child lives with one parent while the other has visitation rights.

4. Children in single-parent families

– Characteristics of children in single-parent families include failure in school and emotional problems such as **depression,** which can lead to **drug abuse, suicide,** and **criminal activity.**
– Children from divorced families often suffer long-term effects such as a **greater likelihood of being divorced** themselves.
– Children who continue to have regular contact with their fathers fare better after divorce than those who have no contact.

III. Family Systems

A. Family-systems theory

- In family-systems theory, individual behavior is explained in terms of interactions between individuals in a family rather than in terms of motivational forces within an individual in a family.
- All causality is regarded as circular, not linear; members of the family influence each other in a reciprocal fashion.
- In systems theory, symptoms such as anxiety, depression, or eating disorders are not signs of individual pathology but, rather, they indicate dysfunction within the family.

B. Interactions in family systems

- Family systems exhibit **homeostasis**; that is, deviations from typical family patterns are kept within a restricted range.
- Family systems are comprised of **subsystems** such as the **executive subsystem**, which is composed of the two parents.
  - **Boundaries** determine who is allowed to participate in the functioning of a particular subsystem and how an individual may participate; that is, parents should not cross the boundary surrounding the executive subsystem and act as "friends" to their children.
- **Mutual accommodation** is the process by which two family members get to know each other's needs and act to meet those needs; for example, newly married people learn the give-and-take of getting along with each other.
- Breakdowns in communication and in mutual accommodation within a **dyad** (relationship between two family members) result in emotional cutoffs and **triangles**.
  - A triangle is a dysfunctional coalition between two family members against a third (i.e., a father and daughter against the mother).
  The **multigenerational transmission process** is a method in which patterns of adaptation in relationships are passed from generation to generation; that is, you interact with your spouse much as your parents interacted with each other.

C. Family therapy

- Family therapy is based on the assumption that even if only one person in the family has been identified as having a psychological or social problem, it is important to involve all members of the family system in the remediation of the difficulty.
- Sessions are usually held once a week for about 2 hours.
- Family therapy includes identification of the dysfunctional behavior, followed by communication and problem-solving training.

IV. Culture in the United States

A. Characteristics

- The United States is comprised of a variety of **minority subcultures** as well as a **large, white, middle class**, the major cultural influence.
- Although many subcultures both in the past and the present have made up the American culture, some people feel that the culture itself has developed certain characteristics.
  - **Independence** is valued at all ages and especially in the elderly.

– Emphasis is placed on **personal hygiene** and cleanliness.
– Characteristics of United States culture include the **nuclear family** with few children.
– Goals in United States culture include financial independence at an early age and **home ownership**.

B. Culture and illness

– **Minority subcultures** in the United States include African (black) Americans, Asian Americans (including Chinese, Japanese, and Korean Americans, and people from the Pacific Islands), Hispanic Americans (including Mexican, Puerto Rican, and Cuban Americans), Native Americans (American Indians) and Eskimos.
– Ethnic groups often have characteristic ways of dealing with illness.
– Although the same major mental disorders such as schizophrenia and depression are seen in all cultures, what is considered abnormal behavior may differ considerably by culture.
  – Differences in presentation of symptoms may be due to the individual characteristic of a patient or to the characteristics of the particular ethnic group.

C. Culture shock

– Culture shock may occur when individuals relocate to a foreign culture. It can be reduced by prior information about the culture, the presence of an intact family, and a geographic clustering of immigrants.
– **Young immigrant men** appear to be at greater risk for psychiatric problems than other sex and age groups.
– In particular, immigrants are more likely to show **paranoid symptoms, schizophrenia and depression,** and be hospitalized for these disorders.

V. Minority Subcultures

A. African Americans

– There are approximately 26 million African Americans, making them the largest ethnic group in the United States.
– The average income of black families is only about half that of white families. This lower socioeconomic status is associated with **increased health risks** and decreased access to health care services.
– When compared to white Americans, black Americans have a shorter life expectancy and **higher rate of hypertension, stroke, and obesity**.
– **Religion** plays a major role in social and personal support among many black Americans.
– **Strong extended kinship networks** are characteristic of many black families.
– Among black Americans, the condition of the **blood** is considered important. "High blood" is thought to be caused by rich foods, and "low blood" is thought to result in symptoms such as tiredness.
– In some groups of black Americans, **hexes and voodoo** imposed by the anger of a friend or relative are believed to cause illness.

B. Mexican Americans

– There are over 10 million Mexican Americans living in the United States, making them the largest group of Hispanic Americans.
– As a group, Hispanic Americans place great value on the nuclear family and on **large families**.

- Mexican Americans are called **Chicanos**, especially in the Southwest where most live.
- Mexican Americans often seek health care from folk healers known as **curanderos**. Treatment provided by curanderos includes magic, herbal medicines, or specific changes in diet.
- "Hot" and "cold" influences are believed to result in illness (e.g., rheumatic fever is a hot illness).
  - Foods considered cold such as cow's milk and corn are taken to treat hot illnesses; foods considered hot such as goat's milk and rice are taken to treat cold illnesses.

C. Puerto Rican Americans

- The second largest group of Hispanics in the United States are Puerto Rican Americans. Most live in the Northeast.
- Puerto Rican Americans often go to folk healers known as **espiritismos**. Treatment by espiritismos (spiritism) takes place in neighborhood centers, or **centros**, by mediums who use magic to **release spirits** that have invaded the patient and caused the illness.
  - Espiritismos work to relieve **nervios** (nervousness), **susto** (soul loss or depression), and **ataque** (symptoms of anxiety), which can mimic psychosis.

D. Asian Americans

- The largest group of Asian Americans are the **Chinese** and **Japanese**; there are over 800,000 Chinese and over 700,000 Japanese living in the United States.
- Although assimilated to a large extent, ethnic differences may still result in different responses to illness in Asian Americans.
  - Chinese children are expected to care for elderly parents.
  - Chinese patients may respond by smiling when they are unhappy or embarrassed.
- In many Asian Americans, the **abdominal-thoracic area** rather than the brain is thought to be the **spiritual core** of the person; thus, the concept of brain death and resulting organ transplant are generally not well accepted.
- Many Asian Americans metabolize alcohol differently from white Americans. When alcohol is consumed, they accumulate more acetaldehyde and show a characteristic flushing reaction.

E. American Indians and Eskimos

- There are about 1.4 million Native Americans (i.e., American Indians) in the United States.
- American Indians have their own program of medical care under the direction of the **Indian Health Service** of the federal government.
- In American Indian culture, the distinction between mental and physical illness is blurred; engaging in forbidden behavior and witchcraft are thought to result in illness.
- Both American Indians and Eskimos have **high rates of alcoholism and suicide**.

F. Other subcultures

- Studies of Americans of Anglo-Saxon, Jewish, and Italian descent indicate that members of these groups respond differently to illness.

- **Anglo-Americans** are less emotional, more **stoic**, and less vocal about pain and illness than members of the Jewish and Italian groups.
- **Italian Americans** are less likely than Jewish or Anglo-Americans to express concern about underlying disease processes once their pain has been relieved.
- **Americans of Jewish descent** are more likely than other groups to **report their medical problems** and visit physicians for help.

Review Test

Directions: Each of the numbered items or incomplete statements in this section is followed by answers or by completions of the statement. Select the **one** lettered answer or completion that is **best** in each case.

1. A physician conducts a physical examination on a new patient, a 35-year-old man. Of the following, the most important predictor of the health of this individual is

(A) age
(B) marital status
(C) race
(D) education
(E) socioeconomic status

2. All of the following statements about health care in the Hispanic American subculture in the United States are true EXCEPT

(A) "hot" and "cold" influences are believed to be important in health
(B) folk healers are commonly utilized
(C) releasing evil spirits is a technique used by folk healers
(D) the condition of the blood is considered of prime importance in health
(E) depression is described as susto or loss of soul

3. Which of the following statements about the family in the United States is true?

(A) Approximately 30% of couples have no children
(B) Approximately 65% of the population marries
(C) Approximately 10% of children live in families with two working parents
(D) Almost half of new marriages end in divorce
(E) The nuclear family commonly includes parents, grandparents, uncles, aunts, and children

4. Risk factors for divorce include all of the following EXCEPT

(A) marriage during teenage years
(B) long courtship period
(C) premarital pregnancy
(D) differences in socioeconomic background
(E) death of a child

5. All of the following statements about single-parent families are true EXCEPT

(A) they have lower incomes than two-parent families
(B) they have less social support than two-parent families
(C) they are more likely to be at risk for health problems than two-parent families
(D) about 15% are headed by men
(E) approximately 20% of black families are headed by a single parent

6. All of the following statements about family therapy are true EXCEPT

(A) it includes problem-solving training
(B) it includes identification of dysfunctional behavioral patterns
(C) therapy sessions are usually held once a month
(D) it includes communication training
(E) all family members should be involved

7. Which of the following statements about the Native American (Indian) subculture is true?

(A) There is a low rate of alcoholism
(B) The suicide rate is lower than in the general population
(C) They have a separate federal medical care program
(D) There is a clear distinction between mental and physical illness
(E) They number about 4 million individuals

8. All of the following statements about Asian American subculture are true EXCEPT

(A) there are over 700,000 Japanese Americans in the United States
(B) Chinese children are expected to care for their elderly parents
(C) inappropriate smiling may occur in Chinese patients when they are sad
(D) Asian Americans are assimilated into the American culture to a large extent
(E) the brain is believed to be the spiritual core of the person

9. All of the following statements about the American culture are true EXCEPT

(A) home ownership is valued
(B) it is characterized by the nuclear family with few children
(C) there is an emphasis on personal hygiene
(D) independence in children is discouraged
(E) independence in old age is encouraged

10. Which of the following is true about black Americans?

(A) They have a shorter life expectancy than white Americans
(B) They have a lower incidence of obesity than white Americans
(C) They have a lower incidence of hypertension than white Americans
(D) The median income of black families is about 90% that of whites
(E) There are about 10 million black Americans

Directions: The group of items in this section consists of lettered options followed by a set of numbered items. For each item, select the **one** lettered option that is most closely associated with it. Each lettered option may be selected once, more than once, or not at all.

Questions 11–14

Match the family interaction with the word or phrase with which it is most closely associated.

(A) Subsystems
(B) Triangles
(C) Emotional cutoff
(D) Mutual accommodation
(E) Multigenerational transmission process

11. A brother and sister learn to get along while living in an apartment together while attending the same college

12. All family members no longer speak to an uncle with whom one of them has had a disagreement

13. A mother and son become confidants, excluding the father

14. A husband interacts with his wife the way his father interacted with his mother

Answers and Explanations

1–B. The best predictor of this patient's future health is marriage.

2–D. "Hot" and "cold" influences are important in health among Hispanic Americans. The condition of the blood is important in health among black Americans.

3–D. In the United States, approximately 95% of the population marry, and almost half of these marriages will end in divorce. Only 10%–15% of couples have no children, and approximately 50% of children live in families with two working parents.

4–B. Risk factors for divorce include less social support, marriage during teen years, premarital pregnancy, short courtship period, differences in religious or socioeconomic background, and serious illness or death of a child.

5–E. Almost half of black families are headed by a single parent; most single-parent families are headed by women. Single-parent families are more limited financially, have less social support, and are at higher risk for health problems than two-parent families.

6–C. Family therapy sessions usually are held once a week for 2 hours.

7–C. The federal government has a separate medical care program for American Indians. Native Americans, who number about 1.4 million, have high rates of alcoholism and suicide. Among American Indians, the distinction between mental and physical illness may not be clear.

8–E. Among many Asian Americans, the abdominal-thoracic area is believed to be the spiritual core of the person.

9–D. In the American culture, independence in both children and old people is encouraged.

10–A. Black Americans have a shorter life expectancy than white Americans, a higher incidence of obesity and hypertension, and a median income of only half that of white Americans. There are about 26 million black Americans.

11–D. Mutual accommodation is the process by which family members get to know each other's needs and act to meet those needs.

12–C. Emotional cutoff results from a breakdown in communication.

13–B. A triangle is a dysfunctional coalition of two family members against a third member of the family.

14–E. Multigenerational transmission process is how patterns of adaptation and interaction are passed from one generation to another.

19
Sexuality and Aggression

I. Sexual Development

– Sex is determined by genetic sex, sex of the gonads, sex of the internal and external genitalia, sex of the brain, and sex of assignment and rearing.

A. Prenatal sex determination

1. Gonads

– Differentiation of the gonads is dependent on the presence or absence of the **Y chromosome,** which contains the testis-determining factor gene.
– Gonadal sex determination occurs by gestational week 7 in males and by gestational week 12 in females.

2. Genitalia

– The hormonal secretions of the **testes** direct the differentiation of the internal and external genitalia of the male.
– In the absence of testicular hormones during prenatal life, internal and external genitalia will be female.

3. Brain

– In addition to their action on the genitalia, differential exposure to sex hormones during prenatal life results in differences in the brains of males and females.
  – Regions of the brain that show sex differences include areas of the hypothalamus, anterior commissure, corpus callosum, and thalamus.

B. Gender identity and sexual orientation

– **Gender identity** is an individual's sense of being male or female; **gender role** is the expression of one's gender identity in society.
  – A child's gender identity is based on genital sex as well as on sex of assignment and rearing.
– **Sexual orientation** is an individual's preference for one gender or the other as a sexual and love object.
– Gender identity and sexual orientation may be affected by genetic and hormonal influences (Table 19-1) as well as by psychological factors (Table 19-2).

Table 19-1. Physiologic Abnormalities of Sexual Development

Syndrome	Genotype	Phenotype	Gender Identity	Sexual Preference for	Associated Characteristics
Turner's	XO	Female	Female	Men	Fibrous or absent ovaries, short stature, webbed neck
Klinefelter's	XXY	Male	Male	Women	Small testes, breast development
Androgen insensitivity (testicular feminization)	XY	Female	Female	Men	Body cells unresponsive to androgen; undescended testicles
Congenital adrenal hyperplasia (adrenogenital)	XX	Female (masculinized) genitalia	Female	One-third lesbian	Adrenal gland cannot produce adequate cortisone; excessive androgen secreted prenatally

A. Hormones and behavior in women

- In some studies, sexual interest and sexual behavior in women have been correlated with phases of the menstrual cycle.
  - Peaks in sexual interest and behavior have been seen in women about the time of ovulation, just prior to menstruation, and just following menstruation.
  - These peaks may correlate with **high estrogen** levels and with **low progesterone** levels.
- **Menopause** (cessation of ovarian estrogen production) and **aging** do not result in decreased sex drive if a woman's general health is good.
- **Testosterone**, which is secreted by the adrenal glands throughout adult life, is believed to play the major role in the **sex drive in women** as well as in men.
  - Drugs with **androgenic activity** may increase sex drive in women primarily by causing clitoral hypertrophy.

Table 19-2. Alterations in Psychological Sexual Development

Category	Genetic Sex	Gender Identity	Sexual Preference For	Associated Characteristics
Transsexual	Male	Female	Men	Sense of being born into the wrong body; seek sex change surgery, low sex drive in males
	Female	Male	Women	
Homosexual	Male	Male	Men	Love interest in same sex individuals
	Female	Female	Women	
Transvestite	Male	Male	Women	Dress in women's clothes for sexual pleasure

Table 19-3. The Sexual Response Cycle

Stage	Male	Female	Both Male and Female
Excitement	Penile erection	Clitoral erection, vaginal lubrication (watery exudate due to increased blood flow); uterus rises in pelvic cavity (tenting effect)	Nipple erection
Plateau	Fifty percent increase in testes' size; testes move upward, scrotal skin thickens, few drops of sperm-containing fluid secreted	Contraction of the outer third of the vagina, forming the orgasmic platform; tenting effect continues	Increased heart rate, blood pressure, respiration, skin flush
Orgasm	Testes, prostate, seminal vesicles, and urethra contract, seminal fluid forcibly expelled in the emission phase	Vagina and uterus contract, same response whether caused by clitoral or vaginal stimulation	Dramatic increase in heart rate, blood pressure, respiration, muscular contractions, and skin flushing
Resolution	Refractory period; restimulation not possible	Little if any refractory period; restimulation possible	Return of sexual organs to prestimulation state over 10–15 minutes if orgasm occurred; decrease in heart rate, blood pressure, and respiration

B. Hormones and behavior in men

– Testosterone levels in men generally are higher than necessary to maintain normal sexual functioning, although **stress** may result in a **reduction in testosterone levels.**

– Testosterone levels show seasonal peaks (higher in the fall) and daily peaks (higher in the morning) that may correlate with increased sexual interest and behavior.

– Medical treatment with estrogens, progesterone, or antiandrogens for conditions such as prostate cancer results in reduced sexual interest and behavior.

III. The Sexual Response Cycle

– Masters and Johnson devised a four-stage model for sexual response in both men and women—the **excitement, plateau, orgasm,** and **resolution stages** (Table 19-3).

IV. Sexual Dysfunction

A. Characteristics (Table 19-4)

– **Sexual dysfunctions** can result from biological, psychological, or interpersonal causes or a combination of causes.

– Dysfunctions may have always been present (**primary** sexual dysfunction), or they may occur after an interval when function has been normal (**secondary** sexual dysfunction).

Table 19-4. *DSM-IV* Categories of Sexual Dysfunction

Dysfunction	Characteristics	Approximate Occurrence
Sexual desire disorder	Reduced interest in or aversion to sex; more common in women	20%
Male erectile disorder		
Primary	No previous erection sufficient for penetration	1%
Secondary	Failure to maintain erection; (normal erections in the past), often due to alcohol abuse; presence of erections during REM sleep indicates a psychogenic cause	10%–20%
Female sexual arousal disorder	Failure to maintain lubrication until the sex act is completed	33%
Female orgasmic disorder	Absence of orgasm	
Primary	No previous orgasm	5%
Primary and secondary	Associated with guilt, fear of rejection, pregnancy, and loss of control	30%
Male orgasmic disorder	Delayed or absent orgasm	5%
Premature ejaculation	Ejaculate too soon, no plateau phase, anxiety present; squeeze technique used in treatment	35% of male sexual disorders
Dyspareunia	Persistent pain associated with sexual intercourse, in women, may be due to insufficient lubrication	. . .
Vaginismus	Spasm of outer third of vagina, causes difficulty during intercourse and gynecologic examination; associated with rape, incest, or strict religious upbringing; vaginal dilators used in treatment	. . .

- Sexual dysfunctions can occur in all situations or only with a certain partner or in a specific location (selective sexual dysfunction).
- Individuals may be completely or only partially dysfunctional.

B. **Therapy**

1. **Dual-sex therapy**

   - **Dual-sex therapy,** in which the couple participates with both a male and a female therapist, was developed by Masters and Johnson. This short-term behavioral therapy, when integrated with psychotherapy, is a very successful treatment modality for sexual problems. Specific exercises are used in dual-sex therapy.

   a. In **sensate-focus exercise,** used to treat arousal and orgasmic disorders, the individual's awareness of touch, sight, smell, and sound stimuli are increased and pressure to have an orgasm is decreased.

   b. In the **squeeze technique,** used to treat premature ejaculation, the man is taught to identify the sensation surrounding ejaculatory inevitability, a point just before the emission phase when ejaculation can no longer be prevented.

      - Being able to identify the moment of ejaculatory inevitability allows the man to slow his sexual response. At this moment, the partner exerts

Table 19-5. Paraphilias and Associations

Type	Sexual Gratification Derived From
Exhibitionism	Exposing the genitals
Fetishism	Inanimate objects (i.e., women's underclothing or shoes)
Frotteurism	Rubbing the penis against the clothing of a woman
Necrophilia	Corpses
Pedophilia (most common)	Children
Sexual masochism	Receiving physical suffering or humiliation
Sexual sadism	Inducing physical suffering or humiliation
Transvestic fetishism	Wearing women's clothing
Voyeurism	Sneaking observations of people dressing or engaging in sexual activity
Zoophilia	Sexual activity involving animals

pressure on the coronal ridge of the glans on both sides of the penis until the erection subsides.

– Circumcised and noncircumcised men have equal sensation in the glans.
– Reports of penile damage have decreased the use of the squeeze technique.

2. **Hypnotherapy**

 – **Hypnosis** is used to reduce the anxiety and stress surrounding sexual activity by using relaxation techniques.

3. **Behavioral therapy**

 – Behavioral approaches to sex therapy such as systematic desensitization and assertiveness training are based on the idea that sexual problems are maladaptive patterns of behavior that have been learned.
 – The patient learns to reduce the anxiety associated with sex through **systematic desensitization**.
 – **Assertiveness training** teaches the patient to talk about sexual feelings and desires with his or her partner.

4. **Group therapy**

 – Psychodrama and role playing are techniques used in group therapy to relieve the guilt and anxiety surrounding sexual problems.

C. **Outcome of sex therapy**

 – If a couple is young, follows instructions about specific exercises, and has a flexible attitude, the likelihood of successful treatment is great.
 – There is a growing tendency for the physician to treat the sexual problems of patients rather than refer patients with sexual problems to specialists.

V. Paraphilia

 – Paraphilias occur almost exclusively in men and involve **unusual objects of sexual desire** or sexual activities (Table 19-5).
 – Fantasies about unusual sexual objects or activities do not qualify as paraphilias; a person must have acted on these fantasies or be very concerned about them and must have problems forming close relationships with others because of them.

VI. Homosexuality

A. Occurrence

- Estimates of the occurrence of homosexuality are **3%–10% in men** and **1%–5% in women**, with no significant ethnic differences in these figures.
- About 50% of all men have had some prepubertal homosexual experience.
- Most homosexuals have experienced heterosexual sex, and 50%–75% of homosexuals have had children.

B. Etiology

- Both biologic and psychosocial factors have been proposed in the etiology of homosexuality.
- **Alterations in prenatal hormones** (i.e., high levels of androgens in females and decreased androgens in males) may contribute to the development of homosexuality; however, homosexual men and women generally have **normal hormone levels in adulthood**.
- Recent evidence indicates a prenatally based difference in hypothalamic responsiveness to estrogen and difference in the size of a sexually dimorphic hypothalamic nucleus between heterosexual and transsexual or homosexual men, phenomena that may be due to decreased fetal androgen levels.
- A higher concordance rate in monozygotic twins than in dizygotic twins and markers recently identified on the X chromosome suggest that **genetic factors** are involved in homosexuality.
- **Cross-gender behavior** during childhood may be predictive of later homosexual orientation, more so in boys than in girls.

C. Intervention

- Although the *DSM-IV* does not consider homosexuality a dysfunction, persistent discomfort about one's sexual orientation is considered a sexual disorder.
- Psychological intervention generally involves helping the person who is uncomfortable about his or her sexual orientation to become comfortable with that orientation.

VII. Common Illness and Sexuality

- **Heart disease and diabetes** affect at least 14 million Americans. Fear of sexual activity can delay complete recovery in these patients.

A. Myocardial infarction

- **Erectile dysfunction and decreased libido** caused by psychological factors are common problems following myocardial infarction (MI).
  - Many patients with cardiac problems fear that the exertion or excitement of sexual activity will lead to another heart attack or to sudden death.
- Some researchers have compared the cardiovascular changes that occur with sexual activity in middle-aged men with familiar partners as that equivalent to climbing two flights of stairs or engaging in ordinary occupational tasks.
  - Generally, if exercise that raises the heart rate to 110–130 beats/minute can be tolerated without severe shortness of breath or chest pain, sexual activity can be resumed after a heart attack.

B. **Diabetes**

1. **Erectile dysfunction**
   - One-quarter to one-half of diabetic men have erectile dysfunction. Orgasm and ejaculation are less likely to be affected, and older patients are more likely to have erectile dysfunction.
   - Erectile problems generally occur several years after diabetes is diagnosed but may be the first symptom of the disease.
   - The major cause of erectile problems in men with diabetes is **diabetic neuropathy**, which involves microscopic damage to nerve tissue as a result of hyperglycemia.
      - Poor metabolic control of diabetes is related to increased incidence of sexual problems.
   - In some men with diabetes, erectile problems may be caused by **vascular changes** that affect the blood vessels in the penis.
   - Although physiologic causes are most important, **psychological factors** may also influence erectile problems associated with diabetes.

2. **Treatment**
   - Treatment of erectile problems in men with diabetes includes identifying both interpersonal problems and evidence of physical damage.
   - Surgical approaches, including penile implants, may be used to treat the problem.
      - Although penile implants may be used, diabetic men often have greater difficulties in wound-healing and greater susceptibility to infection.

VIII. Spinal Cord Injuries and Sexuality

A. **Spinal cord injuries in men**
   - Although sexual functioning in men is frequently affected by spinal cord injury, the sexual **prognosis is better** for men with incomplete rather than complete motor neuron lesions and lower rather than upper motor neuron lesions.
      - When ejaculation does occur, it may be retrograde in men with spinal cord injuries.
      - Testosterone levels and fertility are often reduced after spinal cord injury.

B. **Spinal cord injuries in women**
   - The effects of spinal cord injury in women have not been well-studied. Vaginal lubrication, pelvic vasocongestion, and incidence of orgasm may be reduced, but fertility does not appear to be adversely affected.

IX. Aging and Sexuality

A. **Physical changes**
   - Alterations in sexual functioning normally occur with the aging process.

1. In **men**, these changes include slower erection, diminished intensity of ejaculation, and longer refractory period.

2. In **women**, these changes include vaginal thinning, shortening of vaginal length, and vaginal dryness, changes that can be reversed with estrogen replacement therapy.

B. **Sexual interest and activity**
   - In spite of physical changes and societal attitudes, many older people are interested and continue to engage in sexual activity.

Table 19-6. The Effects of Some Prescription Drugs on Sexuality

Drug Type and Subtype	Effect	Percent Affected
Antihypertensive		
Thiazide diuretic	Erectile dysfunction	5%
Potassium sparing diuretic (spironolactone)	Reduced libido, erectile dysfunction	22%
Central antiadrenergic (methyldopa, clonidine)	Erectile dysfunction	10%–50%
Peripheral antiadrenergic (guanethidine)	Reduced libido, erectile dysfunction, inhibited ejaculation	50%–60%
Vasodilator (hydralazine)	Reduced libido	5%–10%
β-Blocker (propranolol)	Reduced libido, inhibited orgasm	< 5%
Antidepressant		
Tricyclic	Erectile dysfunction, inhibited ejaculation	5%
Selective serotonin reuptake inhibitor	Reduced libido, inhibited orgasm in men and women	20%–50%
MAO inhibitor	Erectile dysfunction, inhibited ejaculation	10%–30%
Lithium carbonate	Erectile dysfunction	< 5%
Trazodone	Priapism	< 5%
Sedative		
Benzodiazepine	Reduced libido, inhibited orgasm	< 5%
Barbiturate	Reduced libido, erectile dysfunction	< 5%
Antipsychotic	Erectile dysfunction, inhibited orgasm	10%–20%
Anticholinergic	Erectile dysfunction, vaginal dryness	...
Anticholesterol (clofibrate)	Reduced libido, erectile dysfunction	...
Histamine-receptor antagonist (cimetidine)	Erectile dysfunction	...
Antihistamine	Erectile dysfunction, vaginal dryness	...
Antiparkinsonism (L-dopa)	Increased libido	...

MAO = monoamine oxidase.

- In people 60–65 years of age, at least 75% of men and 50% of women report that they **continue to have sexual interest**; about 70% of men and 30% of women continue to engage in **sexual activity.**
- Decreasing sexual activity with increasing age is related to death of a spouse, illness, or decreased interest.
- Prolonged absence of sexual activity leads more quickly to physical atrophy of the genital organs in old age ("use it or lose it").

X. Drugs and Sexuality

A. Prescription drugs

- Many commonly used prescription drugs have negative effects on sexuality (Table 19-6).

B. Drugs of abuse

1. **Alcohol** use decreases erection and vaginal lubrication.
   - The negative physiologic effects are counteracted by the uninhibiting properties of alcohol, which may increase sexuality.

– With long-term use, alcohol may cause **liver dysfunction**, resulting in increased estrogen availability and **decreased potency** in men.

2. **Marijuana** appears to enhance the enjoyment of sex by psychological, not physiologic, means.
   – Chronic use of marijuana may reduce **testosterone levels** in men and **pituitary gonadotropin levels** in women.

3. **Heroin and methadone** use are associated with suppressed libido, retarded ejaculation, and failure to ejaculate.
   – Methadone is associated with fewer sexual problems than heroin.

4. **Amphetamine** use often results in increased libido, probably by direct action on the brain.

5. Although **cocaine** use may be sexually stimulating, it is also associated with loss of erection or with priapism (constant erection).

6. **Amyl nitrite** is a vasodilator that is used as an aphrodisiac to enhance the sensation of orgasm; however, cardiovascular accidents may result.

XI. Aggression and Control

A. Theories of aggression

– Some researchers believe that aggression is the result of an innate fighting instinct. Others maintain that aggression is learned rather than innate behavior.

B. Determinants of aggression

1. **Social determinants** include frustration, provocation by others, and exposure to aggression in the media.
   – Other determinants include pain and sexual excitement.
   – **Homicide**, which occurs more often in **low socioeconomic populations**, is increasing; at least half of homicides are accomplished with **guns.**

2. **Environmental determinants** include overcrowded living conditions, noise, and hot weather.

3. **Biologic determinants**

   a. **Hormones**
      – **Testosterone** is closely associated with aggression in animals; in most species and societies, males are more aggressive than females.
      – **Homicide** involving strangers is **committed** almost exclusively by **men**; women may commit homicide in the context of a family situation.
      – **Androgenic or anabolic steroids**, often taken by body builders to increase muscle mass, can result in high levels of aggression and psychosis; severe depression frequently occurs with withdrawal from these hormones.

   b. **Substances of abuse**
      – Drugs linked to aggression include **alcohol and barbiturates**.
      – Low doses of these drugs inhibit and high doses facilitate aggression.
      – While intoxicated, heroin users show little aggression; increased aggression is associated with the use of **cocaine, amphetamines, PCP,** and extremely high doses of **marijuana.**

c. Neural bases of aggression

– Neurotransmitters linked to aggression include the **monoamines** and **GABA**.
   – Serotonin and GABA inhibit and dopamine and norepinephrine facilitate aggression.
   – Abnormalities of the brain (abnormal activity in the amygdala and prepyriform area and psychomotor and temporal lobe epilepsy) and lesions of the temporal lobe, frontal lobe, and hypothalamus are associated with increased aggression.
   – A high percentage of men in prison for serious crimes have a history of **head injury** and/or show abnormal electroencephalograms.

C. Children and aggression

– Children who show high levels of aggression by age 8 are more likely to show violent criminal behavior as adults.
– **Violence on television** correlates directly with increased aggression in children.
– Children at risk for showing aggressive behavior in adulthood frequently have low IQs, poor grades in school, and an inability to defer gratification; their parents frequently are poor, display criminal behavior, and have physically or sexually (or both) abused them.
   – Starting **fires, bed-wetting**, and **cruelty to animals** in childhood also have been associated with criminal behavior in adulthood.

D. Control of aggression

1. Social control

– Punishment may temporarily control aggression in an individual; however, it often can elicit a wish for revenge and ultimately result in increased aggression.
– Teaching aggressive individuals social skills and exposing them to evidence of suffering by their victims can bring a reduction in aggression.

2. Pharmacologic control

– Drugs used to treat aggression include lithium (especially in adolescent boys), female sex hormones and antiandrogens (in male sex offenders), antipsychotics, antidepressants, anticonvulsants, mild tranquilizers, and stimulants (in children).

XII. Rape

A. Definition and occurrence

– **Rape** is an act of aggression demonstrated through sexual activity.
   – By legal definition, rape is the penetration of the outer vulva by the penis; erection and ejaculation do not have to occur.
– **Sodomy** includes nonconsenting fellatio (oral-penile contact) and anal penetration.
   – In most states, **male rape** is legally defined as sodomy.
– Rape often occurs in the context of other criminal activity and is frequently associated with the use of weapons.

B. Characteristics of the rapist

- About half of rapists are white, half are black; both tend to rape women of their own race.
- **Alcohol** is associated with one-third of rapes.
- The majority of rapists are under age 25.

C. Characteristics of the rape victim

- **Females** ranging from 10–29 years of age are most likely to be rape victims, although rape can occur at any age.
- Most often rape occurs inside the victim's home.
- Fifty percent of rapists are known by the victims; seven percent of rapists are close relatives.

D. Emotional results of rape

- Women often suffer the emotional results of rape for 1 year or longer—the **rape trauma syndrome**.
- Factors associated with recovery include immediate support from people in the victim's environment, the opportunity to talk about the intense anger, and the arrest of the rapist.
- **Group therapy** with other rape victims is very effective.

E. Legal aspects of rape

- Only 10%–25% of rapes are reported; about 100,000 rapes were reported in 1990.
- In court, a woman does not have to prove that she resisted the rapist; recently, a rapist was convicted even though the victim had asked him to use a condom.
- In some states, the victim's **previous sexual activities are not admissible as evidence** in trials of rape; also, husbands can be prosecuted for the rape of their wives.

Review Test

Directions: Each of the numbered items or incomplete statements in this section is followed by answers or by completions of the statement. Select the **one** lettered answer or completion that is **best** in each case.

1. A 35-year-old male patient states that he has a strong sex drive and has been living with another man in a stable, sexual, and love relationship for the past 10 years. Which of the following is least likely to be true about this patient?

(A) As a child, he liked to play with girl's toys
(B) He has normal levels of circulating testosterone
(C) He has a homosexual relative
(D) He has experienced sex with a woman
(E) He wants a sex change operation

2. The occurrence of homosexuality in men is about

(A) 0.5%–1%
(B) 3%–10%
(C) 12%–14%
(D) 15%–17%
(E) 17%–20%

3. The major technique used in conjunction with hypnotherapy during sex therapy is

(A) the squeeze technique
(B) sensate focus
(C) relaxation
(D) psychotherapy
(E) behavioral modification

4. A 25-year-old man suffered a spinal cord injury in an automobile accident. Which of the following is true about sexuality in this patient?

(A) Sexual functioning will be better if the lesion is complete
(B) Sexual functioning will be better if the lesion is of the upper motor neurons
(C) Sexual problems rarely occur
(D) Testosterone levels are probably normal
(E) Fertility is likely to be reduced

5. All of the following statements about sexuality in normal aging are true EXCEPT

(A) erection is slower
(B) vaginal dryness occurs
(C) aging men have a longer refractory period following ejaculation
(D) prolonged absence of sexual activity leads more quickly to atrophy of the genital organs
(E) decrease in estrogen with menopause commonly results in reduced sexual interest in women

6. Which of the following antihypertensive drugs is least likely to cause erectile disorder?

(A) Guanethidine
(B) Spironolactone
(C) Propranolol
(D) α-Methyldopa
(E) Clonidine

7. A 34-year-old man has been taking fluoxetine for treatment of depression for 4 months. Which of the following sexual dysfunctions is he most likely to report?

(A) Primary erectile disorder
(B) Secondary erectile disorder
(C) Premature ejaculation
(D) Orgasmic disorder
(E) Dyspareunia

8. All of the following statements about rape are true EXCEPT

(A) half of rapists are white
(B) half of rapists are known by their victims
(C) rapists tend to rape women of the same race
(D) group therapy with other rape victims is an effective treatment
(E) the emotional effects of rape commonly last for approximately 1 month

9. Which of the following statements about rape is true?

(A) Alcohol is frequently involved
(B) It commonly occurs at a woman's work environment
(C) Most rapes are reported to the authorities
(D) It rarely occurs in the context of another criminal activity
(E) For the court to convict a rapist, the female victim must prove that she actively resisted the rapist

10. All of the following statements about sex determination are true EXCEPT

(A) chromosomes direct the early differentiation of the gonads
(B) differentiation of the ovaries takes place about week 12 of gestation
(C) differentiation of the testes takes place about week 7 of gestation
(D) the brains of males and females are affected by gonadal hormones during early development
(E) in the absence of ovarian hormones during prenatal life, the internal and external genitalia of the developing fetus will be masculine

11. Individuals who dress in clothes of the opposite sex for sexual pleasure

(A) are known as transsexuals
(B) are almost always homosexual
(C) are almost exclusively males
(D) usually have a defect in gender identity
(E) believe that they were born the wrong sex

12. All of the following statements about premature ejaculation are true EXCEPT

(A) it is the least common sexual dysfunction
(B) the squeeze technique is useful in treatment
(C) the plateau phase of the sexual response cycle is usually absent
(D) an important factor in its diagnosis is the age of the man
(E) anxiety is characteristic

13. Which of the following statements about the hormonal control of male sexuality is true?

(A) There is no temporal pattern of testosterone release
(B) Stress results in an increase in testosterone levels
(C) Treatment with progesterone increases sexual behavior in men
(D) Treatment with estrogen increases sexual behavior in men
(E) Homosexual men generally have normal testosterone levels

Questions 14 and 15

14. A husband and wife state that they are having serious marital problems. During the interview you discover that, while their sex life has been good, the last time they tried to have intercourse (4 weeks previously), the husband could not maintain an erection. Which of the following is least likely to have caused this problem?

(A) Alcohol
(B) Antihypertensive medication
(C) An endocrine disturbance
(D) Diabetes
(E) Amphetamines

15. If no obvious physical cause for the man's erectile dysfunction is found in this couple, which of the following will be least useful in diagnosis and treatment?

(A) The squeeze technique
(B) Sensate focus
(C) Dual-sex therapy
(D) Hypnotherapy
(E) Monitoring of nocturnal erections

16. Which of the following statements about sexual dysfunction in men is true?

(A) Primary erectile disorder is common
(B) Lack of sexual desire is not considered a sexual dysfunction
(C) Erectile disorder involves failure to maintain erection
(D) Secondary erectile disorder occurs in 1%–2% of men
(E) Absence of nocturnal erections during REM sleep indicates a psychological cause of sexual dysfunction

17. All of the following statements about the etiology of male homosexuality are true EXCEPT

(A) alterations in prenatal hormones may be involved
(B) cross-gender behavior during childhood commonly occurs
(C) most homosexual men have female rather than male siblings
(D) the *DSM-IV* does not consider homosexuality a sexual dysfunction
(E) there is a higher concordance rate among monozygotic twins than among dizygotic twins

18. All of the following statements about sexual activity in heart patients are true EXCEPT

(A) sexual problems after a heart attack frequently have a psychogenic component
(B) fear of sexual activity can delay complete recovery
(C) decreased libido is relatively rare following a heart attack
(D) there is a high occurrence of erectile disorder following a heart attack
(E) if exercise that raises the heart rate to 120 beats/minute can be tolerated, sexual activity can be resumed

19. All of the following statements about erectile dysfunction associated with diabetes are true EXCEPT

(A) penile implants may be used
(B) erectile disorder occurs in one-quarter to one-half of diabetic men
(C) erectile dysfunction occasionally is the first symptom of diabetes
(D) the major causes of erectile disorder in diabetic men are psychogenic
(E) metabolic control of diabetes is related to decreased incidence of sexual problems

20. Brain abnormalities associated with increased aggression include all of the following EXCEPT

(A) temporal lobe lesions
(B) frontal lobe lesions
(C) hypothalamic lesions
(D) cerebellar atrophy
(E) abnormal activity in the amygdala

21. Drugs used in treating aggression include all of the following EXCEPT

(A) stimulants
(B) lithium
(C) antidepressants
(D) calcium channel blockers
(E) antiandrogens

22. Determinants of aggression include all of the following EXCEPT

(A) overcrowded living conditions
(B) sexual excitement
(C) progesterone
(D) alcohol
(E) pain

23. A 26-year-old man who habitually abuses drugs is arrested for attacking and beating another man. Which of the following drugs is he least likely to have just taken?

(A) PCP
(B) Heroin
(C) Amphetamines
(D) Cocaine
(E) Marijuana

Directions: Each group of items in this section consists of lettered options followed by a set of numbered items. For each item, select the **one** lettered option that is most closely associated with it. Each lettered option may be selected once, more than once, or not at all.

Questions 24–28

Match the characteristic to the stage of the sexual response cycle that is most closely associated with it.

(A) Excitement
(B) Plateau
(C) Orgasm
(D) Resolution

24. Erection begins

25. The tenting effect begins

26. Shows the greatest difference between men and women

27. Emission of semen occurs

28. Formation of the orgasmic platform occurs

Questions 29–31

Match the patient to the drug that is most likely being used.

(A) Alcohol
(B) Marijuana
(C) Heroin
(D) Amphetamine
(E) Amyl nitrite

29. A 54-year-old man suffers a heart attack when he has an orgasm

30. A 25-year-old woman cannot become pregnant

31. A 50-year-old man shows breast enlargement

Answers and Explanations

1–E. Transsexual individuals seek sex change surgery. Homosexual individuals, like the patient described, are generally happy with their biological sex and have a sexual and love interest in individuals of the same sex.

2–B. The occurrence of homosexuality in men is about 3%–10%.

3–C. Patients in hypnotherapy are taught relaxation techniques to use before sexual activity begins.

4–E. In spinal cord injury, both testosterone levels and fertility are often reduced. Sexual prognosis is better for men with incomplete rather than complete lesions and with lesions of the lower rather than upper motor neurons.

5–E. Despite decreased estrogen production, menopause is not generally associated with reduced libido in women. Testosterone is the "female libido hormone."

6–C. Sexual problems in patients taking propranolol are relatively rare.

7–D. Fluoxetine [Prozac], a selective serotonin reuptake inhibitor (SSRI), is associated with orgasmic problems in 20%–50% of men and women.

8–E. The emotional effects of rape may continue for a year or longer.

9–A. Rape usually occurs in a woman's own home in the context of another criminal activity and alcohol is often involved. Women no longer have to prove in court that they actively fought against the rapist.

10–E. In the absence of testicular or ovarian hormones during prenatal life, the external genitalia of the fetus will be feminine.

11–C. Transvestites, individuals who dress in clothes of the opposite sex for sexual pleasure, are almost always male, heterosexual, and do not have a defect in gender identity.

12–A. Premature ejaculation is the most common sexual dysfunction.

13–E. Homosexual men generally have normal testosterone levels. Testosterone is released in a cyclic pattern; stress results in decreased testosterone levels; and treatment with estrogen, progesterone, or antiandrogens decreases sexual interest and behavior in men.

14–E. Amphetamines stimulate sexual behavior. Alcohol, antihypertensive drugs, and endocrine disturbances such as diabetes may result in erectile dysfunction.

15–A. The squeeze technique is used to treat premature ejaculation, not erectile dysfunction.

16–C. In erectile disorder, erection cannot be maintained until completion of the sex act. Although primary erectile disorder is rare, secondary erectile disorder occurs in 10%–20% of men. Lack of sexual desire may be considered a sexual dysfunction if it disturbs the individual or partner. The presence of erections during sleep indicates a psychological cause for erectile disorder.

17–C. The sex of siblings is not commonly associated with the occurrence of homosexuality.

18–C. Decreased libido is relatively common following a heart attack.

19–D. One-quarter to one-half of diabetic men eventually have erectile disorder. The major cause of this problem is thought to be physiologic.

20–D. Brain abnormalities associated with increased aggression include temporal lobe and psychomotor epilepsy, abnormal activity in the amygdala, and temporal lobe, hypothalamic, and frontal lobe lesions.

21–D. Drugs used in the treatment of aggression include lithium, antipsychotics, antidepressants, stimulants, anticonvulsants, mild tranquilizers, and antiandrogens.

22–C. Determinants of aggression include pain, sexual excitement, alcohol, overcrowded living conditions, and testosterone.

23–B. People are not aggressive after they have just taken heroin, and while on heroin, aggression is decreased. Amphetamines, cocaine, marijuana, and PCP are associated with increased aggression.

24–A. Erection begins in the excitement stage.

25–A. The tenting effect begins in the excitement stage.

26–D. Restimulation during the refractory period is possible for women but not for men.

27–C. Emission of semen occurs during ejaculation and orgasm.

28–B. Formation of the orgasmic platform occurs during the plateau stage in women.

29–E. Amyl nitrite is a vasodilator used as an aphrodisiac.

30–B. Lowered pituitary gonadotropin levels are associated with use of marijuana in women.

31–A. Increased estrogen availability in men may result from chronic alcohol use.

20

Doctor-Patient Communication

I. Roles
A. Expectations of patients
   - Patients' expectations of doctors include the following: The doctor will be helpful, have expertise concerning the problem, and will permit the patient to become involved in diagnosis and treatment of the illness.
   - Patient expectations are influenced by his or her culture, previous experiences with medical care, physical and mental condition, and personality.

B. Transference reactions
   - Patients have unconscious transference reactions to their doctors, which are based in childhood parent-child relationships.
   1. In **positive transference**, the patient views the doctor as good and has a high level of confidence in the doctor's abilities.
      - Idealization of the doctor can result in the patient having sexual feelings toward the doctor.
      - Idealization of the doctor can lead to disillusionment and negative transference.

   2. In **negative transference**, patients develop resentment or anger toward the doctor if their desires and expectations are not realized, which may result in noncompliance with medical advice.

   3. **Countertransference** refers to doctors' reactions toward patients. Doctors may feel guilty when they are unable to help a patient, or they may have particular feelings toward patients who remind them of a close relative or friend.
      - Countertransference can result in the tendency of physicians to minimize the severity of another physician's illness.

C. Characteristics of the physician
   - The doctor's ethnic background, sex, and age may affect the patient's reaction to the doctor.
      - Although young physicians may initially be viewed as childlike by patients, the power of the role of the physician usually overrides the initial image.
   - The physician's technical skills influence the doctor-patient relationship less than the doctor's relationship with the patient and family.

165

Table 20-1. Models of the Doctor-Patient Relationship

Model	Characteristics	Useful For
Activity-passivity	Doctor is in charge, patient is passive	Acute illness, surgery
Guidance-cooperation	Doctor formulates the treatment plan, patient is permitted choices in following the plan	Acute illness
Mutual participation	Doctor formulates the treatment plan, patient is responsible for carrying it out	Chronic illness

D. Medical practice

– About one-third of individuals with symptoms seek medical care. However, the occurrence of a stressful life event doubles the chances that a person will visit a physician when symptoms are present.
– Most people contend with illnesses at home with over-the-counter (OTC) medications and home treatment.
– Although chronically ill patients are most critical concerning medical care, they seek medical care most often.
– Szasz and Hollender suggested that the doctor-patient relationship is different in acute and chronic illnesses (Table 20-1).
– There is a strong correlation between psychological illness and physical illness; morbidity rates and mortality rates are much higher in patients who need psychiatric attention.

E. "The sick role"

– A sick person assumes a particular role in society and certain behavioral patterns when ill (the "sick role," described by T. Parsons), which includes lack of responsibility for becoming ill, exemption from usual responsibilities, expectation of care by others, working towards becoming healthy, and cooperation with health care personnel in getting well.
– Critics of the sick role theory argue that it applies only to middle-class patients with acute physical illness, and that it emphasizes the power of the doctor and undervalues the individual's social support network in getting well.

II. The Clinical Interview

A. Communication and skills

– Patient compliance with medical advice, detection of both physical and psychological problems, and patient satisfaction with the physician are improved by good doctor-patient communication.
– One of the most important skills that a physician must learn is how to interview patients. In the interview, the physician must first establish **trust and confidence** in the patient and then gather physical, psychological, and social information to identify the patient's problem.

B. Interviewing techniques

1. **Facilitation** is a basic interviewing technique used by the interviewer (the doctor) to encourage the patient to elaborate on an answer. For example, "And then what happened?"

    – **Reflection** is a variation of facilitation in which the physician repeats the response of the patient to encourage elaboration of the answer. For example, "You said that your pain increased after you washed the floor?"

2. **The open-ended question**
   – Although direct questioning can elicit information, the open-ended type of question and interview is most likely to produce a good clinical relationship, aid in obtaining information about the patient, and not close off potential areas of pertinent information.
   – Using open-ended questions, the interviewer gives little structure to the patient, encourages the patient to speak freely, and elicits a great deal of information. For example, "Tell me about your fall."

3. **Direct questions** are used to elicit specific information when time is limited. For example, "Where on your side do you feel the most pain?"

4. **Support** is used to express the physician's interest and concern for the patient. For example, "That must have been a frightening experience for you."

5. **Empathy** is used to express the physician's personal understanding of the patient's problem. For example, "I understand that you are worried about the financial consequences of this injury."

6. The physician can use the technique of **silence**, the least controlling interview technique, to increase the patient's responsiveness.

7. The technique of **confrontation** calls the patient's attention to inconsistencies in his or her responses or body language. For example, "You seem really upset about the circumstances under which the fall took place."

8. In **validation**, the doctor gives credence to the patient's feelings. For example, "Many people would feel the same way if they had been injured as you were."

9. In **recapitulation**, the physician sums up the information obtained during the interview. For example, "Let's go over what happened. You fell last night and hurt your side. You then were really upset and became concerned about whether you would be able to go back to work."

III. Compliance

A. Definition

    – **Compliance** is the extent to which a patient follows the instructions of the physician and includes taking medications on schedule, keeping appointments, and following directions for changes in life-style such as diet or exercise.

B. Patient characteristics associated with compliance

    – Approximately one-third of patients are compliant with treatment, one-third comply some of the time, and one-third do not comply with treatment. Factors that increase and decrease compliance are listed in Table 20-2.
    – Because their illness is generally asymptomatic, about half of hypertensive patients initially comply with treatment; however, many who initially complied have stopped complying within 1 year of diagnosis.
    – Group support may increase compliance.
       – One-third of former smokers in support groups versus less than one-fourth who quit smoking without support remain abstinent for at least 1 year.

Table 20-2. Factors Associated with Patient Compliance with Medical Advice

Increase Compliance
Good doctor-patient relationship: most important factor
Physician knowledge of and sensitivity to the patient's beliefs
Physician enthusiasm, permissiveness, and time given to the patient
Physician experience and older physician age
Patient feels ill
Patient's knowledge of how the medication will help
Short waiting room time
Written instructions for taking medication
Understanding instructions for taking medication
Acute illness

Decrease Compliance
Perception of the physician as cold and unapproachable
Physician's failure to explain the diagnosis or cause of symptoms
Complex treatment schedule (i.e., frequent doses of medication daily)
Increased behavioral changes (i.e., diet, stop smoking, begin exercising)
Verbal instructions for taking medication
Visual problems reading prescription labels (particularly in the elderly)
Chronic illness

  – There is little relationship between compliance and a patient's sex, religion, socioeconomic or marital status, race, intelligence, or education.

C. The "Health Belief Model" and compliance

  – In the "Health Belief Model," whether individuals seek health care and then comply with the advice they are given depends on factors such as their subjective feelings of illness and whether their usual activities have been disrupted by illness.
  – Other factors include how practical it is to obtain health care, possibly feeling that the benefits of care outweigh the costs, and surmounting the obstructions to obtaining needed care.

IV. The Psychobiology of Chronic Pain

A. Psychosocial factors

  – **Chronic pain** is a commonly encountered complaint of patients. It may be caused by physical or psychological factors.

  1. Psychological factors associated with chronic pain include depression, alcohol and drug abuse, childhood neglect, physical and sexual abuse, and life stress.

  2. Patients with borderline or narcissistic personality disorders or those with hypochondriasis are at risk for developing **chronic pain syndrome**.

  3. Religious, cultural, and ethnic factors may influence the patient's expression of pain and the responses of the patient's support systems to the pain.

  4. Psychological "uses" of chronic pain include attention from others, financial gain, and justification of inability to establish social relationships.

B. Perception and tolerance of pain

  – Most people **perceive** pain in a similar manner, although pain tolerance may differ among individuals.

    – **Tolerance to pain** may be altered by biofeedback, physical therapy or physical activity, optimistic emotional state, relaxation, meditation, guided imagery, electrical stimulation of pain transmission pathways, suggestion, and hypnosis.
    – Extreme sensitivity to pain is associated with depression, anxiety, and hypochondriasis.
    – In the **gate control theory**, the perception of pain can be blocked by electrical stimulation of large diameter afferent nerves.

C. Depression and chronic pain

    – Depression may predispose a person to develop chronic pain, which in turn frequently leads to depression; however, relief can be achieved by use of antidepressant and antipsychotic drugs.

D. Treatment

  1. If chronic pain is caused by cancer or other chronic medical disease, pain relief is best achieved by **analgesics** (the first line of treatment) or **nerve-blocking** surgical procedures.

  2. Behavior modification and deconditioning may be helpful for controlling pain caused by physical illnesses such as cancer.
    – Patients with chronic pain benefit from **psychotherapy** and **behavioral therapy** by needing less pain medication, becoming more active, and showing increased attempts to return to a normal life-style.

  3. In physical illness, a **medication schedule** that separates the experience of pain from the receipt of medication through the scheduled administration of medication rather than medication on demand can help control pain.
    – Many patients with chronic pain are **undermedicated** because of the physician's fears of the patient becoming addicted to the medications. Recent evidence indicates that patients with chronic pain do not become addicted to opiate drugs as addicts do; they are able to discontinue the use of drugs easily as the pain remits.

Review Test

Directions: Each of the numbered items or incomplete statements in this section is followed by answers or by completions of the statement. Select the **one** lettered answer or completion that is **best** in each case.

1. A 46-year-old man presents to the emergency department with chest pain. Which of the following statements will elicit the most information from this patient?

(A) "Point to the area of pain in your chest"
(B) "Tell me about the pain"
(C) "Tell me about the pain in your chest"
(D) "Have you been to a physician within the past 6 months"
(E) "Is there a history of heart disease in your family"

2. A 50-year-old woman presents complaining of gastric distress. She seems agitated and says that she is afraid she has cirrhosis of the liver but then stops speaking. Which of the following will best encourage her to continue speaking?

(A) "Please go on"
(B) "How much liquor do you drink"
(C) "Do you drink"
(D) "Why did you wait so long to come in"
(E) "I see that the situation upsets you"

3. Which of the following is an example of the interviewing technique known as confrontation?

(A) "Tell me again about the pain in your chest"
(B) "What happened then"
(C) "I'll be there to help you"
(D) "You look terrified"
(E) "How do you feel about giving up your job"

4. Patients do not comply with medical advice for all of the following reasons EXCEPT

(A) an asymptomatic illness
(B) deliberate misuse of medication
(C) misunderstanding of the instructions for taking the medication
(D) denial of the severity of the illness
(E) the treatment schedule is complex

5. All of the following statements about transference in the doctor-patient relationship are true EXCEPT

(A) in positive transference, the patient may develop an overly strong confidence in the doctor
(B) overidealization of the physician can lead to negative transference
(C) transference reactions are based in the parent-child relationship
(D) patients are consciously aware of their transference reactions toward the doctor
(E) in a negative transference reaction, patients may develop resentment if their expectations of the doctor are not realized

6. Which of the following is true about medical practice?

(A) Most people who have symptoms of illness visit physicians
(B) Chronically ill patients are the least critical about medical care
(C) Over-the-counter medications are rarely used by people with serious illnesses
(D) Morbidity rate is high in groups needing psychiatric care
(E) Mortality rate is equivalent in psychiatric and nonpsychiatric populations

7. Which of the following characteristics of the patient is most likely to be associated with compliance?

(A) Race
(B) Socioeconomic status
(C) Attitude toward the physician
(D) Intelligence
(E) Gender

8. Which of the following is associated with decreased compliance?

(A) Verbal instructions for taking medications
(B) Older age of the physician
(C) Acute illness
(D) Severe symptoms of the disease
(E) Decreased waiting room time

9. All of the following are true about chronic pain EXCEPT

(A) it is associated with childhood sexual abuse
(B) it may be used to justify an individual's inability to establish social relationships
(C) it may involve social gain
(D) it is rarely influenced by cultural factors
(E) financial gain may be involved

10. All of the following statements about chronic pain are true EXCEPT

(A) it is a relatively rare complaint of patients
(B) it is commonly associated with depression
(C) it frequently results in depression
(D) it can be treated with phenothiazines
(E) it is associated with substance abuse

11. Which of the following statements about chronic pain and pain relief is true?

(A) Patients are at high risk for drug addiction
(B) Pain medications should be given only when the patient is experiencing severe distress
(C) Deconditioning is the first line of treatment in pain caused by cancer or chronic disease
(D) Behavior modification is useful for pain caused by cancer
(E) Many patients being treated for pain are overmedicated

12. All of the following statements about patients with chronic pain who receive psychotherapy and behavioral therapy are true EXCEPT

(A) they need less pain medication
(B) they become overly dependent on the therapist
(C) they become more active
(D) they show increased attempts to return to their normal lives
(E) behavioral therapy and psychotherapy are generally beneficial to chronic pain patients

13. The "sick role" as described by Parsons

(A) applies mainly to low socioeconomic groups
(B) overvalues people's support networks
(C) includes acceptance of responsibility for becoming ill
(D) includes exemption from usual responsibilities
(E) applies mainly to chronic illness

14. Which of the following psychological problems is least likely to be associated with chronic pain syndrome?

(A) Hypochondriasis
(B) Borderline personality disorder
(C) Narcissistic personality disorder
(D) Paranoid personality disorder
(E) Depression

Answers and Explanations

1–B. The most open-ended of these questions, "Tell me about the pain," gives little structure to the patient and can therefore elicit the most information.

2–A. The interview technique known as facilitation is used by the interviewer to encourage the patient to elaborate on an answer. The phrase, "Please go on," is a facilitative statement.

3–D. The physician's statement, "You look terrified," calls the patient's attention to his or her own response or body language.

4–B. Deliberate misuse of medication is rarely the reason for noncompliance with medical advise.

5–D. Transference reactions are unconscious reactions.

6–D. About one-third of people who have symptoms seek medical help. Most people treat their illnesses with over-the-counter medication and home treatment. Although the chronically ill are critical of medicine, they seek medical help more frequently than other groups. Both morbidity rates and mortality rates are high in groups needing psychiatric care.

7–C. Although a patient's attitude toward the physician is very important, there is no clear association between compliance and a patient's sex, marital status, race, religion, socioeconomic status, intelligence, or educational level.

8–A. Written rather than verbal instructions increase compliance. Compliance also is associated with being treated by a physician who is older, acute illness, simple treatment schedule, decreased waiting room time, and how ill the patient feels.

9–D. Cultural, religious, and ethnic factors can influence a patient's expression of pain and the responses of the support system of the patient to the pain.

10–A. Chronic pain is a commonly encountered complaint of patients. Chronic pain, which is associated with depression, substance abuse, childhood neglect and abuse, and stress can be treated with antidepressants and phenothiazines.

11–D. Although medication is the preferred method of treatment, behavior modification and deconditioning have been used to treat pain caused by cancer or chronic diseases. For pain relief in chronic diseases, the medication schedule should be separated from the experience of pain (i.e., medication should be scheduled at regular intervals rather than given on demand). Many patients are undermedicated even though they are at low risk for addiction.

12–B. Patients with chronic pain benefit from psychotherapy and behavioral therapy by needing less pain medication, becoming more mobile, and showing increased attempts to return to their normal lives.

13–D. The "sick role" applies mainly to middle-class patients with acute physical illnesses, undervalues support networks, and includes the expectation of care by others, lack of responsibility for becoming ill, and exemption from the patient's usual responsibilities.

14–D. Patients with narcissistic or borderline personality disorders and patients with hypochondriasis and depression are at risk for developing chronic pain syndrome.

21

Emotional Reactions to Illness

I. Emotional Responses

A. Coping with illness

– **Defense mechanisms** can help patients cope with serious illness.

1. **Denial**: Refusing to accept or minimizing the severity of an illness; occurs in the initial stages of illness and is the most common defense mechanism used by patients.
   – Reducing stress by limited use of denial, particularly in patients with coronary disease, can help in recovery. However, excessive use of denial can decrease compliance with medical advice and thus pose a danger to the patient.

2. **Regression**: Returning to immature ways of dealing with psychological stress by crying or having tantrums; frequently occurs with physical illness.

B. Depression, fear, anxiety, and anger in illness

1. **Depression** caused by illness may result in expressions of sadness such as crying or withdrawal.

2. **Illness** almost always results in fear and anxiety since illness is perceived as a dangerous occurrence.
   – **Fears** associated with illness include fear of loss or injury to parts of the body, loss of function, being separated from family, loss of love and approval by family, and fear of strangers.

3. Patients often express **anger** at health care personnel and family members when they are fearful about their illness.

C. Patient personality and illness

– A patient's psychological reactions to illness are dependent on the patient's psychological resources, social resources, and personality style. Personality types are divided into the following categories:

1. The **dependent personality** is afraid of being helpless and has a need to be cared for, resulting in the need for attention during an illness.

173

2. The **passive-aggressive personality** may ask for help from the physician and then not comply with the physician's advice.

3. The **compulsive personality** fears loss of control and may in turn become controlling during illness.

4. The **histrionic personality** may be dramatic, emotionally changeable, and act sexually inappropriate toward the physician during illness.

5. The **narcissistic personality** feels that the perfect self-image is threatened by illness. Narcissistic patients often feel that they are better than others and may request that only the most famous physicians be involved in their treatment.

6. The **masochistic personality** may see illness as a retribution for real or imagined misdeeds and may prolong illness to receive affection and attention.

7. The **paranoid personality** often blames the doctors for the illness and is supersensitive to a perceived lack of attention or caring.

8. The **schizoid personality** becomes anxious and even more withdrawn with illness.

II. The Hospitalized Patient

A. Consultation-liaison psychiatry

1. Psychological problems in medical patients
- The most common problems seen in hospitalized medical patients needing psychiatric care are **depression, anxiety, and disorientation**, all of which can negatively affect health.
- Other problems are agitation, attempted suicides or threats of suicide, hallucinations, sleep disorders, noncompliance, and refusal to consent to necessary medical procedures.

2. Treatment
- Techniques used by the consultation-liaison psychiatrist include support, devising methods for dealing with real problems, and informing and organizing the patient's social support system.
- If psychotherapy is used, it is usually of the short-term, dynamic type (patients who receive psychotherapy are released about 2 days sooner than patients who do not receive psychotherapy).
- Behavioral therapy or hypnosis may also be used.

B. At risk patients
- Patients at greater risk for developing psychological reactions in response to illness, hospitalization, or surgery are those with a prior history of psychosis or other psychiatric illness and those whose relationships with their families or with the medical staff become strained during the illness.

C. Intensive care unit
- Because of the seriousness of the illness of patients in intensive care units (ICUs), psychological problems can be life threatening or influence the likelihood of recovery.
- Patients in ICUs may suffer initial shock and fear, which is often followed by denial of the illness, acting out, anger and hostility, and excessive dependence.

- Allowing patients to take as much control of their environment as possible (e.g., letting them make choices as to when to take pain medication) gives them reassurance.
- Because of the absence of orienting cues, patients in ICUs are at increased risk for delirium, known as **ICU psychosis.**
- ICU nurses are at high risk for anxiety, depression, and changing jobs.

D. **Patients on renal dialysis**

- Patients on a renal dialysis unit must confront a chronic illness that requires dependence on other people and on machines. **Depression** and **suicide** are not uncommon in dialysis patients.
- Dialysis patients often suffer from **sexual problems** that have both physical and psychological causes.
- **Self-help groups** and **home dialysis units** are associated with successful psychological adaptation to chronic renal disease.

E. **Surgical patients**

- Surgical patients at relatively greater risk for developing psychological problems include patients who have **unrealistic expectations** regarding a surgical procedure, **depressed** patients who are convinced they will not survive surgery, and patients who **deny** that they are seriously worried prior to the surgery.
- When surgical patients are able to **express their depression and anxiety** and when they have a positive attitude toward the surgery, they are at relatively lower risk for morbidity and mortality.
- Other factors contributing to an improved outcome for surgical patients include knowing what to expect during and following the procedure in terms of pain, possible disorientation, tubes and machines, and the presence of family support.

IV. The Patient with AIDS

A. **Response to the diagnosis**

- Intense anxiety is frequently the response to a diagnosis of AIDS. Hopelessness and suicidal depression may then develop.
- Patients respond well to reassurances that they will not be abandoned by the physician, family members, and friends.

B. **Psychological intervention**

- Psychotherapy can help patients with AIDS deal with the guilt they may have over their risk-taking behaviors that may have led to the disease.
- Psychotherapy may help homosexual patients with AIDS **"come out"** to family members.
- Individuals in high risk groups may be extremely anxious about getting AIDS despite negative test results. For these patients, psychotherapy is frequently useful.
- Although the actual risk is relatively low, **health care workers** dealing with patients with AIDS may suffer from fear of becoming infected. Other problems include depression and a high attrition rate, which commonly occur in health care workers dealing with patients who will die.

Table 21-1. Illnesses Associated with Psychosomatic Factors

Illness	Associated Psychological Factors
Bronchial asthma	Excessive dependency
Cancer	Separation and loss, inability to express feelings
Coronary artery disease	Type A personality
Diabetes mellitus	Psychological stress, dependent, passive
Hypertension	Repressed rage
Hyperthyroidism	Psychological stress, dependent, fear of rejection
Infectious disease	Depression and anger
Migraine headache	Obsessive personality
Obesity	Oral fixation and regression
Pruritus	Repressed anger and anxiety
Tension headache	Anxiety, depression, type A personality
Ulcerative colitis	Psychological stress, compulsive personality

V. Stress and Illness

A. Psychosomatic disorders

– Psychological stress may initiate or exacerbate physical disorders such as congestive heart failure, cardiac arrhythmias, peptic ulcer disease, ulcerative colitis, rheumatoid arthritis, low back pain, tension and migraine headaches, diabetes mellitus, and immune system disorders.

– Other psychological factors associated with the development of physical disorders are found in Table 21-1.

B. Effects of stress on the body

– **Hans Selye** described the stages that the body goes through in response to stress as the **general adaptation syndrome**, which involves the alarm reaction, followed by adaptation in the form of psychosomatic illness, and finally exhaustion.

– According to Selye, stress results in the classic stress response of the **endocrine system,** which is characterized by rapid release of adrenocorticotropic hormone (ACTH), followed by the release of corticosteroids.

  – Corticosteroids, in turn, suppress immune responses as measured by impaired lymphocyte function and lowered lymphocyte mitogen responses.

– Stress also is associated with increased heart rate, respiratory rate, blood pressure, body oxygen consumption, and skin conductance and resistance (measured by galvanic skin response).

VI. Stress and Life Events

–Correlations between life stress and both physical and emotional illness have been demonstrated. Everyone has a threshold of vulnerability to life stress and an inborn ability to deal with it.

A. Negative and positive stressors

– Stressful life events may be **negative**, such as the death of a spouse; they may also be **positive**, such as the birth of a wanted child.

– Life stressors have been categorized by Holmes according to a **point value system**, with 100 points (death of a spouse) being the highest stress and the birth of a child and vacations having stress values of 39 and 15, respectively.

Table 21-2. *DSM-IV* Severity of Psychosocial Stressors

| Stressor | | Scale | Severity |
Adults	Children/Adolescents		
No immediate stressor	No immediate stressor	1	None
Child leaves home; graduation	School transfer	2	Mild
Marriage; separation; loss of employment; retirement; miscarriage	Suspension from school; birth of sibling	3	Moderate
Divorce; birth of first child	Divorce of parents; unwanted pregnancy; trouble with law enforcement authorities	4	Severe
Death of spouse; serious medical illness; rape	Sexual or physical abuse; death of parent	5	Extreme
Death of child; suicide of spouse; overwhelming natural disaster	Death of both parents	6	Catastrophic

– One study indicates that 80% of individuals who accumulated 300 points in 1 year were at risk of illness within the next few years.

B. *DSM-IV* categories of psychosocial stressors

– In the *DSM-IV* categorization of mental disorders, there is a 6-point rating scale for coding psychosocial stressors—from 1 (no stress) to 6 (catastrophic stress)—as they affect the development or exacerbation of mental disorders in adults and children or adolescents (Table 21-2).

Review Test

Directions: Each of the numbered items or incomplete statements in this section is followed by answers or by completions of the statement. Select the **one** lettered answer or completion that is **best** in each case.

1. A patient tells the physician that he forgot to take the medicine prescribed and did not know that he was supposed to return for a checkup in 1 month. This behavior is characteristic of which one of the following personality types?

(A) Schizoid
(B) Passive-aggressive
(C) Paranoid
(D) Histrionic
(E) Dependent

2. All of the following factors about life stress and illness are true EXCEPT

(A) marriage and separation from a spouse are equally stressful for an adult
(B) birth of a sibling is a moderate life stress for a child
(C) each individual has a threshold of vulnerability to life stress
(D) only negative life events are likely to cause stress to the individual
(E) death of a spouse is an extreme stressor for an adult

3. A psychiatrist is called to conduct a psychiatric consultation on a 55-year-old man in the surgical ICU. Which one of the following problems is the physician least likely to encounter in this patient?

(A) Agitation
(B) Noncompliance
(C) Sleep disorders
(D) Disorientation
(E) Schizoid personality disorder

4. Which of the following is considered the most extreme stressor for children and adolescents?

(A) Divorce of parents
(B) Change of school
(C) Being arrested
(D) School suspension
(E) Physical abuse

5. All of the following statements about patients in an intensive care unit (ICU) are true EXCEPT

(A) the initial emotion is frequently fear
(B) excessive dependence is characteristic
(C) hostility toward health care personnel may occur
(D) the nurses should relieve the patient of making any decisions
(E) denial of serious illness is common

6. All of the following are associated with the general adaptation syndrome EXCEPT

(A) responses of the body to stress
(B) the sick role theory
(C) alarm reaction
(D) adaptation
(E) exhaustion

7. All of the following are physiologic consequences of stress EXCEPT

(A) decreased mitogen responses
(B) release of ACTH
(C) suppression of the immune response
(D) decreased body oxygen consumption
(E) increased skin conductance

8. Which of the following is most likely to be the first defense mechanism that a patient with pancreatic cancer will use when he learns the diagnosis?

(A) Repression
(B) Regression
(C) Denial
(D) Projection
(E) Acting out

9. Surgical patients at relatively greater risk for developing psychological problems include all of the following EXCEPT

(A) a patient who believes he will not survive surgery
(B) a patient who says that he is not worried about a serious surgical procedure he faces the next day
(C) a patient who has unrealistic expectations of surgery
(D) a patient who has been told that he will be on a respirator after surgery
(E) a patient without family support

10. All of the following are true about psychiatric problems in medical inpatients EXCEPT

(A) psychotherapy can shorten the hospital stay of medical inpatients
(B) when psychotherapy is used, it is usually of the dynamic short-term type
(C) the most common psychiatric disorder is schizophrenia
(D) psychological problems can affect a patient's health
(E) behavioral therapy may be used

11. The first response of patients who have just received a diagnosis of AIDS is usually

(A) depression
(B) anxiety
(C) guilt
(D) hopelessness
(E) feeling of abandonment

12. All of the following statements about renal dialysis patients are true EXCEPT

(A) they must adapt to dependency on others and on machines
(B) sexual problems frequently occur
(C) self-help groups are useful
(D) their life-styles are rarely affected
(E) use of home dialysis units is associated with successful psychological adaptation

13. A 55-year-old male patient has a competitive, driven (Type A) personality. Which of the following physical problems is most likely to be seen in this patient?

(A) Coronary artery disease
(B) Cancer
(C) Obesity
(D) Pruritus
(E) Bronchial asthma

Directions: The group of items in this section consists of lettered options followed by a set of numbered items. For each item, select the **one** lettered option that is most closely associated with it. Each lettered option may be selected once, more than once, or not at all.

Questions 14–17

Match each of the descriptions below with the personality type that is most closely associated with it.

(A) Compulsive
(B) Narcissistic
(C) Masochistic
(D) Paranoid
(E) Dependent
(F) Schizoid
(G) Passive-aggressive

14. A 40-year-old businessman insists on making a phone call to his office just as the physician is about to examine him

15. A patient in the waiting room becomes extremely angry when the physician must take an emergency case before him

16. Although a mastectomy is indicated, a 45-year-old woman refuses to consent to surgery because it will alter her appearance

17. A 30-year-old male patient calls the physician's office daily to speak about relatively minor health complaints

Answers and Explanations

1–B. The passive-aggressive personality type may ask for help from the physician and then not comply with the physician's advice.

2–D. Positive as well as negative life events can cause stress to the individual.

3–E. Agitation, noncompliance, sleep disorders, and disorientation are commonly seen in hospitalized medical and surgical patients.

4–E. Sexual or physical abuse is rated as an extreme stressor in the life of a child or adolescent.

5–D. Allowing patients some control over their environment, such as choosing when they will take their pain medication, can reassure patients in the ICU.

6–B. The general adaptation syndrome, described by Hans Selye, describes the stages that the body goes through in response to stress. It involves an initial alarm reaction, followed by adaptation, and finally exhaustion.

7–D. Physiologic consequences of stress include rapid release of ACTH followed by release of corticosteroids, which in turn suppress the immune response (lowered lymphocyte mitogen response). Stress is also associated with increased heart rate, respiratory rate, blood pressure, and body oxygen consumption, and skin conductance and resistance.

8–C. Denial is the most common initial defense mechanism seen in very ill patients.

9–D. Surgical patients at relatively greater risk for developing psychological problems include those who have unrealistic expectations about the surgery, those who are depressed and convinced that they will not survive the surgery, those who deny that they are seriously worried about the surgery, and those without family support. Patients who know what to expect have a better recovery after surgery.

10–C. Psychiatric disorders commonly seen in medical inpatients are depression, agitation, and sleep disorders. Psychological problems can put medical patients at risk and are usually treated with brief dynamic therapy.

11–B. Intense anxiety is frequently the initial response to a diagnosis of AIDS.

12–D. The life-styles of patients on renal dialysis are often severely affected by the disease and by the time required for dialysis.

13–A. Coronary artery disease has been linked with the Type A personality.

14–A. This businessman, a compulsive personality type, fears loss of control and is trying to gain control over this interaction by insisting on making a phone call.

15–D. This paranoid patient is supersensitive and suspicious about giving up his place to another patient.

16–B. This narcissistic woman will risk death to avoid disfiguring surgery that can save her life.

17–E. This dependent patient has a strong need for personal attention.

22

Epidemiology and Statistical Methods

I. Epidemiology: Incidence and Prevalence

– **Epidemiology** is the study of the factors determining the occurrence and distribution of diseases in human populations.

A. Incidence

– **Incidence rate** is the number of new individuals that develop an illness in a given time period (commonly 1 year) divided by the total number of individuals at risk for the illness during that time period (e.g., the number of drug abusers newly diagnosed as HIV positive in 1993 divided by the number of drug abusers in the population during 1993).

B. Prevalence

– **Prevalence** is the number of individuals in the population who have an illness (e.g., the number of people in the United States who currently are HIV positive divided by the total population).

– **Point prevalence** is the number of individuals who have an illness at a specific point in time (e.g., the number of people who are HIV positive on July 4, 1994, divided by the total population on that date).

– **Period prevalence** is the number of individuals who have an illness during a specific time period (e.g., the number of people who are HIV positive in 1994 divided by the total population in 1994).

C. Relationship between incidence and prevalence

– Prevalence is equal to incidence multiplied by the length of the disease process (assuming that incidence and length of the disease process are stable).

– Prevalence is higher than incidence if the disease is long term (e.g., while the prevalence of diabetes, which lasts for the life of the person, is much higher than the incidence, the prevalence of influenza, an acute illness, is approximately equal to the incidence).

D. Risk factors

– Risk factors are variables that are linked to the cause of a disease (e.g., smoking is a risk factor for lung cancer).

– Ways of identifying risk factors (**causality**) include association of the factor with only one disease (**specificity**); observation of the factor prior to the emergence of the disease (**temporality**); demonstration of the presence of the factor in many studies; and demonstration that the disorder is absent if the factor is removed.

E. Person-years

- The denominator for rates are sometimes calculated as **person-years**.
- To arrive at this measure, the number of years of exposure to a risk factor in members of a population is added (e.g., if one woman has smoked for 6 months, another has smoked for 9 months, and another has smoked for 15 months, the sum is 2.5 person-years of exposure to smoking).

II. Research Study Design

A. Prospective studies

- **Prospective,** or **cohort, studies** begin with the identification of specific populations (cohorts), which are free of illness at the start of the study.
- Following assessment of exposure to the risk factor, exposed and nonexposed members of a cohort are compared to see who becomes ill (e.g., healthy adults are followed through middle age to compare the health of those who smoke versus those who do not smoke).
- Prospective studies can be **concurrent** (taking place in the present time) or **nonconcurrent** (some activities may have taken place in the past).
- **Clinical treatment trials** are prospective studies in which a cohort receiving one treatment is compared with a cohort receiving a different treatment or a placebo (e.g., differences in survival between men with lung cancer who receive a new cancer drug and men with lung cancer who receive a standard cancer drug).

B. Retrospective studies

- In retrospective studies, or **case-control studies**, subjects who have the disorder (cases) and subjects who do not have the disorder (controls) are identified and information on their prior exposure to risk factors is obtained and compared using odds ratios.

C. Cross-sectional studies

- Cross-sectional studies provide information on possible risk factors and health status of a group of individuals at one specific point in time.

III. Relative and Attributable Risk

A. Relative risk

- Relative risk compares the incidence rate of a disorder among individuals exposed to a risk factor with the incidence rate of the disorder in unexposed individuals.

$$\text{Relative risk} = \frac{\text{Incidence rate of lung cancer among smokers}}{\text{Incidence rate of lung cancer among nonsmokers}}$$

- For example, if the chance of getting lung cancer is 15 times higher for heavy smokers than for nonsmokers, the relative risk is 15.
- Relative risk can provide information on how much higher an individual's risk of lung cancer is if he or she smokes.
- Relative risk can be calculated **only for prospective** (cohort) **studies.**

Example 22-1. Calculating the Odds Ratio

Of 200 patients in the hospital, 50 have lung cancer. Of these 50 patients, 45 are smokers. Of the remaining 150 hospitalized patients who do not have lung cancer, 60 are smokers. Use this information to calculate the odds ratio for smoking and the risk of lung cancer.

	Smokers	Nonsmokers
People with lung cancer	A = 45	B = 5
People without lung cancer	C = 60	D = 90

$$\textbf{Odds ratio} = \frac{(A)\,(D)}{(B)\,(C)} = \frac{(45)\,(90)}{(5)\,(60)} = 13.5$$

An odds ratio of 13.5 means that the risk of lung cancer is 13.5 times higher in people who smoke than in those who do not smoke.

B. Attributable risk

- In attributable risk, the incidence rate of the illness in nonexposed individuals is subtracted from the incidence rate of the illness in those who have been exposed to the risk factor.

    Attributable risk = Incidence rate of lung cancer in smokers − incidence rate of lung cancer in nonsmokers

    - For example, 50 people out of a group of 1000 smokers and 2 people out of a group of 1000 nonsmokers have lung cancer. Therefore, the risk of lung cancer attributable to smoking (the attributable risk) is 50/1000 − 2/1000 or 48/1000.
- Attributable risk is useful for determining what would happen in a study population if the risk factor was removed (e.g., how common lung cancer would be in a study if people did not smoke).

C. Odds ratio

- The **odds** (or odds risk) **ratio** is an estimate of the relative risk when incidence data are not available.
- The odds ratio is calculated for **retrospective (case-control)** studies (Example 22–1).

IV. Testing

- To be useful, testing instruments must be bias-free, reliable, and valid (i.e., sensitive and specific).

A. Bias

- A biased test is constructed so that one outcome is more likely to occur than another.
- Bias can flaw research and can occur if the individual administering the test knows how the results are expected to turn out and subtly influences subjects' responses.

B. Reducing bias

– Blind, crossover, and randomized studies and placebos are used to reduce bias.

1. Blind studies

– In a single-blind study, the subject does not know what drug he or she is receiving.
– In a double-blind study, neither the subject nor the experimenter knows what drug the subject is receiving.

2. Placebo responses

– In a blind drug study, a patient may receive a placebo (an inactive substance) rather than the active drug.
– People receiving the **placebo** are the **control group;** those receiving the **active drug** are the **experimental group.**
– At least one-third of patients respond to treatment with placebos (the placebo effect); in psychiatric illnesses, the placebo effect is even greater.
– Placebo effects, which are more likely to occur in cases in which pain and anxiety are severe, are increased by the presence of positive social support systems and feelings of mastery over the disorder.
– Placebo effects appear to be mediated by the **endogenous opioid system** and in some instances may be blocked by treatment with an opiate receptor blocker such as naloxone.

3. Crossover studies

– A variation of a double-blind study is a crossover study.
– In a crossover study, subjects in Group 1 first receive the drug and subjects in Group 2 first receive the placebo.
– Later in the crossover study, the groups switch; those in Group 1 receive the placebo, and those in Group 2 receive the drug.
– Because subjects in both groups receive both drug and placebo, each subject acts as his or her own control.

4. Randomization

– In order to ensure that the number of sick and well people is proportionate in treatment and control (placebo) groups, patients are randomly assigned to these groups.

C. Reliability and validity

– Reliability refers to the reproducibility of results.
– **Interrater reliability** means that the results of the test are the same when the test is administered by a different rater or examiner.
– **Test-retest reliability** means that the results are the same when the person is tested a second or third time.
– **Validity** is a measure of whether the test assesses what it was designed to assess; sensitivity and specificity are components of validity.

D. Sensitivity and specificity (Example 22-2)

1. Sensitivity measures how well a test identifies truly ill people.

– **True positives** are ill people whom a test has correctly identified as being ill.
– **False negatives** are ill people whom a test has incorrectly identified as being well.

Example 22-2. Sensitivity, Specificity, Predictive Value, and Prevalence

A new blood test to detect the presence of HIV was given to 1000 patients. Although 200 of the patients were actually infected with the virus, the test was positive in only 160 patients (true +); the other 40 infected patients had negative tests (false −) and thus were not identified by this new test. Of the 800 patients who were not infected, the test was negative in 720 patients (true −) and positive in 80 patients (false +).

Use the following information to calculate sensitivity, specificity, positive predictive value, and negative predictive value of this new blood test and the prevalence of HIV in this population.

	Patients infected with HIV	Patients not infected with HIV	Total patients
Positive HIV blood test	160 (true +)	80 (false +)	240 (those with + test)
Negative HIV blood test	40 (false −)	720 (true −)	760 (those with − test)
Total patients	200	800	1000

$$\text{Sensitivity} = \frac{160 \text{ (true +)}}{160 \text{ (true +)} + 40 \text{ (false −)}} = \frac{160}{200} = 80.0\%$$

$$\text{Specificity} = \frac{720 \text{ (true −)}}{720 \text{ (true −)} + 80 \text{ (false +)}} = \frac{720}{800} = 90.0\%$$

$$\text{Positive predictive value} = \frac{160 \text{ (true +)}}{160 \text{ (true +)} + 80 \text{ (false +)}} = \frac{160}{240} = 66.67\%$$

$$\text{Negative predictive value} = \frac{720 \text{ (true −)}}{720 \text{ (true −)} + 40 \text{ (false −)}} = \frac{720}{760} = 94.7\%$$

$$\text{Prevalence} = \frac{200 \text{ (total of those infected)}}{1000 \text{ (total patients)}} = 20.0\%$$

- **Sensitivity** is calculated by dividing the number of true positives by the sum of the number of true positives and false negatives.

2. **Specificity** measures how well a test identifies truly well people.
    - **True negatives** are well people whom a test has correctly identified as being well.
    - **False positives** are well people whom a test has incorrectly identified as being ill.
    - **Specificity** is calculated by dividing the number of true negatives by the sum of the number of true negatives and false positives.

E. **Predictive value** (see Example 22-2)
    - The **predictive value** of a test is a measure of the percentage of test results that match the actual diagnosis.
    - **Positive predictive value** is the probability that someone with a positive test actually has the illness.

- **Negative predictive value** is the probability that a person with a negative test is actually well.
- If the prevalence of a disease in the population is low, even tests with very high sensitivity and specificity will have low positive predictive value.

V. Statistical Analyses

A. Statistics in epidemiology

- Statistical tests are used to analyze data from medical epidemiologic studies; those frequently used are listed in Table 22-1.

B. Variables

- A **variable** is a quantity that can change under different experimental situations; variables may be independent or dependent.
  - An **independent variable** is a characteristic that an experimenter can change (e.g., giving a drug to reduce blood pressure or giving a placebo).
  - A **dependent variable** is the outcome that reflects the effects of changing the independent variable (e.g., the blood pressure reading following treatment with the drug or the placebo).

C. Measures of dispersion

- **Variance** is used to analyze the variation among factors such as subjects and treatment outcomes.

Table 22-1. Commonly Used Statistical Tests

A consumer group would like to evaluate the success of three different commercial weight loss programs. To obtain this information, three groups of people (Group 1, Group 2, and Group 3), whose average weight is not significantly different at the start of the study (Time 1), are put on three different diet regimens. At Time 1 and at the end of the 6-week study (Time 2), all of the subjects are weighed and their blood pressures, cholesterol levels, and serum uric acid levels are obtained. Examples of how statistical tests can be used to analyze the results of this study are given below.

t-test: **Difference between means of two samples**

Independent (non paired): Tests the difference between mean body weights of people in Group 1 and people in Group 2 at Time 1 (two groups of people are sampled on one occasion).
Dependent (paired): Tests the difference between mean body weights at Time 1 and Time 2 of people in Group 1 (the same people are sampled on two occasions).

Analysis of variance: **Differences between means of more than two samples**

One-way: Tests the difference among mean body weights of Group 1, Group 2, and Group 3 at Time 2 (one variable, group).
Two-way: Tests differences between mean body weights of men and women and among mean body weights of Group 1, Group 2, and Group 3 at Time 2 (two variables, group and sex).

Chi-square test: **Differences between frequencies in a sample**

Tests the difference between the percentage of people with body weight at or under 140 lbs and the percentage of people with body weight over 140 lbs in Group 1 at Time 2.

Correlation: **Mutual relationship between two continuous variables**

Tests the relationship between blood pressure and body weight at Time 2.

Multiple regression: **Relationship between many measures**

Tests the relationship between weight loss at Time 2 and blood pressure at Time 2 controlling for blood pressure at Time 1, cholesterol level at Time 1, and serum uric acid level at Time 1.

– **Standard deviation** is obtained by squaring each variation or deviation from the mean in a group of scores, adding the squared deviations, dividing by the number of scores in the group minus one, and taking the square root of the result.

– **Standard error** is the standard deviation divided by the square root of the number of scores in that group.

D. Measures of central tendency

– The **mean** is the average and is obtained by adding a group of numbers and dividing by the number of scores in the group.

– The **median** is the middle value in a sequentially ordered group of numbers.

– The **mode** is the value that appears most often in a group of numbers.

E. Normal distribution

1. A **normal** distribution, also referred to as a **Gaussian** or **bell-shaped** distribution, is a theoretical distribution of scores that is symmetric.

– The mean, median, and mode are equal in a normal distribution.

– The highest point in the distribution of scores is the **modal peak**. In a **bimodal distribution,** there are two modal peaks (e.g., two distinct populations).

– In a normal distribution, approximately 68% of the population scores fall within one standard deviation of the mean; approximately 95% of scores fall within two, and 99.7% of scores fall within three standard deviations of the mean (Figure 22-1).

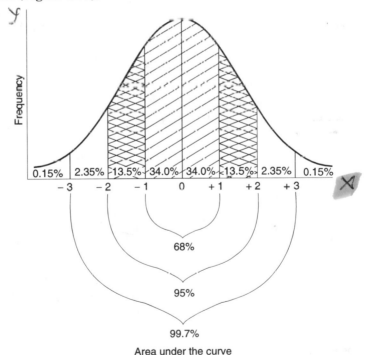

Figure 22-1. The normal distribution. The number of standard deviations (–3 to +3) from the mean is found on the x axis. The percentage of the population that falls within each standard deviation is shown.

2. A **skewed distribution** means that the modal peak is off to one side (Figure 22-2).
   – In a **positively-skewed** distribution (skewed to the right), the tail is toward the right and the modal peak is toward the left side (i.e., scores cluster toward the low end).
   – In a **negatively-skewed** distribution (skewed to the left), the tail is toward the left and the modal peak is toward the right side (i.e., scores cluster toward the high end).

F. Nonparametric statistical tests
   – If the distribution of scores in a population is not normal (or in the case of small sample sizes), **nonparametric** statistical tests must be used to evaluate the presence of statistically significant differences between groups.
   – Nonparametric tests include the Mann-Whitney U test and the Wilcoxon matched-pairs signed-rank test.

G. Correlation
   – The degree of relationship between two variables can be assessed using correlation coefficients that range between **–1 and +1**.

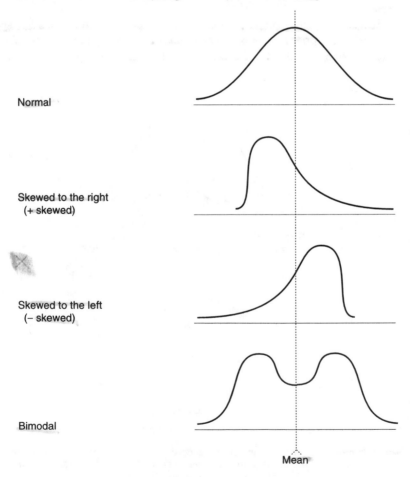

Figure 22-2. Frequency distributions.

- If the two variables move in the same direction, the correlation coefficient is **positive** (e.g., as height increases, body weight increases).
- If the two variables move in opposite directions, the correlation coefficient is **negative** (e.g., as time spent exercising increases, body weight decreases).

1. **Hypothesis testing**

   a. An **hypothesis** is a statement based on inference, the literature, or preliminary studies and postulates that a difference exists between two groups. The possibility that this observed difference occurred by chance is tested using statistical procedures.

   b. The **null hypothesis,** which postulates that there is no difference between the two groups, can either be rejected or not rejected following statistical analysis.

2. **Example of the null hypothesis**

   a. A group of 20 patients who have similar systolic blood pressures at the beginning of a study (Time 1) is divided into two groups of 10 patients each. One group is given daily doses of an experimental drug (experimental group); the other group is given a placebo daily (placebo group). Blood pressure is measured 2 weeks later (Time 2).

   b. The null hypothesis assumes that there are no significant differences in blood pressure between the two groups at Time 2.

   c. If, at Time 2, patients in the experimental group show systolic blood pressures similar to those in the placebo group, the null hypothesis (there is no significant difference between the groups) is not rejected.

   d. If, at Time 2, patients in the experimental group have significantly lower blood pressures than those in the placebo group, the null hypothesis is rejected.

3. **Type I and type II errors**

   - A **type I error** occurs when the null hypothesis is rejected although it is true (e.g., the drug really does not lower blood pressure).
   - A **type II error** occurs when the null hypothesis is not rejected although it is false (e.g., the drug really does lower blood pressure).

4. **Probability**

   - The p (probability) value is the chance of a type I error. If a p value is equal to or lower than 0.05, it is unlikely that a type I error has been made; that is, a type I error will be made 5 times or less out of 100.
     - A p value equal to or less than 0.05 is generally considered to be statistically significant; lower p values (e.g., $p < 0.01$) may be required for statistical significance in studies with large sample sizes.

Review Test

Directions: Each of the numbered items or incomplete statements in this section is followed by answers or by completions of the statement. Select the **one** lettered answer or completion that is **best** in each case.

1. The number of people who have lung cancer on January 1, 1994, divided by the total population on that date is the

(A) point prevalence
(B) period prevalence
(C) incidence
(D) odds ratio
(E) relative risk

2. A new test for HIV does not detect the presence of the virus in someone who is infected. This is known as

(A) a false-positive result
(B) a false-negative result
(C) a true-positive result
(D) a true-negative result
(E) a predictive result

3. In which of the following infectious illnesses is prevalence most likely to exceed incidence?

(A) Rhinovirus
(B) Influenza
(C) Leprosy
(D) Rubella
(E) Rabies

4. A study designed to determine the relationship between emotional stress and ulcers used the records of patients diagnosed with peptic ulcer disease versus controls over the period from July 1978–July 1988. This is an example of what kind of study?

(A) Cohort
(B) Cross-sectional
(C) Retrospective
(D) Prospective
(E) Crossover

Questions 5 and 6

5. Twelve patients are given a drug or a placebo to determine the effect of medication on blood pressure. The dependent variable in this study is

(A) the experimenter's bias
(B) giving the patients the drug
(C) giving the patients a placebo
(D) the patient's blood pressure following treatment with the drug
(E) the daily variability in the patient's blood pressure before the drug treatment

6. The study described in the preceding question is

(A) case-control
(B) retrospective
(C) prospective
(D) nonconcurrent
(E) cross-sectional

7. In testing, the term interrater reliability means that

(A) structured interviews are involved
(B) an assessment instrument is being used
(C) the test actually measures what it was designed to measure
(D) the results are the same when the test is administered a second or third time
(E) the results are the same when the test is used by a different examiner

8. Each of the following factors reduces test bias EXCEPT

(A) errors in construction
(B) single-blind studies
(C) double-blind studies
(D) crossover studies
(E) randomization of the sample

9. On a gross anatomy quiz, test scores of 10, 10, 10, 20, 40, 70, and 90 are obtained by seven students in a laboratory group. Which of the following statements correctly describes these quiz scores?

(A) Mean is 50
(B) Median is 10
(C) Negatively skewed
(D) Mode is 10
(E) Modal peak is the same as the mean

Questions 10–12

A study was undertaken to determine if prenatal exposure to marijuana is a cause of low-birth weight. Mothers of 50 infants weighing less than 5 lbs (low-birth weight) and 50 infants weighing more than 7 lbs (high-birth weight) were questioned about their use of marijuana during pregnancy. The study found that 20 mothers of low-birth weight infants and only 2 mothers of high-birth weight infants used the drug during pregnancy.

10. In this study, the odds ratio associated with smoking marijuana during pregnancy is

(A) 2
(B) 16
(C) 20
(D) 30
(E) 48

11. An odds ratio of X, calculated in the preceding question, means that

(A) the incidence of low-birth weight in infants whose mothers smoke marijuana is X
(B) an infant whose mother uses marijuana during pregnancy is X times as likely to be of low-birth weight as an infant whose mother does not use the drug
(C) a child has a 1/X chance of being born of low-birth weight if its mother uses marijuana
(D) the risk of low-birth weight in infants whose mothers use marijuana is no different from that of infants whose mothers do not use the drug
(E) the prevalence of low-birth weight in infants whose mothers smoke marijuana is X

12. This study is

(A) case-control
(B) cross-sectional
(C) double-blind
(D) prospective
(E) cohort

Questions 13 and 14

13. If systolic blood pressure is normally distributed with a mean of 120 mmHg and a standard deviation of 10, what percentage of people have systolic blood pressure at or above 140 mmHg?

(A) 1.9%
(B) 2.5%
(C) 13.5%
(D) 34.0%
(E) 64.2%

14. Among 500 people, how many will have systolic blood pressure between 110 and 120 mmHg?

(A) 80
(B) 100
(C) 125
(D) 170
(E) 250

Questions 15 and 16

15. A blood test to detect prostate cancer was given to 1000 male members of a large HMO. Although 50 of the men actually had prostate cancer, the test was positive in only 15; the other 35 patients with prostate cancer had negative tests. Of the 950 men without prostate cancer, the test was positive in 200 men and negative in 750. The specificity of this test is approximately

(A) 15%
(B) 30%
(C) 48%
(D) 79%
(E) 86%

16. The positive predictive value of this blood test is

(A) 7%
(B) 14%
(C) 21%
(D) 35%
(E) 93%

Directions: The group of items in this section consists of lettered options followed by a set of numbered items. For each item, select the **one** lettered option that is most closely associated with it. Each lettered option may be selected once, more than once, or not at all.

Questions 17–20

Match the studies described below with the appropriate statistical test.

(A) Paired *t*-test
(B) Analysis of variance
(C) Chi-square test
(D) Correlation
(E) Independent *t*-test

17. Used to evaluate differences among mean body weights of women in three different age groups

18. Used to evaluate the difference in the percentage of women who lose weight on a protein-sparing diet versus the percentage who fail to lose weight on the diet

19. Used to evaluate differences between initial body weight and final body weight of women on a protein-sparing diet

20. Used to evaluate the relationship between body weight and systolic blood pressure in a group of 25-year-old women

Answers and Explanations

1–A. Point prevalence is the number of people who have an illness at a specific point in time (i.e., January 1, 1994).

2–B. A false-negative result occurs if a test does not detect HIV in someone who truly is HIV positive.

3–C. In leprosy, a long-lasting infectious illness, the number of people in the population who have the illness (prevalence) is likely to exceed the number developing the illness in a given year (incidence).

4–C. Retrospective (case-control) studies are based on past events such as hospital admissions records, from July 1978–July 1988, of patients with peptic ulcer disease.

5–D. The dependent variable is a measure of the outcome of an experiment. In this case, blood pressure following treatment with the drug or placebo is the dependent variable.

6–C. The study described is a clinical treatment trial, a prospective study in which a cohort receiving the blood pressure drug is compared with a cohort receiving a placebo.

7–E. Interrator reliability describes how likely it is that test findings are the same when used by a different examiner.

8–A. Bias results from errors in test construction. Bias is reduced by randomization of the sample and by use of single-blind, double-blind, and crossover studies.

9–D. The mean of the quiz scores is 35.7, the median is 20, and the mode is 10. Because of all the low scores, the distribution of these test scores is skewed to the right (positively skewed).

10–B. The odds ratio is 16 and is calculated as follows:

	Mother smoked marijuana	Mother did not smoke marijuana
Low-birth weight babies	A = 20	B = 30
High-birth weight babies	C = 2	D = 48

$$\textbf{Odds ratio} = \frac{(A)(D)}{(B)(C)} \text{ or } \frac{(20)(48)}{(30)(2)} = \frac{960}{60} = 16$$

11–B. The odds ratio of 16 means that an infant whose mother uses marijuana during pregnancy is 16 times as likely to be of low-birth weight as an infant whose mother does not use the drug.

12–A. This study is a retrospective (or case-control) study; the risk factor here is exposure to marijuana during prenatal life.

13–B. Systolic blood pressure of 140 mmHg is 2 standard deviations above the mean (120 mmHg). The area under the curve between 2 and 3 standard deviations above the mean is about 2.35% plus about 0.15% (everything above 3 standard deviations). Thus, a total of about 2.50% of the people will have blood pressure of 140 mmHg and above.

14 D. Systolic blood pressure between 110–120 mmHg is one standard deviation below the mean. The percentage of people in this area on a normal curve is 34%. Thus, 34% of 500 people, or 170 people, will have systolic blood pressure in the range of 110–120 mmHg.

15–D. Calculations shown below indicate that the specificity of this blood test is 79%.

	Those who have prostate cancer	Those who do not have prostate cancer	Total
Positive blood test	15 (true +)	200 (false +)	215
Negative blood test	35 (false −)	750 (true −)	785
Total patients	50	950	1000

Specificity:

$$\frac{750 \text{ (true } -)}{750 \text{ (true } -) + 200 \text{ (false } +)} - 78.9\%$$

16–A. The calculations shown below indicate that the positive predictive value of this test is 7%.

Positive predictive value:

$$\frac{15 \text{ (true } +)}{15 + 200 \text{ (those with } + \text{ test)}} = 7.0\%$$

17–B. Analysis of variance is used to examine differences among means of more than two samples. In this case, there are three samples (i.e., age groups).

18–C. The chi-square test is used to examine differences between frequencies in a sample: In this case, the percentage of women who lose weight versus those who fail to lose weight on the diet.

19–A. The *t*–test is used to examine differences between means of two samples. This is an example of a paired *t*–test because the same women are examined on two different occasions.

20–D. Correlation is used to examine the relationship between two variables—in this case, systolic blood pressure and body weight.

23

Systems of Health Care Delivery

I. Levels of Health Care

- Health care in the United States can be classified into three levels by the mode of delivery: **primary, secondary,** and **tertiary** (Table 23-1).

II. Hospitals

A. History

- The development of modern hospitals coincided with the development of the **germ theory** of disease and the introduction of aseptic technique in the mid-nineteenth century.
  - Prior to 1900, people typically died of acute respiratory or gastrointestinal infections, problems treated largely with preventive health measures.
  - Since 1900, chronic diseases such as heart disease and cancer have been responsible for most deaths.

B. Current status

- There are about **6700 hospitals** in the United States with a total capacity of about 1,000,000 beds.
- The United States hospital system has excess capacity. Currently, about 10% of hospital beds are not needed; most of these extra beds are in urban hospitals.

C. Utilization

- Approximately 75% of the adult population has been hospitalized on at least one occasion.
- Most stays in general hospitals average **6–7 days.**
- Hospital patients are **more likely to be women** than men and are more likely to be old than young.

D. Hospital ownership

- **Investor-owned hospitals,** which may be oriented to general or to specialty care, are for-profit ventures and total about 12% of the hospitals in the United States.
- Not-for-profit hospitals, or **voluntary hospitals,** are owned privately or sponsored by churches, universities, or community governments.
  - Most of the population receives care in voluntary hospitals.

Table 23-1. Levels in the Health Care System

Level	Facilities
Primary care	Hospital outpatient departments Community mental health centers School and industrial health centers
Secondary care	Hospital inpatient departments Hospital emergency rooms
Tertiary care	Specialty hospitals (e.g., chronic disease, mental)

- The **federal government** owns and operates Veterans Administration and military hospitals.
- **State governments** own and operate **long-term psychiatric hospitals**.
- Municipal governments own and operate city hospitals, which are often teaching hospitals affiliated with medical schools.
  - To qualify as a **general teaching hospital**, a hospital must have at least four active residency training programs and must provide clinical training for medical students.

E. **Short-term care and long-term care**
- Hospitals may be classified as providing **acute** (short-term) care or **chronic** (long-term) care.
- Usually, length of stay in an acute care hospital is less than 30 days; in a chronic care or rehabilitation hospital, stays exceed 30 days.
- Although the number of short-term care hospitals has remained the same over the last few years, the number of long-term care hospitals has increased.

F. **General and specialty hospitals**
- **General hospitals** offer a wide range of medical and surgical services.
- **Specialty hospitals** provide care in one medical specialty (e.g., pediatrics, psychiatry) and may be for-profit or not-for-profit.
  - There are about 875 short-term and long-term specialty hospitals in the United States.

III. Nursing Homes
- There are currently about 25,000 **nursing homes** with a capacity of 1,500,000 beds in the United States.

A. **Types of nursing homes**
- Nursing homes provide long-term care and can be classified according to the level of care offered.
  - A **skilled nursing facility** offers the services of practical nurses 24 hours a day and registered nurses during the daytime hours.
  - An **intermediate care facility** provides limited nursing care, typically restorative nursing care and assistance with self-care.
  - A **residential care facility** is basically a sheltered environment that does not provide nursing care.

B. **Related care facilities**
- An **extended care facility** of a hospital functions like a skilled nursing facility or an intermediate care facility for patients who do not need more than nursing care.

- **Halfway houses** and similar rehabilitation centers provide help for hospitalized patients to reenter society.

IV. Health Care Delivery

A. Managed care

- **Managed care** describes a health care delivery system in which all aspects of an individual's health care are coordinated or managed by a group of providers to enhance cost effectiveness.

1. Health maintenance organizations (HMOs)

- An **HMO** is a prepaid insurance and service managed care plan in which physicians and other health care personnel are paid by salary to provide medical services to a group of people who are enrolled voluntarily and who have paid an annual premium.
- Because fewer patient visits result in lower costs, the philosophy of HMOs stresses **prevention** rather than acute treatment.
- Benefits of HMOs include hospitalization, physician services, preventive medicine services, and often dental, eye, and podiatric care.
- Currently, there are over **600 HMOs** in the United States covering **32 million people.**

2. Independent practice associations (IPAs) and preferred provider organizations (PPOs)

- Variants of HMOs, **IPAs** and **PPOs,** are formed by groups of physicians who establish contracts to provide services to specific groups of patients.
- Physicians in private practice who participate in IPAs or PPOs receive a fee or **capitation** for each patient they see.
- In **IPAs,** physicians in private practice are hired by an HMO to provide services to HMO patients.
- In **PPOs,** a **third-party payor,** often a union trust fund or an insurance company, contracts with doctors and hospitals to provide medical care to its subscribers.
  - PPOs guarantee doctors a certain volume of patients and provide reduced costs for patients.
  - There are currently about **200 PPOs** in the United States.

B. Visiting nurse care

- Visiting nurse associations provide services in a patient's home.
- Home care for some elderly is funded by Medicare as a **less expensive** alternative to hospitalization or institutionalization.
- Home care services include nursing, physical and occupational therapy, psychiatric nursing, and social work services.

C. Hospices

- Hospices use physicians, nurses, social workers, and volunteers to provide **inpatient and outpatient** supportive care to **terminally ill patients** (i.e., those expected to live less than 6 months).
- Primary features of hospice care include grief counseling, group support, and administration of pain medication as needed.
- Currently, there are about **1700 hospice programs** in the United States.
- In 1983, the federal government began to pay for hospice care under Medicare.

V. Physicians

A. Demographics

- Currently, there are **126 medical schools** and **16 colleges of osteopathic medicine** in the United States, graduating annually over 15,000 medical doctors (M.D.) and 1800 doctors of osteopathy (D.O.).
  - Training and practice are essentially the same for **DOs** as for MDs, however, the philosophy of osteopathic medicine stresses the **interrelatedness of body systems** and the use of **musculoskeletal manipulation** in the diagnosis and treatment of physical illness.
- There are currently about **643,000 physicians** in the United States; about 35,000 of these are D.O.s, and 139,000 are foreign medical school graduates.
- A physician earns an average of **$200,000 annually.**
  - Psychiatrists, pediatricians, and family practitioners earn about $150,000 annually, while plastic surgeons, orthopedic surgeons, and neurosurgeons typically earn more than $350,000 annually.

B. Geographic distribution of physicians

- Although the ratio of physicians to patients is high in the Northeastern states and in California, the ratio is low in the Southern and Mountain states.
- Although inner cities and rural areas commonly do not have an adequate number of physicians, government attempts to equalize geographic distribution have generally failed.

C. Medical specialization

- Primary care physicians, including family practitioners, internists, and pediatricians, provide initial care to patients and comprise one-third of all doctors.
- Approximately **80%** of physicians are **specialists.**
- By the year 2000, physician surpluses are projected in surgery, ophthalmology, obstetrics and gynecology, internal medicine, and neurosurgery; physician shortages are expected in psychiatry, preventive medicine, emergency medicine, and hematology and oncology.
- An adequate number of physicians are expected in family practice, dermatology, pediatrics, and otolaryngology.

D. Patient consultations

- Two-thirds of doctors are in private practice and are paid in the form of **fee-for-service**; most doctor-patient interaction occurs in this setting.
- People in the United States average **5.5 visits** to physicians per year, significantly fewer visits than people in developed countries with systems of socialized medicine.
- Seventy-five percent of people visit physicians in a given year; patients tend to be **children,** the **elderly**, and **women**.
- High-income patients are more likely to seek treatment in private doctor's offices; low-income patients are more likely to seek treatment in emergency departments.
  - In order of frequency, the most common reasons for office visits are general physical examination, prenatal visits, treatment for nose and throat problems and hypertension, and postoperative consultations.

VI. Other Health Care Personnel

A. Overview

- The ratio of other health care workers to physicians has increased twentyfold since 1900.
- Nonphysician health care personnel include nurses, nurse clinicians and nurse practitioners, physician's assistants, dentists, podiatrists, pharmacists, clinical psychologists, dietitians, physical and occupational therapists, radiologic technicians, and medical technologists.
- **Physician's assistants** (PAs) are certified by a national commission; however, certification is not required in all states.
- There are about **60 dental schools** in the United States with a total enrollment of about 22,000.
- There are approximately **six colleges of podiatry** and about 9000 podiatrists in the United States.

B. Regulation of paramedical personnel

- **Licensing**, which specifies the scope of practice and determines the qualifications necessary for practice, is done by **states.**
- **Certification** defines the qualifications necessary for the use of a specific title.
- **Registration** simply lists those individuals who are using a title.
  - Certification and registration may be done by the state or by governing groups for each category of paramedical personnel.

Review Test

Directions: Each of the numbered items or incomplete statements in this section is followed by answers or by completions of the statement. Select the **one** lettered answer or completion that is **best** in each case.

1. The percentage of physicians in the United States who are specialists is

(A) 20%
(B) 40%
(C) 50%
(D) 60%
(E) 80%

2. Each of the following statements about health care in the United States is true EXCEPT

(A) there are currently about 6700 hospitals
(B) there are about 1,000,000 hospital beds
(C) prior to 1900, people generally died from infections
(D) the number of short-term hospitals has increased substantially over the last few years
(E) since 1900, heart disease and cancer have been responsible for most deaths

3. Each of the following settings is a primary care facility EXCEPT

(A) psychiatric hospitals
(B) school health centers
(C) hospital outpatient departments
(D) industrial health centers
(E) community mental health centers

4. Which of the following statements about hospitalization in the United States is true?

(A) The average hospital stay is 2 days
(B) Rates of hospitalization increase with age
(C) Men are hospitalized more often than women
(D) There is presently a shortage of hospital beds in urban areas
(E) Approximately 10% of adults have been hospitalized on at least one occasion

5. Each of the following statements about financing of hospitals in the United States is true EXCEPT

(A) voluntary hospitals may be owned by churches
(B) voluntary hospitals are not-for-profit
(C) about 12% of hospitals are designed to earn a profit for investors
(D) municipal hospitals are often affiliated with medical schools
(E) long-term psychiatric hospitals are commonly owned by the federal government

6. Each of the following statements about nursing homes is true EXCEPT

(A) nursing homes generally provide long-term care
(B) an intermediate care facility provides some nursing care
(C) a residential care facility usually provides nursing care
(D) there are approximately 25,000 nursing homes in the United States
(E) a skilled nursing care facility has both practical and registered nurses

7. Each of the following statements about hospice care is true EXCEPT

(A) pain medication is given as needed
(B) care is provided in a patient's own home
(C) Medicare covers the cost for the elderly
(D) hospices primarily serve chronically ill people
(E) there are currently about 1,700 hospice programs in the United States

8. Which of the following statements about physician visits is true?

(A) Most patients are middle-aged
(B) Patients are more likely to be male than female
(C) Patients average 25 visits to physicians per year
(D) Americans are more likely to visit doctors than people in countries that have socialized medicine
(E) High-income patients are likely to seek treatment in private doctor's offices rather than in hospital emergency departments

9. The most common reason for office visits to physicians is

(A) prenatal care
(B) hypertension
(C) nose and throat problems
(D) general physical examination
(E) postoperative consultations

10. Which of the following specialties is likely to have a shortage of physicians by the year 2000?

(A) Psychiatry
(B) Neurology
(C) Ophthalmology
(D) Neurosurgery
(E) Surgery

11. Health maintenance organizations (HMOs) typically provide benefits for all of the following EXCEPT

(A) hospitalization
(B) optometrist's services
(C) physician's services
(D) long-term nursing home care
(E) preventive medicine services

12. Patients pay a fixed amount in advance for medical services in each of the following care settings EXCEPT

(A) HMOs
(B) IPAs
(C) PPOs
(D) systems of managed care
(E) community-based hospitals

13. Which of the following statements about physicians in the United States is true?

(A) Average income is $100,000
(B) Overall, there are about 200,000 physicians
(C) About one-fifth are graduates of foreign medical schools
(D) A high ratio of physicians to patients is common in the Mountain states
(E) A high ratio of physicians to patients is common in the Southern states

Answers and Explanations

1–E. About 80% of physicians in the United States are specialists.

2–D. The number of short-term hospitals in the United States has remained approximately the same over the last few years.

3–A. Primary care facilities include hospital outpatient departments, community mental health centers, and school and industrial health centers. Psychiatric hospitals are tertiary care facilities.

4–B. Rates of hospitalization increase with age. Women are hospitalized more often than men; approximately 75% of adults have been hospitalized on at least one occasion; the average hospital stay is 6–7 days; and there is an oversupply of hospital beds in the United States, particularly in urban areas.

5–E. Long-term psychiatric hospitals are owned and operated by state governments.

6–C. A residential care facility does not usually provide nursing care.

7–D. Hospice care provides services mainly to terminally ill people.

8–E. Higher income patients have fewer visits to emergency departments. Patients average 5.5 visits to physicians per year; patients tend to be children, the elderly, and women. Americans make fewer visits to physicians than people in developed countries using socialized medicine.

9–D. The most common reason for office visits to physicians is for general physical examination.

10–A. There will most likely be a shortage of psychiatrists by the year 2000. Other areas that probably will experience a shortage of physicians include emergency medicine, preventive medicine, and hematology and oncology.

11–D. HMOs do not provide long-term nursing home care for subscribers.

12–E. In HMOs, subscribers pay an annual premium for health care benefits. Independent practice associations and preferred provider organizations are variants of HMOs, and all are systems of managed care.

13–C. Low physician-to-patient ratios are typical of the Mountain states as well as the Southern states. There are approximately 643,000 physicians in the United States; 21% of these are foreign medical school graduates.

24

Issues in Health Care Delivery

I. Costs of Health Care

A. Health care expenditures

- Health care expenditures in the United States reached approximately $675 billion in 1990; this figure represents slightly over **12% of the gross domestic product** (GDP).
- This figure is expected to reach **over 16% of the GDP** by the year 2000.
- Of personal health care expenses, federal and state governments pay about 40%, private health insurance pays 31%, individuals pay 28%, and industry and charity pay 1%.

B. Allocation of health care funds

- Hospitalization is the most expensive element of health care in the United States, accounting for 44% of total expenditures. Physicians (22%), nursing homes (9%), medications and medical supplies (11%), mental health services (10%), and dental and other care (4%) consume the remaining portion of U.S. health care expenses.
  - The most commonly treated mental health problems are anxiety disorders (12.6%), depressive disorders (9.5%), substance abuse disorders (9.5%), cognitive impairment (2.7%), antisocial personality disorder (1.5%), and schizophrenia (1.1%).
- Health care expenditures have been rising because of the **increasing age of the population,** advances in medical technology, and the ready availability of health care to old and poor people through Medicare and Medicaid.

II. Health Insurance

A. Health insurance coverage

- Up to 85% of Americans have health insurance; approximately 35 million Americans have no health care coverage.
- Health insurance typically covers **80% of hospital costs** and over 50% of physician costs (less is covered for psychiatry).

B. Health insurers

- **Blue Cross/Blue Shield,** a nonprofit private insurance carrier, is regulated by insurance agencies in each state and pays for hospital costs (Blue Cross) or

204 / *Behavioral Science*

doctor and diagnostic tests in the hospital (Blue Shield) for about 30%–50% of working people in the United States.
- Individuals can also contract with one of about 1000 commercial insurance companies to pay for their medical costs.
- These "self-pay" patients pay a specific amount based on either their individual health record or, if they are part of a group, the group rate.
- Insurance companies may require **co-payments**, a percentage (typically 20%) of the total bill that the patient must pay.

C. **Medicare**
- In 1966, the federal government established the **federally funded** health insurance programs **Medicare** and **Medicaid** as an amendment to the Social Security Act.
- Medicare provides hospital and medical costs for all people eligible for Social Security (persons **over 65** years of age regardless of income or persons with permanent disabilities or chronic debilitating illness).
    - **Part A** of Medicare covers inpatient hospital costs, home health care, medically necessary nursing home care following hospitalization, dialysis, and hospice care.
    - **Part B** is optional and is bought by the patient to cover therapy, medical supplies, laboratory tests, outpatient hospital care, doctor bills, ambulance service, and medical equipment.
- Medicare is financed by federal tax monies under the Social Security system.
- Medicare recipients must pay an annual deductible (amount the patient must pay before Medicare begins to pay) for physician services and 20% of other charges.
- Medicare pays hospital bills based on the **diagnosis-related group** (**DRG**) [an estimate of how much hospitalization for each illness should cost rather than the actual charges incurred].

D. **Medicaid**
- **Medicaid** (Med-Cal in California) is **funded** by both **federal and state governments** and pays for health care primarily for **low-income groups**.
- Each state decides who is eligible for Medicaid.
- The percentage of costs that the federal government pays depends on the per capita income in each state and ranges from 40%–79%.
- Medicaid pays for inpatient and outpatient hospital costs, home health care, physician services, laboratory tests, prescription drugs, and long-term nursing home care; there are no deductibles associated with Medicaid.
- One-third of Medicaid money is allocated for nursing home care for elderly indigent people.

III. Socioeconomics of Health Care

A. **Life style and health**

- A variety of factors affect health and health care delivery.
- Life style and poor dietary and other habits, particularly smoking, are responsible for about **70% of mental and physical illness**; for example, cancer is frequently related to poor diet, to smoking tobacco, or to both.

B. Socioeconomic status and health

- Socioeconomic status is based **primarily on occupation** with secondary emphasis on educational level.
- Approximately 85% of poor people are black or hispanic.
- People in low-socioeconomic groups typically experience decreased life expectancy and poorer mental and physical health, with increased incidence of obesity, hypertension, arthritis, and upper respiratory illnesses.

C. Race and health

- **Whites** visit doctors' offices **10 times more often** than blacks.
- Blacks have higher rates of heart disease, hypertension, obesity, and diabetes than whites.

D. Gender and health

1. Women

- Women visit physicians and are hospitalized more frequently than men.
- Women are most often hospitalized for childbirth, cancer, and heart disease.
- The most common chronic medical conditions in women are arthritis, heart disease, and hypertension.
- The rate of lung cancer in women has risen steadily in recent years; female smokers now outnumber male smokers.
  - Although the reasons are not clear, women smokers are at higher risk for hypertension, heart attack, and high cholesterol than male smokers.

2. Men

- Men are most frequently hospitalized for heart disease, cancer, and fractures.
- The most common chronic conditions in men are heart disease, arthritis, and back or spine problems.

E. Age and health

- The most common illnesses occurring in all age groups are upper respiratory ailments, influenza, and injuries.
- **Older** people (over age 65) and **younger** people (20–30 years) experience **more health problems** and need more health care than middle-aged people.
- The likelihood of mental illness as well as physical illness and hospitalization increases with age.
- Over 75% of individuals over age 65 suffer from at least one chronic medical condition.
- The leading medical conditions among the elderly are arthritis, hypertension, and heart disease.
- **Five percent of elderly people** need care in **nursing homes**.
- Although the **elderly** comprise only 12% of the population, they currently incur over **30% of all health care costs**; this figure is expected to rise to 50% by the year 2020.

IV. Life Expectancy and Causes of Death

A. Life expectancy

- The average life expectancy in the United States is currently **75.5 years**; however, this figure varies greatly by gender and race (Table 24-1).
- Differences in life expectancies by gender and race have been decreasing over the past few years.

Table 24-1. Life Expectancy (Years) in the United States by Sex and Race

	Overall	Black	White
Males	72.0	64.6	72.9
Females	78.9	73.8	79.6

B. **Causes of death in adults**
  - The death rate for adults, 8600 per 1,000,000, is lower than in previous years.
  - The three leading causes of death in 1993 were **heart disease** (34%), **cancer** (23%), and **stroke** (7%), followed by chronic obstructive pulmonary diseases and accidents.
  - **AIDS** is now the ninth leading cause of death in the United States.
    - In the **25 to 44-year-old** age group, AIDS is the **leading cause of death** in men; it is the third leading cause of death in black women and the sixth in white women.
  - **Lung cancer** is the first leading cause of death from cancer, and **colorectal cancer** ranks third in both men and women; the second leading cause is **prostate cancer** in men and **breast cancer** in women.

C. **Causes of death in children and adolescents**
  - In descending order, the most common causes of **death in infants** are congenital anomalies, respiratory distress syndrome, and sudden infant death syndrome (SIDS).
  - In descending order, the most common causes of **death in children** under age 14 are accidents, cancer (leukemia and cancer of the central nervous system are most likely to result in death), and congenital anomalies.
  - In descending order, the most common causes of **death in adolescents** (ages 15–24 years) are **accidents** (approximately 75% result from automobile accidents), **suicide, and homicide**.

V. Legal Issues in Health Care

A. **Definition of death**

  - When an individual dies, a physician must certify the cause of death and sign the **death certificate.**
  - The death is classified as natural, suicide, accident, homicide, or due to unknown causes.
  - If death occurs when a physician is not involved in the case, the body must be examined by the coroner, medical examiner, or pathologist to determine cause of death.
  - **Brain death**, the standard of death in the United States, is defined as irreversible cessation of brain (including the brain stem) function.
    - Life-prolonging medical care, including food and water, can be withheld from a patient who is brain dead.

B. **Malpractice**
  - Malpractice is generally defined as professional negligence or deviation from normal standards of professional care.
  - Malpractice is a **tort or civil wrong**, not a crime.
  - To successfully argue a claim, a patient must be able to prove that the doctor demonstrated the "four Ds" of malpractice: **dereliction** (negligence) of a **duty**

(there was an established doctor-patient relationship) causing **damages** (the patient was injured in some way) **directly** (also known as "proximate cause," meaning that the damages were caused by the negligence) to the patient.
  - **Compensatory damages** pay the patient money to compensate for suffering as well as for medical bills and lost salary.
  - **Punitive damages** are awarded only in cases of wanton carelessness or gross negligence in order to punish the doctor and alert the medical community.
  - Surgical specialists and anesthesiologists are the physicians most likely to be sued for malpractice; psychiatrists and family practitioners experience relatively few malpractice suits.

C. **Informed consent**
  - The possibility of a malpractice suit can be reduced by the informed consent process.
  - Informed consent must be obtained prior to any medical procedure; a formal document is not strictly required.
    - The patient must understand the diagnosis, treatment, alternatives to treatment, and risks and benefits of a procedure.
    - The patient must understand what will happen if he or she does not consent to the procedure.
    - The patient must also understand that he or she can withdraw consent at any time prior to the procedure.

  1. **Adults**
    - The legally **competent** patient voluntarily signs a document of agreement prior to submitting to a procedure such as surgery.

  2. **Minors**
    - **Parents** usually must **give consent** for medical procedures involving minor children.
    - Parents **do not have to consent** to treatment of minors in emergency situations or under certain conditions such as medical care in pregnancy, for sexually transmitted diseases, and for drug and alcohol dependence.
    - Twenty-three states require the consent of one or both parents when a minor seeks an **abortion.**
    - Married or self-supporting minor children generally are considered **emancipated minors**, have the rights of adults, and do not require parental consent for medical care.

D. **Confidentiality**
  - The 1974 **Tarasoff decision** stated that mental health clinicians may break the usual rules of doctor-patient confidentiality to warn intended victims and notify law enforcement officials of threats by their patients toward others.
  - In a related manner, doctor-patient confidentiality may be breached if HIV-positive patients habitually put others at risk by engaging in unprotected sex.
  - Other exceptions to traditional confidentiality restrictions include cases of child abuse, life-threatening situations, or when there is significant risk of suicide.

E. **Advance directives**
  - Hospitals receiving Medicare payments are required to inquire about and assist patients in writing advance directives such as a living will or a durable power of attorney.

– In a **living will**, the patient gives directions for future care in the event that he or she is no longer competent to do so.

– In a **durable power of attorney**, patients designate legal representatives who will make decisions concerning their health care when they can no longer do so.

– When critical care decisions are required for a patient who is incompetent or otherwise unable to give consent, providers and family members must determine what the patient would have done if competent.

F. **Involuntary treatment and right to die**

– For a patient to be committed for involuntary treatment, the patient must be proven to be both mentally ill and dangerous to self or others.

– In general, even if death will result, **competent patients may refuse medical treatment**.

– Recent test cases suggest that **doctor-assisted patient suicide**, while not "strictly legal" in any state, is not generally an indictable offense. However, in a late-1993 case, a Michigan physician was ordered to stand trial for violating a state law prohibiting assisted suicide.

Review Test

Directions: Each of the numbered items or incomplete statements in this section is followed by answers or by completions of the statement. Select the **one** lettered answer or completion that is **best** in each case.

1. The percentage of the GDP spent on health care in 1990 was about

(A) 1%
(B) 8%
(C) 12%
(D) 22%
(E) 30%

2. Which of the following sources pays the largest percentage of personal health care expenses?

(A) Federal and state governments
(B) Private health insurance
(C) Industry
(D) Charity
(E) Personal funds

3. In the United States, most health care expenditures are for

(A) physician fees
(B) nursing homes
(C) hospitals
(D) drugs
(E) dental services

4. The percentage of mental and physical illness due to poor personal habits and life style is

(A) 20%
(B) 30%
(C) 50%
(D) 70%
(E) 90%

5. The most common cause of death in children aged 2–14 years is

(A) leukemia
(B) CNS cancer
(C) congenital anomalies
(D) accidents
(E) respiratory distress syndrome

6. The average life expectancy for black women in the United States is

(A) 65.4 years
(B) 71.1 years
(C) 73.8 years
(D) 78.3 years
(E) 79.6 years

7. The percentage of hospital costs typically paid for by health insurance in the United States is

(A) 10%
(B) 20%
(C) 50%
(D) 80%
(E) 100%

8. Which of the following statements about Medicare is true?

(A) It is funded by individual states
(B) It has no deductibles
(C) It is financed under the Social Security system
(D) It is designed primarily for welfare recipients
(E) States decide who is eligible to receive Medicare

9. Medicare Part B generally covers all of the following medical costs EXCEPT

(A) inpatient hospital costs
(B) medical supplies
(C) ambulance service
(D) doctor bills
(E) therapy

10. Each of the following statements about Medicaid is true EXCEPT

(A) it pays outpatient hospital costs
(B) it has a $100 deductible for physician services
(C) it is funded by both federal and state governments
(D) it is designed primarily for people with low incomes
(E) individual states decide who is eligible to receive Medicaid

11. The rates of all of the following conditions are higher among blacks than among whites EXCEPT

(A) obesity
(B) schizophrenia
(C) diabetes
(D) heart disease
(E) hypertension

12. Which of the following is the third leading cause of death in the United States?

(A) AIDS
(B) Heart disease
(C) Cancer
(D) Spinal cord injuries
(E) Stroke

13. The most common cause of cancer death in the United States is cancer of the

(A) lung
(B) colon
(C) breast
(D) prostate
(E) liver

14. The usual standards of doctor-patient confidentiality apply to which of the following patients?

(A) A man tells his physician that he plans to strangle his wife
(B) A bereaved woman tells her physician that she has had thoughts of suicide
(C) A man tells his physician that he has been sexually abusing his 10-year-old step-daughter
(D) An HIV-positive man is engaging in sexual intercourse without condoms
(E) A depressed woman tells her physician that she has saved up 50 secobarbital tablets and wants to die

15. A woman sues her physician for malpractice. For this claim, the patient must prove that the doctor

(A) committed a criminal act
(B) deliberately caused the injury
(C) significantly overcharged her for the care
(D) had established a professional relationship with her
(E) did not have the appropriate credentials to practice medicine

16. A 15-year-old patient consults her family physician because she has contracted chlamydia. Prior to treating her for the infection, the physician should

(A) notify her parents
(B) notify her sexual partner
(C) get written permission from her parents
(D) counsel her on safe sex practices
(E) report the case to the local health authorities

Answers and Explanations

1–C. Approximately $675 billion was spent on health care in the United States in 1990. This represents over 12% of the GDP for 1990.

2–A. The federal and state governments pay about 40% of personal health care expenses; private insurance pays about 31%.

3–C. Hospital costs represent 44% of health care expenditures and physicians fees represent 22%. Nursing home, drug, mental health, and dental services make up the remaining percentage.

4–D. About 70% of mental and physical problems are due to poor personal habits and life style such as smoking, overeating, and sedentary life style.

5–D. Accidents are the most common cause of death in children aged 2–14 years.

6–C. The average life expectancy for black women in the United States is 73.8 years. This figure is less than the life expectancy for white females, 79.6 years.

7–D. About 80% of hospital costs are typically paid by health insurance.

8–C. Medicare, financed and managed under the Social Security system, was primarily designed for people over 65 or for individuals with permanent disabilities. Medicare recipients must pay an annual deductible of 20% for medical services.

9–A. Medicare Part B is optional and covers doctor bills, medical supplies, outpatient hospital health care, ambulance services and therapy. Part A covers inpatient hospitalization.

10–B. Medicaid has no deductibles and is funded by both the federal and state governments. It is designed for poor people, and pays for all medical costs including outpatient care. Each individual state determines which residents are eligible for Medicaid.

11–B. Rates of schizophrenia are similar in blacks and whites. Rates of obesity, diabetes, heart disease, and hypertension are higher among blacks than whites.

12–E. Stroke is the third leading cause of death in the United States, with heart disease and cancer being the first and second. The rates of the three leading causes of death are highest among black males. Women in all age groups have lower mortality rates than men.

13–A. Cancer of the lung is responsible for most cancer deaths in the United States.

14–B. A bereaved woman with thoughts of suicide but has no plans is currently not at high risk to kill herself. Exceptions to confidentiality include patients who commit child abuse, put their sexual partners at risk for HIV infection, indicate that they plan to harm someone, or those at significant risk for suicide by having a suicidal plan.

15–D. For a claim of malpractice, the patient must prove that the doctor was derelict or negligent, caused damages (not necessarily deliberately), and had a duty to the patient because they had a professional relationship. Malpractice is a civil wrong or tort, not a crime.

16–D. Prior to treating the patient, the physician should counsel her on safe sexual practices. Parental consent is generally not required for treating minors in cases of sexually transmitted disease, pregnancy and substance abuse.

Comprehensive Examination

Directions: Each of the numbered items or incomplete statements in this section is followed by answers or by completions of the statement. Select the **one** lettered answer or completion that is **best** in each case.

1. A woman who has religious beliefs that preclude blood transfusion is scheduled for major surgery. Prior to the surgery, she is clearly mentally competent and states that the physician is not to give her a blood transfusion, although she may need it during surgery. If a transfusion becomes necessary during surgery, the physician should

(A) get a court order to do the transfusion
(B) get permission from the woman's family to do the transfusion
(C) replace body fluids but not give the woman the transfusion
(D) give the woman the transfusion but not tell her about it
(E) give the woman the transfusion and inform her of it when she recovers from the anesthetic

2. When compared with the general population, suicide in the elderly occurs

(A) one-third as often
(B) half as often
(C) equally as often
(D) twice as often
(E) four times as often

3. A 45-year-old woman who usually drinks two cups of coffee each morning is hospitalized and placed on intravenous fluids. After 2 days, this patient is most likely to complain of all of the following signs EXCEPT

(A) headache
(B) insomnia
(C) depression
(D) hunger
(E) lethargy

4. The percentage of women who suffer postpartum reactions following the birth of a child is approximately

(A) 5%–10%
(B) 15%–25%
(C) 30%–50%
(D) 75%–85%
(E) 90%–95%

5. A physician outlines a treatment plan for a 57-year-old woman with rheumatoid arthritis. The patient then assumes the responsibility for carrying out the plan. This is an example of which model of the doctor-patient relationship?

(A) Sick role
(B) Gate control
(C) Activity-passivity
(D) Mutual-participation
(E) Guidance-cooperation

6. Blockade of which of the following receptors is useful in the treatment of anorexia nervosa?

(A) H_1
(B) H_2
(C) D_1
(D) D_2
(E) Muscarinic

7. Characteristics of patients with Alzheimer's disease include all of the following EXCEPT

(A) apathy
(B) severe memory loss
(C) personality changes
(D) cognitive deficits
(E) clouding of consciousness in the early stages

8. A 24-year-old man who uses crack cocaine is likely to show all of the following signs EXCEPT

(A) hyposexuality
(B) aggressiveness
(C) euphoria
(D) irritability
(E) impaired judgment

9. The electroencephalogram of a 28-year-old patient shows mainly alpha waves. This patient is most likely to be

(A) awake and concentrating
(B) awake and relaxing
(C) in Stage 1 sleep
(D) in Stage 4 sleep
(E) in REM sleep

10. A 30-year-old man presents with an injured hand. During the interview, he states that he believes that his hand was injured when aliens took him aboard their ship the previous night, as they have done many times in the past. The patient has no history of psychiatric illness. He has good social and work relationships. Except for his comments about the alien spaceship, he speaks clearly, logically, and appropriately. The most likely diagnosis is

(A) schizophrenia
(B) bipolar disorder
(C) delusional disorder
(D) somatization disorder
(E) schizoid personality disorder

11. Visual hallucinations, tachycardia, and sweating are most likely seen following withdrawal from which of the following drugs?

(A) Alcohol
(B) Cocaine
(C) Opioids
(D) Amphetamines
(E) Barbiturates

12. Which individual has the highest risk of developing schizophrenia?

(A) The dizygotic twin of a schizophrenic person
(B) The child of two schizophrenic parents
(C) The monozygotic twin of a schizophrenic person
(D) The child of one schizophrenic parent
(E) A child raised in an institutional setting when neither biological parent was schizophrenic

13. Although a 12-year-old girl has been promoted to the sixth grade, she only shows the mental ability of an 8-year-old (second grade). The IQ of this child can be classified as

(A) mildly mentally retarded
(B) borderline
(C) low-average
(D) average
(E) high-average

14. Which area of the brain is associated mainly with memory function?

(A) Cerebellum
(B) Temporal lobes
(C) Frontal lobes
(D) Parietal lobes
(E) Occipital lobes

15. An 18-year-old man using marijuana regularly is likely to show all of the following signs EXCEPT

(A) decreased heart rate
(B) increased appetite
(C) impaired memory
(D) lack of motivation
(E) abnormal time perception

16. Erectile dysfunction is LEAST likely to be associated with

(A) diabetes
(B) alcohol abuse
(C) Alzheimer's disease
(D) major depressive disorder
(E) antihypertensive medication

17. Which of the following neurotransmitters is most likely to facilitate aggression?

(A) Endorphins
(B) Dopamine
(C) Serotonin
(D) Histamine
(E) GABA

18. In the United States, the cost of raising a child in a middle-class environment to age 17 is approximately

(A) $25,000–$45,000
(B) $50,000–$75,000
(C) $90,000–$180,000
(D) $190,000–$250,000
(E) $350,000–$450,000

19. The rate of suicide is similar in white men and black men in which age group?

(A) 15–19 years
(B) 20–24 years
(C) 31–35 years
(D) 48–52 years
(E) 62–66 years

20. Which of the following defense mechanisms is the LEAST mature?

(A) Humor
(B) Denial
(C) Altruism
(D) Suppression
(E) Sublimation

21. Which group of drugs is associated with the highest incidence of sexual problems?

(A) Sedatives
(B) Tranquilizers
(C) Antipsychotics
(D) Antihistamines
(E) Antihypertensives

22. Caffeine is commonly found in all of the following substances EXCEPT

(A) tea
(B) cola
(C) cough medicine
(D) nonprescription diet drugs
(E) nonprescription stimulants

23. In the United States, the incidence of childhood physical abuse cases reported each year is approximately

(A) 100,000
(B) 200,000
(C) 500,000
(D) 800,000
(E) 1,000,000

24. At the close of a long interview with an elderly male patient, the physician states, "Let's see if I have taken all of the information correctly," and then sums up the information that the patient has given. This interviewing technique is known as

(A) support
(B) reflection
(C) validation
(D) facilitation
(E) recapitulation

25. Which of the following patients is most likely to be obese?

(A) A 35-year-old black man
(B) A 50-year-old black woman
(C) A 50-year-old black man
(D) A 50-year-old white man
(E) A 50-year-old white woman

26. In which of the following states does the federal government pay the highest percentage of Medicaid costs?

(A) Alabama
(B) California
(C) New Jersey
(D) New York
(E) Pennsylvania

27. The type of reinforcement that produces the highest rate of response is

(A) variable ratio
(B) variable interval
(C) continuous
(D) fixed ratio
(E) fixed interval

28. The percentage of all health care costs incurred by the elderly is approximately

(A) 15%
(B) 30%
(C) 50%
(D) 65%
(E) 75%

29. A 65-year-old woman whose husband died 3 weeks previously cries much of the time and eats and sleeps poorly. Also, she states that she thinks that she saw her husband walking down the street the day before. The physician should first

(A) recommend a vacation
(B) provide support and reassurance
(C) prescribe antipsychotic medication
(D) prescribe antidepressant medication
(E) recommend a psychiatric evaluation

30. According to the *DSM-IV*, which of the following is the LEAST severe life stressor?

(A) Marriage
(B) Birth of a child
(C) A child leaving home
(D) A serious medical illness
(E) Divorce

31. In the United States, the leading cause of death in men aged 25–44 years is

(A) AIDS
(B) suicide
(C) homicide
(D) hypertension
(E) pancreatic cancer

32. Differences between frequencies in a sample are tested using

(A) *t*-test
(B) analysis of variance
(C) chi-square test
(D) correlation
(E) regression

33. Which of the following statements is an expression of a mood-congruent delusion in a depressed 49-year-old man?

(A) "I am an inadequate person"
(B) "I am a worthless human being"
(C) "I will never get better"
(D) "I am a failure in my profession"
(E) "I am personally responsible for the economic recession"

34. The largest percentage of health-care dollars is spent on

(A) hospitalization
(B) physicians
(C) nursing care facilities
(D) medications
(E) medical supplies

35. A 7-year-old child requires surgery within 24 hours for a life-threatening injury. If, because of religious reasons, the father refuses to allow the surgery, the physician should

(A) operate on the child anyway
(B) obtain a court order for the operation
(C) obtain permission from another family member
(D) have the child moved to another hospital
(E) not operate

36. Which of the following statements best describes the relationship between the incidence and prevalence of AIDS in the United States?

(A) Incidence is higher than prevalence
(B) Prevalence is higher than incidence
(C) Prevalence and incidence are equal
(D) There is no relationship between incidence and prevalence
(E) If incidence decreases, prevalence increases

37. All of the following statements concerning visits to physicians are true EXCEPT

(A) most patients are middle-aged
(B) patients are more likely to be female than male
(C) each patient averages 5.5 visits per year to a physician
(D) patients who are poor are more likely to seek treatment in emergency departments
(E) the most common reason to see a physician in an office is for a general physical examination

38. The average life expectancy for black women in the United States is approximately

(A) 65 years
(B) 74 years
(C) 79 years
(D) 82 years
(E) 85 years

39. All of the following are characteristic of a manic patient at the height of mania EXCEPT

(A) delusions
(B) flight of ideas
(C) increased appetite
(D) decreased need for sleep
(E) increased activity level

40. The percentage of smokers who quit smoking without the help of a support group and remain abstinent for at least 1 year is approximately

(A) 10%
(B) 25%
(C) 33%
(D) 60%
(E) 80%

41. Which of the following ethnic groups is most likely to be the most stoic about pain?

(A) Mexican-American
(B) Puerto Rican-American
(C) Jewish-American
(D) Anglo-American
(E) Italian-American

42. A patient who has suffered a major psychological stress is examined because of severe hearing loss. No medical cause can be found. Which of the following is likely to be true about this patient?

(A) The patient is old
(B) The patient is male
(C) The patient is well educated
(D) The hearing loss appeared suddenly
(E) The patient is very upset about the hearing loss

43. Long-term psychiatric hospitals in the United States are owned and operated primarily by

(A) universities
(B) private investors
(C) state governments
(D) municipal governments
(E) the federal government

44. A 60-year-old man from New Jersey whose wife has just died wakes up in Akron, Ohio. He does not know how he arrived there. This patient is probably suffering from

(A) localized amnesia
(B) psychogenic fugue
(C) anterograde amnesia
(D) generalized amnesia
(E) depersonalization disorder

45. All of the following statements about the family in the United States are true EXCEPT

(A) approximately 10% of children live in families with two working parents
(B) approximately 15% of couples are childless
(C) approximately 15% of single-parent families are headed by a man
(D) approximately 20% of children live in families where the father works outside the home and the mother manages the home
(E) approximately 95% of the population marries during their lifetimes

46. The dexamethasone suppression test (DST) is LEAST likely to be positive in

(A) obesity
(B) pregnancy
(C) schizophrenia
(D) Alzheimer's disease
(E) obsessive-compulsive disorder

47. The most common adverse effect of benzodiazepines is

(A) tremor
(B) dry mouth
(C) akathisia
(D) drowsiness
(E) urinary hesitancy

48. Which of the following genetic conditions commonly becomes apparent in the fourth or fifth decade of life?

(A) Down's syndrome
(B) Klinefelter's syndrome
(C) Turner's syndrome
(D) Cri-du-chat syndrome
(E) Huntington's disease

49. Retinal pigmentation is associated with the use of which one of the following antipsychotic agents?

(A) Chlorpromazine
(B) Haloperidol
(C) Perphenazine
(D) Trifluoperazine
(E) Thioridazine

50. Which of the following personality disorders is seen more frequently in men than in women?

(A) Histrionic
(B) Antisocial
(C) Borderline
(D) Dependent
(E) Avoidant

51. A person who was buried under rubble for 24 hours after a major earthquake is likely to later suffer from all of the following EXCEPT

(A) flashbacks
(B) nightmares
(C) hallucinations
(D) guilt
(E) memory impairment

52. A woman in REM sleep is likely to show all of the following EXCEPT

(A) dreaming
(B) increased pulse
(C) clitoral erection
(D) skeletal muscle relaxation
(E) delta waves on the electroencephalogram

53. A 23-year-old man states that he often hears the voice of Elvis Presley talking to him. Although somewhat anxious, his mood is normal. The most likely diagnosis is

(A) schizophrenia
(B) bipolar disorder
(C) schizoid disorder
(D) schizotypal disorder
(E) schizoaffective disorder

54. Intravenous infusion of sodium lactate is most useful in the diagnosis of

(A) schizophrenia
(B) panic attacks
(C) major depression
(D) schizoaffective disorder
(E) obsessive-compulsive disorder

55. Negative predictive value is the probability that a person with a

(A) negative test is actually well
(B) positive test is actually well
(C) negative test is actually ill
(D) positive test is actually ill
(E) positive test will eventually show signs of the illness

56. The tenting effect first occurs in which stage of the sexual response cycle?

(A) Excitement
(B) Plateau
(C) Orgasm
(D) Emission
(E) Resolution

Questions 57 and 58

57. In a prospective study, the ratio of the incidence of miscarriage among women who use LCD computer screens to the incidence of miscarriage among women who do not use LCD computer screens is the

(A) attributable risk
(B) odds-risk ratio
(C) incidence rate
(D) prevalence rate
(E) relative risk

58. The study was carried out to determine whether exposure to LCDs in the first trimester of pregnancy results in miscarriage. To do this, 50 women who had miscarriages and 100 women who carried to term were questioned the day after miscarriage or delivery, respectively, about their exposure to LCDs during pregnancy. If 10 women who had miscarriages and 8 women who carried to term used LCDs during their pregnancies, the odds-risk ratio associated with LCDs in pregnancy is approximately

(A) 1.9
(B) 2.9
(C) 10.0
(D) 20.4
(E) 46

59. Harry Harlow's studies of development in infant monkeys showed that infant monkeys reared by surrogate artificial mothers show

(A) long-lasting negative effects
(B) normal mating behavior as adults
(C) normal maternal behavior as adults
(D) normal social behavior as adults
(E) fewer effects if they are male

Questions 60 and 61

In a study, the incidence rate for tuberculosis in people who have someone living in their home with tuberculosis is 5 per 1000. The incidence rate for tuberculosis in people who have no one living in their home with tuberculosis is 0.5 per 1000.

60. What is the risk for getting tuberculosis attributable to living with someone who has tuberculosis (attributable risk)?

(A) 1.5
(B) 4.5
(C) 7.5
(D) 9.5
(E) 10.0

61. How much higher is the risk of getting tuberculosis for people who live with a patient with tuberculosis than for people who do not live with a tuberculosis patient (relative risk)?

(A) 1.5
(B) 4.5
(C) 7.5
(D) 9.5
(E) 10.0

62. The most effective drug for treating obsessive-compulsive disorder is

(A) clomipramine
(B) alprazolam
(C) diazepam
(D) clozapine
(E) clonidine

63. To estimate the relative risk in a retrospective study, which of the following is calculated?

(A) Attributable risk
(B) Odds-risk ratio
(C) Incidence rate
(D) Prevalence rate
(E) Sensitivity

64. Which statement about affective disorders is true?

(A) The lifetime prevalence of unipolar disorder is about 5% in women
(B) The lifetime prevalence of unipolar disorder is higher in men than in women
(C) The genetic influence in bipolar disorder is higher than in schizophrenia
(D) The concordance rate for unipolar disorder is higher than that for bipolar disorder
(E) A child with two parents who have bipolar disorder has a 20% likelihood of having the disorder as an adult

65. The number of people who developed diabetes in 1991 divided by the total number of people at risk for diabetes in 1991 is the

(A) prevalence
(B) point prevalence
(C) period prevalence
(D) incidence rate
(E) odds-risk ratio

Directions: Each group of items in this section consists of lettered options followed by a set of numbered items. For each item, select the **one** lettered option that is most closely associated with it. Each lettered option may be selected once, more than once, or not at all.

Questions 66–69

For each patient described, select the most closely associated illness.

(A) Schizophrenia
(B) Tourette's syndrome
(C) Alzheimer's disease
(D) Delirium
(E) Korsakoff's syndrome
(F) Pseudodementia
(G) Schizoaffective disorder
(H) Pick's disease

66. A 75-year-old woman who lives alone develops a high fever and is brought to the hospital by a neighbor. Although the woman can state her name, she is not oriented to place or time and mistakes the orderly for her nephew.

67. A 19-year-old man is brought to the hospital by the police. The policeman states that when stopped for a minor traffic violation, the man cursed at him and showed bizarre grimacing.

68. A 50-year-old man with a history of alcoholism is being interviewed by the physician. While his level of consciousness is normal, the patient states that he graduated from high school in 1989. He also invents nonexistent life events.

69. An 85-year-old man whose previous functioning has been normal becomes very forgetful shortly after his wife of 50 years dies suddenly.

Questions 70–74

For each characteristic, select the most closely associated stage of life.

(A) Infancy
(B) Toddler
(C) Preschool
(D) Latency
(E) Adolescence
(F) Young adulthood
(G) Middle adulthood
(H) Old age

70. Ventricular enlargement

71. Imaginary companions

72. Acquisition of the capacity for abstract thought

73. Intimacy versus isolation

74. The oedipal stage

Questions 75–78

For each quotation, select the interview technique most likely used by the doctor.

(A) Empathy
(B) Validation
(C) Recapitulation
(D) Facilitation
(E) Reflection
(F) Direct question
(G) Support

75. "And then what happened"

76. "You say that you felt the pain more in the evening"

77. "That must have been terrifying for you"

78. "Many people feel the way you do when they first need hospitalization"

Questions 79–81

For each symptom of a thought disorder, select the most closely associated statement.

(A) "I think I saw my father who died last year just go around that corner"
(B) "If I am seated at a table in the center of a restaurant rather than against the wall, I get dizzy and feel like I cannot breathe"
(C) "I believe that there are people spying on me from my television set"
(D) "I often hear the voice of God speaking directly to me"
(E) "I am afraid that I will die if I leave my home"

79. Hallucination

80. Delusion

81. Illusion

Questions 82–84

For each clinical situation, select the most appropriate diagnostic technique.

(A) Computed tomography (CT)
(B) Magnetic resonance imaging (MRI)
(C) Evoked potentials
(D) Electroencephalogram (EEG)
(E) Galvanic skin response
(F) Positron emission tomography (PET)
(G) Dexamethasone suppression test (DST)

82. Hearing loss in a 3-month-old infant

83. Levels of stress and anxiety in a 29-year-old woman

84. Brain oxygen use during the translation of a written passage from Spanish to English

Questions 85–87

For each patient described, select the most closely associated psychiatric disorder.

(A) Psychogenic fugue
(B) Derealization
(C) Factitious disorder
(D) Malingering
(E) Conversion disorder
(F) Multiple personality disorder
(G) Depersonalization disorder
(H) Body dysmorphic disorder

85. A patient states that she often feels like an observer rather than a participant in her life

86. A woman pretends that she is paralyzed following an automobile accident in order to collect from the insurance company

87. A woman pretends that she is paralyzed following an automobile accident in order to gain attention from her doctor

Questions 88–90

For each patient described, select the most closely associated sleep disorder.

(A) Narcolepsy
(B) Kleine-Levin syndrome
(C) Insomnia
(D) Obstructive sleep apnea
(E) Night terrors

88. A 53-year-old woman who is depressed awakens at 4 a.m. every morning and cannot fall back asleep

89. When a 30-year-old man falls asleep when at work, he loses muscle control and drops to the ground

90. A 40-year-old man who is overweight reports that he feels tired all day despite having 8 hours of sleep each night

Questions 91–94

For each patient described, select the most closely associated personality disorder.

(A) Passive-aggressive
(B) Schizotypal
(C) Antisocial
(D) Paranoid
(E) Schizoid
(F) Obsessive-compulsive
(G) Avoidant
(H) Borderline

91. A 25-year-old man has an abnormal electroencephalogram and history of head injury

92. A 30-year-old man is a recluse who has no interest in socializing with others

93. A 25-year-old woman states that although she would like to have a relationship with a man, she is uncomfortable meeting any new people, so she does not date.

94. A new patient is instructed to avoid salt in her diet and to take medication for her hypertension. When the woman returns for a follow-up visit, she states that she forgot to fill the prescription and is still using salt.

Questions 95–98

For each clinical characteristic, select the most closely associated drug.

(A) Nortriptyline
(B) Alprazolam
(C) Amoxapine
(D) Diazepam
(E) Desipramine
(F) Triazolam
(G) Imipramine
(H) Trazodone
(I) Amitriptyline

95. Least sedating antidepressant

96. Heterocyclic antidepressant least likely to cause orthostatic hypotension

97. Priapism

98. Antianxiety agent with antidepressant properties

Questions 99–105

For each person described, select the most closely associated defense mechanism.

(A) Rationalization
(B) Acting out
(C) Splitting
(D) Identification
(E) Displacement
(F) Suppression
(G) Denial
(H) Undoing
(I) Reaction formation
(J) Intellectualization
(K) Sublimation
(L) Regression

99. A 26-year-old man's arm was severed in an accident at age 18 when he drove his father's car recklessly. He says that the loss was really a "blessing" since he would otherwise have ended up in jail

100. A patient, although angry at her doctor because he canceled her previous appointment at the last minute, tells him at her next appointment that she really likes his tie

101. A 59-year-old man recently diagnosed with lung cancer stops smoking and starts an exercise and diet program

102. A first-year medical student is very upset when he sees his cadaver on the first day of gross anatomy lab. He pushes this feeling aside and joins in the dissection with his lab group

103. A patient ignores a large axillary lump for more than 6 months

104. A professional baseball player who was a petty thief as a teenager is team leader in stolen bases

105. When hospitalized for a pelvic infection, a female lawyer watches "Leave It to Beaver" reruns on television, orders hot dogs and Jell-O from the hospital menu, and reads "Archie" comic books

Questions 106–110

For each patient described, select the most closely associated behavioral technique.

(A) Conditioned response
(B) Unconditioned stimulus
(C) Systematic desensitization
(D) Flooding
(E) Intermittent reinforcement
(F) Fixed ratio reinforcement
(G) Negative reinforcement
(H) Habituation
(I) Stimulus generalization
(J) Implosion
(K) Sensitization

106. A 28-year-old woman terrified of dogs has been taught relaxation techniques and is instructed to relax while she is shown a photograph of a German shepherd dog

107. A 28-year-old woman terrified of dogs is brought into a dog kennel and instructed to remain there until she is no longer afraid

108. When he is first hired for a position in a furniture factory, a 21-year-old man is extremely disturbed by the noise of the machinery. After 6 months, he barely notices the noise

109. A 56-year-old man who has received one intravenous chemotherapy treatment becomes nauseous at the beginning of the second treatment, although the medication has not yet begun to flow

110. Each time a 35-year-old man receives physical therapy for a shoulder injury, his pain lessens. This makes him return for more physical therapy sessions

Questions 111–113

For each quoted statement, select the most closely associated stage of dying.

(A) Denial
(B) Anger
(C) Acceptance
(D) Depression
(E) Bargaining

111. "I will go to church every day if only I can get rid of this illness"

112. "The doctor is to blame for my illness"

113. "I have made my peace and am ready to die"

Questions 114–116

For each situation described, select the most closely associated type of learning.

(A) Operant conditioning
(B) Aversive conditioning
(C) Spontaneous recovery
(D) Modeling
(E) Stimulus generalization

114. A 9-year-old girl states that she wants to be just like her mother when she grows up

115. A mother puts a bitter substance on her 9-year-old son's fingernails in order to break his nail-biting habit

116. A dog learns to turn a doorknob because this behavior has been rewarded with a treat

Questions 117–120

For each psychiatric condition, select the most closely associated neurotransmitter.

(A) Serotonin
(B) Dopamine
(C) Acetylcholine (ACh)
(D) GABA
(E) Histamine

117. Schizophrenia

118. Depression

119. Anxiety

120. Alzheimer's disease

Answers and Explanations

1–C. The physician should use alternative means of replacing body fluids but not give the patient the blood transfusion. Mentally competent patients may refuse treatment.

2–D. In the elderly, suicide occurs twice as often as it occurs in the general population.

3–B. Psychological and physical dependence may occur with chronic use of caffeine. Withdrawal symptoms include headache, lethargy, depression, and increased appetite. Insomnia is associated with the use of caffeine rather than with caffeine withdrawal.

4–C. Approximately 30%–50% of women suffer postpartum reactions following the birth of a child.

5–D. In the mutual-participation model of the doctor-patient relationship, which is generally used for patients with chronic illnesses, the doctor formulates the treatment plan, and the patient is responsible for carrying it out.

6–B. Blockade of H_2 receptors with drugs such as cyproheptadine leads to weight gain; thus, cyproheptadine may be useful in the treatment of anorexia nervosa.

7–E. Characteristics of Alzheimer's disease include apathy, severe memory loss, personality changes, and cognitive deficits. Level of consciousness is normal in the early stages of Alzheimer's disease.

8–A. Use of crack cocaine is associated with hypersexuality (not hyposexuality), aggressiveness, euphoria, irritability, and impaired judgment.

9–B. Alpha waves are associated with the awake relaxed state.

10–C. In persons with delusional (paranoid) disorder, delusions are present without abnormal thought processes. Absence of affective symptoms makes the diagnosis of bipolar disorder unlikely. Good social and work relationships make the diagnosis of schizophrenia unlikely.

11–A. Withdrawal from alcohol is associated with the occurrence of delirium tremens, including hallucinations, sweating, tachycardia, tremor, nausea, and hypertension.

12–C. The monozygotic twin of a schizophrenic person has a 35%–58% chance of developing the disease. The child of one schizophrenic parent has a 10%–13% chance of developing the disease; the dizygotic twin of a schizophrenic patient has a 9%–26% chance; and the child of two schizophrenic parents has a 30%–40% chance.

13–A. A 12-year-old child with the mental age of an 8-year-old (second grader) has an IQ of 8 (mental age) divided by 12 (chronological age) = 66, which falls into the category of mild mental retardation (IQ of 50–70).

14–B. Memory is a function mainly of the temporal lobes.

15–A. Tachycardia, increased appetite, impaired memory, lack of motivation, and abnormalities in perception of time occur with use of marijuana.

16–C. In persons with Alzheimer's disease, erectile function and sexual behavior are rarely affected until the last stages of the illness. Erectile dysfunction is associated with major depressive disorder and diabetes, as well as with the use of antihypertensive medication and alcohol abuse.

17–B. Dopamine and norepinephrine facilitate aggression. GABA and serotonin inhibit aggression.

18–C. The cost of raising a child in a middle-class environment to age 17 is about $90,000–$180,000.

19–B. White people commit suicide more frequently than black people; however, the suicide rate is increasing so rapidly in young black men that the rate is now equivalent in white and black men ages 20–24 years.

20–B. Denial is the least mature of these defense mechanisms.

21–E. Antihypertensive agents are associated with the highest incidence of sexual problems.

22–C. Caffeine is commonly found in tea, cola, nonprescription stimulants, and nonprescription diet drugs. Cough medicine often contains opiates.

23–E. The incidence of childhood physical abuse cases reported each year in the United States is approximately 1,000,000.

24–E. Using recapitulation, the interviewer sums up all of the information given by the patient.

25–B. Obesity is more common in women than in men; also, it is more common in black people than in white people.

26–A. Medicaid costs are shared by the state and federal governments. Because Alabama has the lowest per capita income of the listed states, the federal government makes a higher contribution toward Medicaid costs in that state.

27–A. Variable ratio reinforcement (e.g., a slot machine) results in the highest rate of response.

28–B. The elderly incur over 30% of health care costs, a figure that is expected to rise to 50% by the year 2020.

29–B. The physician should provide support and reassurance since this patient probably is experiencing a normal grief reaction. While limited use of benzodiazepines for sleep is appropriate, antipsychotic or antidepressant medications are not indicated as treatment for normal grief.

30–C. According to the *DSM-IV*, marriage is the most severe life stressor; a child leaving home is the least severe of those life stressors listed.

31–A. AIDS is the leading cause of death in men aged 25–44 years.

32–C. Differences between frequencies in a sample are tested using a chi-square test.

33–E. A person feeling responsible for the negative state of the economy suffers from mood-congruent delusion. All of the other choices are typical of the negative thoughts commonly expressed in people who suffer from severe depression.

34–A. Hospitalization represents 44% of health-care expenditures.

35–B. Parental consent is not strictly required in the case of an emergency involving a minor child. However, because there is some time before this child's operation, a court order can be obtained.

36–B. Prevalence of AIDS is higher than incidence since people with the disease commonly live for years after the diagnosis.

37–A. Most medical patients are either very young or very old (not middle-aged).

38–B. The average life expectancy for black women in the United States is 73.8 years.

39–C. At the height of mania, patients show little interest in eating and have a decreased need for sleep.

40–B. The percentage of former smokers who remain abstinent for 1 year without the help of a support group is approximately 25%. About 33% remain abstinent if they are members of a support group.

41–D. Among the listed ethnic groups, Anglo-Americans are the most stoic about pain.

42–D. Sensory loss in patients with conversion disorder appears suddenly. Patients with this disorder are more likely to be young, female, and less educated. They frequently show "la belle indifferencea" lack of concern about the condition.

43–C. Long-term psychiatric hospitals are owned and operated primarily by state governments.

44–B. Patients with psychogenic fugue wander away from their homes and do not know how they got to another destination.

45–A. Approximately 40% of children live in families with both parents working outside the home.

46–A. The DST may be positive in the following conditions: severe weight loss, anorexia nervosa, pregnancy, schizophrenia, Alzheimer's disease, obsessive-compulsive disorder, and endocrine disturbances as well as in major depression.

47–D. The most common adverse effect of benzodiazepines is drowsiness.

48–E. Huntington's disease first appears between the ages of 35 and 45 years.

49–E. Retinal pigmentation is associated with the use of thioridazine.

50–B. Antisocial personality disorder, like schizoid, paranoid, and obsessive-compulsive personality disorders, is seen more frequently in men than in women. Histrionic, borderline, dependent, and avoidant personality disorders are seen more frequently in women.

51–C. Flashbacks, nightmares, guilt, and memory impairment for the traumatic event characterize post-traumatic stress disorder.

52–E. Delta waves are seen in sleep stages 3 and 4. Penile and clitoral erection; increased pulse, increased respiration, and elevated blood pressure; dreaming; and complete relaxation of skeletal muscles are all seen in REM sleep.

53–A. This patient is probably suffering from schizophrenia. Hallucinations are not seen in persons with schizoid or schizotypal personality disorder, and this man has no mood problems to suggest bipolar or schizoaffective disorder.

54–B. Infusions of sodium lactate, as well as inhalation of carbon dioxide, can induce panic attacks in susceptible people; therefore, sodium lactate is used as a diagnostic tool.

55–A. Negative predictive value is the probability that a person with a negative test is actually well.

56–A. The tenting effect first occurs during the excitement phase of the sexual response cycle.

57–E. In a prospective study, the ratio of the incidence of a condition (e.g., miscarriage) in exposed people to the incidence in nonexposed people is the relative risk.

58–B. The odds-risk ratio (odds ratio) is 2.9 and is calculated as follows.

	LCD exposure	No LCD exposure
Women who miscarried	A = 10	B = 40
Women who carried to term	C = 8	D = 92

$$\text{Odds ratio} = \frac{(A)(D)}{(B)(C)} = \frac{(10)(92)}{(40)(8)} = 2.9$$

59–A. Infant monkeys reared by surrogate artificial mothers have many social problems and are more likely to be adversely affected if they are male.

60–D. The attributable risk is the incidence rate in exposed people (5.0) minus the incidence rate in unexposed people (0.5) = 4.5. Therefore, 4.5 is the additional risk of getting tuberculosis associated with living with someone with tuberculosis.

61–E. The relative risk is the incidence rate in exposed people (5.0) divided by the incidence rate in unexposed people (0.5) = 10.0. Therefore, the chances of getting tuberculosis are 10 times greater when living with someone who has tuberculosis than when living in a household in which no one has tuberculosis.

62–A. The most effective drug for treating obsessive-compulsive disorder is clomipramine. Other tricyclic antidepressants have also proven useful.

63–B. The odds-risk ratio is used to estimate the relative risk in a retrospective study.

64–C. The genetic influence in bipolar disorder is higher than in schizophrenia. A child with two parents who have bipolar disorder has a 50%–75% likelihood of developing the disease in adulthood; a child with both parents who have schizophrenia has a 30%–40% likelihood of developing the disease. The concordance rate for bipolar disorder is higher than that for unipolar disorder, and the lifetime prevalence of unipolar disorder is higher in women (about 15%) than in men (about 10%).

65–D. The incidence rate is the number of individuals who develop an illness in a given time period divided by the total number of individuals at risk for the illness during that period.

66–D. This woman most likely is suffering from delirium.

67–B. Facial tics, cursing, and grimacing seen in this patient are symptoms of Tourette's syndrome.

68–E. Korsakoff's syndrome (alcohol amnestic disorder), a cognitive disorder seen in alcoholics, includes lying to cover up memory loss (confabulation).

69–F. In the elderly, depression is often characterized by memory loss (pseudodementia), which may be confused with dementia.

70–H. The ventricles of the brain show enlargement in old age.

71–C. Imaginary companions are common during the preschool years.

72–E. The individual acquires the capacity for abstract thought in adolescence.

73–F. Erikson's stage of intimacy versus isolation is found in young adulthood.

74–C. The oedipal stage is seen in the preschool years.

75–D. "And then what happened?" is an example of the interviewing technique known as facilitation.

76–E. "You say that you felt the pain more in the evening?" is an example of the interviewing technique known as reflection.

77–G. The statement, "That must have been terrifying for you," is an example of support.

78–B. In validation, the doctor gives credence to the patient's feelings and fears.

79–D. A hallucination is a false sensory perception, such as hearing a voice when no one is there.

80–C. A person with a delusion has a false belief that is not shared by others. In this case, the person believes that people are spying on him from the television set.

81–A. In an illusion, an individual misperceives a real external stimulus. In this case, the individual has seen someone but has interpreted the person as being her father.

82–C. Auditory evoked potentials, the response of the brain to sound as measured by electrical activity, are used to evaluate loss of hearing in infants.

83–E. Galvanic skin response, a reflection of sweat gland activity, is altered with arousal of the sympathetic nervous system.

84–F. PET scans, used mainly as research tools, can localize metabolically active brain areas in persons assigned specific tasks.

85–G. In depersonalization disorder, the patient feels detached from her social situation.

86–D. In malingering, the patient pretends that she is ill in order to gain financially.

87–C. In factitious disorder, the patient simulates illness for attention. The gain to this patient is not as obvious as it is in the malingering patient.

88–C. Early morning awakening is a type of insomnia that is commonly seen in people with major depression.

89–A. Narcolepsy (sleep attacks) is characterized by cataplexy (loss of muscle control).

90–D. Patients with obstructive sleep apnea are frequently unaware that they have awakened often during the night because they cannot breathe. They may become chronically tired.

91–C. In persons with antisocial personality disorder, the electroencephalogram is often abnormal because there is a high incidence of early head injury in these individuals.

92–E. Patients with schizoid personality disorder show lifelong social withdrawal and little interest in others.

93–G. Because this patient is oversensitive to rejection, she has become socially withdrawn. In contrast to the schizoid patient, this patient with an avoidant personality disorder is interested in meeting people but is unable to do so because of her shyness, inferiority complex, and timidity.

94–A. Individuals with passive-aggressive personality disorders appear to be agreeable to changes in their behavior but frequently have an underlying anger at the physician and do not comply with advice given.

95–E. Of the listed antidepressants, desipramine is the least sedating.

96–A. Nortriptyline is the heterocyclic antidepressant least likely to cause orthostatic hypotension.

97–H. Priapism is associated with the use of trazodone.

98–B. Alprazolam is an antianxiety agent with antidepressant properties.

99–A. In rationalization, an irrational happening such as the loss of an arm in an accident, is made to appear reasonable (i.e., he would have ended up in jail if it had not happened).

100–I. In reaction formation, the angry feelings that the patient has for the doctor because he canceled her previous appointment are denied. Instead, the patient adopts the opposite behavior and compliments the doctor.

101–H. In undoing, the patient believes that a change of behavior at this time can reverse or undo something irreversible (his lung cancer caused by years of not taking good care of his health).

102–F. The first-year medical student must consciously suppress his emotions so that he can work effectively at the initially unpleasant task of cadaver dissection.

103–G. This patient is practicing denial and does not admit to the reality of a serious medical symptom.

104–K. Using sublimation, the player's unacceptable desire to steal is rerouted into the socially acceptable action of stealing bases in a baseball game.

105–L. In regression, the lawyer shows a return to childlike patterns of behavior when she is hospitalized.

106–C. This is an example of the treatment technique known as systematic desensitization, in which the patient is exposed to increasing doses of the fear-producing stimulus (dogs) while relaxed.

107–D. In flooding, rather than escaping from the feared stimulus, the person must confront the stimulus until the fear subsides. In the related technique of implosion, the person mentally but not physically confronts the feared stimulus.

108–H. By habituation, this man has become accustomed to a stimulus (noise) because of repeated exposure. In a reverse way, in sensitization a person becomes hypersensitive to a stimulus so that even a weak or subthreshold exposure elicits a response.

109–A. This patient has learned to associate the intravenous setup with nausea, which is now the conditioned or learned response.

110–G. In this example of negative reinforcement, a patient increases his behavior (e.g., going to physical therapy sessions) in order to reduce an aversive stimulus (e.g., his shoulder pain).

111–E. This statement is an example of bargaining.

112–B. This statement is an example of anger.

113–C. This statement is an example of acceptance.

114–D. In modeling, the girl adopts the behavior of her mother, whom she admires.

115–B. In aversive conditioning, an unwanted behavior (nail biting) is paired with a noxious-tasting substance.

116–A. In operant conditioning, a nonreflex behavior, such as a dog turning a doorknob, is learned by using a reward (a treat).

117–B. A hyperdopaminergic state may be involved in the etiology of schizophrenia.

118–A. Reduced availability of serotonin may be involved in the pathophysiology of affective disorders.

119–D. Decreased GABA activity is thought to be involved in the pathophysiology of anxiety.

120–C. Degeneration of cholinergic neurons is involved in Alzheimer's disease.

Index

neuroleptic

(Antipsychotic) same drugs

- neuroleptic
- anti psychotic
- anti depressant

block muscarinic
receptors → anti cholinergic
effects
↓

1 dry mouth
2 Blurred vision
3 Urinary retention
4 constipation
5 delirium